PRESIDENTIAL LEADERSHIP AND AFRICAN AMERICANS

"In this highly original and timely inquiry, eminent social psychologist and leadership scholar George Goethals traces the formative role that presidential judgment and initiative have played in the progress of African Americans in this country—from the beginnings of slavery to the election of its first African American president. The points are incisively argued and the narrative masterfully wrought. This is a major achievement and one that sets the bar for future scholarship in this important and neglected area."
> —*Roderick M. Kramer, William R. Kimball Professor of Organizational Behavior, Stanford University Graduate School of Business, USA*

"Professor Goethals' brilliant and pioneering book is a penetrating examination of the leadership, values, and policy decisions of eight American presidents in relation to the plight as well as the progress of African Americans in the United States. Deeply engaging, brimming with original insights, I could hardly put it down."
> —*Susan Dunn, author of* 1940: FDR, Willkie, Lindbergh, Hitler—the Election Amid the Storm, *Williams College, USA*

"Provocative and compelling. When it came to issues of racial equality, many of our illustrious presidents, including Jefferson, Teddy Roosevelt and Woodrow Wilson, Psychologist Al Goethals tellingly concludes, were conflicted followers of the status quo rather than leaders."
> —*Tom Cronin, Colorado College, USA*

Presidential Leadership and African Americans examines the leadership styles of eight American presidents and shows how the decisions made by each affected the lives and opportunities of the nation's black citizens. Beginning with George Washington and concluding with the landmark election of Barack Obama, Goethals traces the evolving attitudes and morality that influenced the actions of each president on matters of race and shows how their personal backgrounds as well as their individual historical, economic, and cultural contexts combined to shape their values, judgments, and decisions, and ultimately their leadership, regarding African Americans.

George R. Goethals, PhD, is the E. Claiborne Robins Distinguished Professor in Leadership Studies at the University of Richmond. He is a fellow of the American Psychological Association, the Society of Experimental Social Psychology, and the Association for Psychological Science. He is also a member of the Society for Personality and Social Psychology.

Leadership: Research and Practice Series

A James MacGregor Burns Academy of Leadership Collaboration

Series Editors

Georgia Sorenson, PhD, Research Professor in Leadership Studies, University of Maryland, and Founder of the James MacGregor Burns Academy . . . and the International Leadership Association.

Ronald E. Riggio, PhD, is the Henry R. Kravis Professor of Leadership and Organizational Psychology and former Director of the Kravis Leadership Institute at Claremont McKenna College.

Scott T. Allison and George R. Goethals
Heroic Leadership: An Influence Taxonomy of 100 Exceptional Individuals

Michelle C. Bligh and Ronald E. Riggio (Eds.)
Exploring Distance in Leader-Follower Relationships: When Near Is Far and Far Is Near

Michael A. Genovese
Building Tomorrow's Leaders Today: On Becoming a Polymath Leader

Michael A. Genovese and Janie Steckenrider (Eds.)
Women as Political Leaders: Studies in Gender and Governing

Jon P. Howell
Snapshots of Great Leadership

Aneil Mishra and Karen E. Mishra
Becoming a Trustworthy Leader: Psychology and Practice

Ronald E. Riggio and Sherylle J. Tan (Eds.)
Leader Interpersonal and Influence Skills: The Soft Skills of Leadership

Dinesh Sharma and Uwe P. Gielen (Eds.)
The Global Obama: Crossroads of Leadership in the 21st Century

Nathan W. Harter
Leadership and Coherence: A Cognitive Approach

George R. Goethals
Presidential Leadership and African Americans: "An American Dilemma" from Slavery to the White House

PRESIDENTIAL LEADERSHIP AND AFRICAN AMERICANS

"An American Dilemma" from Slavery to the White House

by George R. Goethals

Routledge
Taylor & Francis Group

NEW YORK AND LONDON

First published 2015
by Routledge
711 Third Avenue, New York, NY 10017

and by Routledge
27 Church Road, Hove, East Sussex BN3 2FA

Routledge is an imprint of the Taylor & Francis Group, an informa business

Library of Congress Cataloging-in-Publication Data
Goethals, George R.
    Presidential leadership and African-Americans : "an American dilemma"
from slavery to the White House / by George R. Goethals.
        pages cm. — (Leadership : research and practice series)
    Includes bibliographical references and index.
    1. Presidents—Relations with African Americans—History.
2. Presidents—United States—Racial attitudes—History.   3. Slavery—
Political aspects—United States—History.   4. African Americans—Civil
rights—History.   5. Political leadership—United States—Psychological
aspects—History.   6. United States—Race relations—Political aspects—
History.   7. United States—Politics and government.   I. Title.
    E176.472.A34G63 2015
    323.1196'073—dc23
    2014041473

ISBN: 978-1-138-81424-0 (hbk)
ISBN: 978-1-138-81425-7 (pbk)
ISBN: 978-1-315-74762-0 (ebk)

Typeset in Bembo
by Apex CoVantage, LLC

Printed and bound in the United States of America by Publishers Graphics,
LLC on sustainably sourced paper.

To BB, for a half-century of love and support

CONTENTS

LIST OF ILLUSTRATIONS
AND CREDITS

SERIES EDITOR FOREWORD

Are leaders event-making or do they just happen to live in eventful times? Is our president responsible for the mess we're in, or is he steadily handling a mounting portfolio of intractable problems? As we look for guidance, we have pondered Lincoln's assertion: "I claim not to have controlled events, but confess plainly that events have controlled me."

It hardly seems plausible that a less deft leader than Lincoln could have restored the nation and ended slavery. Still, our view of Lincoln is partly our bias to attribute the favorable outcome to one person—"the romance of leadership." We love to love the leader. But we also killed him.

As this remarkable book details, the complex situational forces that shape the values, priorities, and ultimately the actions of presidents are highly relevant. In so many ways, the presidency is not occupied by a person so much as a container for our wishes, projections, and history.

This book examines one issue—race—and a broad historical trajectory of presidents: Washington, Jefferson, Lincoln, Grant, Wilson, Theodore Roosevelt, Truman, Johnson, and Obama. Its narrative encompasses an emergent presidency rooted in slavery—when George Washington was born, approximately half of the population of Virginia were slaves— and ends with our first black president.

The author, eminent leadership scholar Al Goethals, with his lens as a social psychologist, examines all the complexity of leadership and the myriad of situational and social factors that affect it. His unique approach gives the subject of his study—the presidency—a fresh new way of understanding the complexities and complicities of the role as the fundamental corruption of inequality unfolds.

Presidential scholars study the intricacies of the persons in the role, but seldom do the actions of the presidents reflect their attitudes and aspirations. Other forces are at hand—economic, historical—as are other psychological processes, such as fundamental attribution errors and correspondence bias. How are we to understand Jefferson's original draft of the Declaration of Independence denouncing slavery with his own ownership of slaves, one of whom was his wife's half-sister? How could Wilson's high-mindedness on so many things allow segregation of offices in federal agencies? Or a president, William Clinton, termed "the first Black President" by Toni Morrison, embark on a 1992 strategic "Sister Souljah" southern strategy?

These are the types of questions taken up in this astute and beautifully written, historically nested book.

Georgia Sorenson, PhD
Visiting Professor of Leadership Studies
Carey School of Law, University of Maryland

Ronald E. Riggio, PhD
Henry R. Kravis Professor of Leadership and Organizational Psychology
Kravis Leadership Institute
Claremont McKenna College

PREFACE

I am a social psychologist. It may seem odd or even presumptuous for someone with my background to author a book on presidential leadership and African Americans. A word of explanation. This work combines my lifelong fascination with US presidents and my professional study of the psychology of leadership with more recent interests in how different presidents used their office to address issues pertaining to race in America. My interest goes back to 78 rpm records with songs about the first eight presidents I heard in third grade and then to the presidential biography I read that year, Bessie Rowland James and Marquis James's *The Courageous Heart: A Life of Andrew Jackson for Young Readers.* The next year, a five-dollar bribe from my father convinced me to memorize the presidents, vice presidents, and defeated candidates. Then in high school I read James MacGregor Burns's *John Kennedy: A Political Profile* and subsequently got hooked on Theodore H. White's *The Making of the President* series, starting with his first volume on the 1960 Kennedy-Nixon election. While I studied psychology in college and graduate school, my interest in history and the presidents never diminished. On a sabbatical from Williams College at the University of Virginia in 1978–79, I read several books about the Civil War and encountered there for the first time critiques of Lincoln's Emancipation Proclamation. I became more curious about how Lincoln and others dealt with equality and race when further study led me to read about Ulysses S. Grant's presidency as well as his military leadership. Who knew about Grant's key role in passing the crucial Fifteenth Amendment to the Constitution when "scandal" was just about the only word closely linked to his administration? Further study of presidential leadership and slavery, emancipation, Reconstruction, Jim Crow, and then civil rights and voting rights led me to encounter numerous stories relating both inspirational and profoundly depressing successes and failures of presidential moral leadership. The former include the ringing words in Washington's will directing that his slaves be freed after his wife died "without evasion, neglect, or delay" and Harry Truman's powerful directives "to secure" at long last civil rights for African Americans. The latter include Thomas Jefferson's tortuous retreat from eloquent champion of the proposition that "all men are created equal" to wary guardian of the Southern states' rights to own slaves as property and Woodrow Wilson's segregation of federal offices during the repressive Jim Crow era.

The subtitle of this book borrows the phrase "An American Dilemma" from Gunnar Myrdal's classic 1944 study of race relations and democracy in the United States. Those issues persist as an American dilemma. The story continues to evolve. The United States elected an African American president in 2008 but has recently seen its Supreme Court undoing some of the most important protections for black voting rights. Perhaps the arc of history is bending backward. Time will tell.

No matter the future, this project has been entirely engaging. The lives and administrations of Washington, Jefferson, Lincoln, Grant, Theodore Roosevelt, Wilson, Truman and finally Lyndon Johnson and Barack Obama offer a wonderful education about leadership at its best and at its most disappointing. I very much hope that what I have absorbed and pondered will be of interest to those of you who read this book.

I have been very fortunate in the support and instruction I have received from interested friends and colleagues over the years. When I started on the Williams faculty in 1970, I quickly sought out Jim Burns, whose book on Kennedy had inspired me in high school. From then until his recent death, Jim and I had many illuminating discussions of presidential leadership. He frequently and most helpfully prodded and guided. Later, I began research on presidential debates with Williams colleagues Steve Fein, Saul Kassin, and Matthew Kugler. Once again at the urging of Jim Burns, I developed a course on leadership and initiated a program in Leadership Studies. Doing so eventually led me to move to the Jepson School of Leadership Studies at the University of Richmond in 2006. Since Burns had played a leading role in forming the Jepson School in the early 1990s, he was supportive when I left Williams, his *alma mater*.

Being at Jepson has been crucial in developing this book. First, moving to Virginia from Massachusetts reminded me how turbulent race relations remain in the United States and how issues that many thought had been settled during the Civil War still fester. The Jepson curriculum has allowed me to develop courses on Presidential Leadership and Civil War Leadership in addition to classes focusing on the psychology of leadership. The 2008 presidential election in Virginia was eye-opening. An African American, Barack Obama, became the first Democrat to carry Virginia since 1964. I seemed to have been at the right place at the right time to begin a book on the presidency's intersection with the concerns of African Americans.

At Richmond, many faculty colleagues and staff members have enlightened and supported me. I am very much in the debt of Michele Bedsaul, Joanne Ciulla, Dick Couto, Don Forsyth, Julian Hayter, Gill Hickman, Crystal Hoyt, Peter Kaufman, Pam Khoury, Gary McDowell, Sandra Peart, Terry Price, Susan Taylor, Tammy Tripp, Tom Wren, and Eric Yellen. All have been extremely helpful. My collaborator Scott Allison has been very patient in waiting for me to finish this book so we can resume our studies of heroic leadership. Thank you. Most of my writing happens during summers in Raquette Lake, New York. I am sustained by many family members and friends there at Indian Point,

Pine Island, Raquette Lake Supply, the Tap Room, the Raquette Lake Library, Raquette Lake Navigation, R. Matson Mechanical, Central Adirondack Shipping, Waldron Construction, and the post office. Closer to home, my neighbor and running buddy Stephen Hayes, a willing but nevertheless captive audience, has listened more than almost anyone else to musings about my hopes for this book, and my fears. I am very grateful. Finally, my wife Marion has been my most loving and supportive collaborator. Without her, nothing good could be done.

Finally, I wish to thank series editors Georgia Sorenson and Ron Riggio for their encouragement, and the men and women at Taylor and Francis who helped bring this book to completion: Paul Dukes, Elizabeth Graber, Denise Power, Lauren Verity, Helen Evans, and Maddy Hamlin, as well as Sheri Sipka of Apex CoVantage.

George R. Goethals, October 2014

INTRODUCTION

Presidential Leadership and the American Dilemma: Psychological Dimensions

Figure 0.1 On the *River Queen* at City Point, Virginia, in 1865, Abraham Lincoln discussed lenient terms for the South after the Civil War with General William Tecumseh Sherman, General Ulysses S. Grant, and Admiral David Porter.

George Peter Alexander Healy, "The Peacemakers," 1868, oil on canvas. The White House, Washington, DC. Public domain, via Wikimedia Commons.

In August of 1864, the prospects of Union victory in the Civil War, and Abraham Lincoln's prospects for re-election in November, were at an all-time low. In May of that year, hopes had been high. In Virginia, the Army of the Potomac, now directed by the most successful Union general, Ulysses S. Grant, would finally make good on the cry, "On to Richmond." Further south, General William

T. Sherman was preparing to leave Chattanooga, Tennessee, with the object of capturing Atlanta, thereby severing crucial rail connections in the heart of the Confederacy. By August, such high hopes had turned bitter. Both Grant and Sherman were stalled by their Confederate counterparts, Robert E. Lee and Joseph Johnston. People in the north were appalled at the mounting casualties. Many had reluctantly come to believe that the carnage was too great, the costs too high, and that peace would have to be negotiated. On the South's terms. The Civil War was lost, and the Confederate States of America would gain its independence.

The Southern strategy was clear. While it was not going to be possible to defeat the massive Northern armies or break the strangling Union blockade of Confederate ports, if the war had reached a stalemate, Lincoln would lose the election and the Democratic candidate, most likely former Union General George B. McClellan, would make peace and give the South its independence. In this context, rumor and propaganda flourished. The so-called Copperhead Democrats in the North, long opposed to the president's war efforts—especially his Emancipation Proclamation—sought to defeat Lincoln by claiming it was only his insistence on "the abandonment of slavery" that prolonged the war. If only Lincoln would retract his Proclamation, the South would peaceably return to the Union. Perhaps the Copperheads feared Northern victory and free blacks more than Southern independence. Regardless, they repeated the false story that only Lincoln's "abolition crusade" stood in the way of peace and reunion. However, Lincoln and most Republicans knew that the South would never return of its own volition to the Union. Only total defeat would save the United States of America. And loyal voices attempted to paint Confederate President Jefferson Davis's insistence on independence as the stumbling block to peace. There was, in effect, a contest of causal attribution.[1] Was it Lincoln's insistence on emancipation or Davis's insistence on independence that prolonged the war?

Under tremendous pressure from an ever-larger chorus of criticism, Lincoln was twice tempted to test Davis's willingness to make peace if the slavery issue were put aside. Although he had several times declared that the promise of emancipation "once made, must be kept," Lincoln edged toward exploring the possibility of reunion without abolition. On August 17, he drafted one letter saying, "if Jefferson Davis wishes . . . to know what I would do if he were to offer peace and reunion, saying nothing about slavery, let him try me."[2] If such a letter were made public, the freedom African Americans longed for would likely be forever lost. But Lincoln reconsidered and resisted that dangerous temptation. Still, a week later, he drafted a second such letter to be carried to Richmond by negotiators trying to assess Davis's position on both reunion and slavery. In this one, Lincoln proposed "that upon the restoration of the Union and the national authority, the war shall cease at once, all remaining questions to be left for adjustment by peaceful modes."[3] Again, it seemed that Lincoln might be willing to break the promise, to sacrifice the cause of freedom—which had done so much to transform the war and to potentially transform the nation—for peace.

2

By the next day, Lincoln had again changed his mind. He would not give up the struggle for "a new birth of freedom."[4] If he lost the election, so be it. He reaffirmed first principles. As he wrote the previous year: "[A]nd the promise being made, must be kept."[5]

Fortunately for Lincoln and the nation, the military situation, "upon which all else chiefly depends,"[6] Lincoln asserted later, soon turned dramatically for the better. On September 3, Lincoln received a cherished telegram from Sherman: "Atlanta is ours, and fairly won."[7] Shortly thereafter, Union General Philip Sheridan won decisive battles in the Shenandoah Valley, and Lincoln's war strategy prevailed. He defeated McCellan decisively in the November election.

Psychological Dimensions of Presidential Leadership

The pressures that Lincoln was under, and his apparent temptation to sacrifice the cause of African Americans for peace, are but two examples of the cross-currents of opinion, context, and stress that have challenged presidential leadership in America since the administration of George Washington. Such conflicting forces have often involved black Americans. In combination with the psychological resources of American leaders, they have produced decisions that made conditions better or worse for our countrymen. In this book, we tell the story of those contingencies and how a number of American presidents have responded to them at crucial turning points in US history. How did those presidents think, feel, and act as the external forces that pressed upon them interacted with their own motives, values, goals, and beliefs?

There are a number of perspectives that guide our exploration. First, while presidential decision making, or what Fred Greenstein called "the presidential difference," provides the framework as we go forward, it is far from the only piece to the puzzle.[8] What presidents think and do has been immensely important, but seldom do their actions simply reflect their attitudes and aspirations. Their policies exist and evolve in the midst of the turmoil of events. Other actors' behavior affects their actions and thus American history at least as much as their own. Importantly, as we explore presidential decision making regarding African Americans—from questions of slavery, emancipation, suffrage, segregation, and equal protection of the laws to civil rights and voting rights—the actions of individual African Americans and groups of African Americans weigh heavily. We shall see for example that Abraham Lincoln's Emancipation Proclamation of January 1, 1863, was shaped, perhaps indeed forced, by what slaves and other blacks did for themselves. Lincoln was well aware of this, as he said in a famous letter, "I claim not to have controlled events, but confess plainly that events have controlled me."[9]

We will also see that the decisions and actions of both black Americans and American presidents unfold in a society that, like many others, has a consistent history of racial prejudice and racial exploitation. The history of slavery, emancipation, Jim Crow, and civil rights, for example, reflects deep strains of racism.

3

This is true both for the events in these struggles and in the telling of them. Race prejudice, at times in the background and at times at the forefront, has strongly influenced the course of American history and the history of presidential leadership. It matters greatly.

These considerations underline the importance of several lines of social psychological research on the way human beings understand each other. Studies on what is called the "fundamental attribution error" show that observers of behavior have a tendency to attribute what they see to something about the person performing the action, even when the behavior they observe is very likely caused by something in the situation or the environment.[10] For example, a politician states that she is strongly opposed to raising taxes while another declares that he opposes the death penalty. We make the attribution that their positions reflect their values and dispositions. But we may be wrong. Though their statements could reflect what the office seekers really believe, their true attitudes, it's just as likely that they reflect the prevailing political pressures. These instances of the fundamental attribution error reflect something called "the correspondence bias."[11] We have a strong tendency to see behavior as corresponding to an underlying trait or disposition. We do not consider the circumstances.

In considering presidential decisions affecting the lives of African Americans, it is easy to fall into the trap of attributing either racist or unusually egalitarian attitudes to the president, depending on whether his action advanced or impeded the welfare of black citizens. However, in many cases, the decision will be affected by a whole range of pressures and circumstances. This does not imply that their actions are forced or beyond their control or that they do not bear responsibility for them, only that what they do is affected by much more than their own preferences, beliefs, and morality.

Closely related to the fundamental attribution error is a bias toward attributing group success or failure to the leader, especially the leader's personality and abilities. When groups do well, we think they have been led well and that the leader is the responsible party. This bias is called "the romance of leadership."[12] But it applies to cases of group failure as well as success. We praise or blame the leader for the group's outcomes. People have "leader schemas" or "implicit leadership theories" that encapsulate their knowledge or beliefs about what leaders are like, how they act, and what role they play in influencing or determining events and outcomes.[13] The "romance of leadership" is part of those schemas or theories. It is the common belief that what leaders do causes their groups to win or lose, or succeed or fail. This bias can affect thinking about such questions as how much of the march to Jim Crow segregation and oppression in the early twentieth century is attributable to the leadership of Presidents Theodore Roosevelt, William Howard Taft, and Woodrow Wilson and how much Presidents John F. Kennedy and Lyndon B. Johnson were responsible for the passage of the Civil Rights Act of 1964.

Pointing out these biases does not make students of leadership immune to them. In each case of presidential leadership, he or she makes the best assessments possible considering as much of the relevant circumstance and personal character and capacity as possible. One difficulty is while we can be aware of, if we choose to look, the external pressures acting on a president, we cannot get inside their heads, nor could we even if they were alive, to study the conflicting internal pressures with which they wrestled. George Washington's decisions about slavery reflected not only the political and constitutional constraints on the actions he contemplated. They also balanced his financial interests, his need for control, his feelings about his wife Martha, his sense of responsibility to other family members, his abiding concern with his reputation, and his place in history all against what he believed at the time about the morality of slavery. Abraham Lincoln weighed the goals of union, peace, and ending the war's blood-letting against his public promises and his own sense of right and wrong. In both cases, their decisions reflected multiple external pressures and often conflicting internal considerations.

The different internal impulses decision makers must weigh underline an important distinction between moral thought and moral behavior.[14] In considering the former, we note that different presidents arrive at different points along a scale of moral development. Lawrence Kohlberg's[15] studies of moral development, and its closely related counterpart cognitive development, led him to propose "post-conventional morality" as the most advanced stage of moral thinking. At this level, individuals make moral judgments based on carefully thought-out ethical principles based on universal values such as freedom and justice. Both George Washington and Abraham Lincoln had life experiences that prompted moral development to higher levels than many other presidents. Washington, a slave owner in a society dominated by and constructed for slave owners, had experiences with African Americans that disturbed and challenged the values and beliefs with which he was raised.[16] Lincoln's wartime experiences, and his contact with individual African Americans such as Frederick Douglass, also set in motion moral thinking that would not have otherwise taken place. Presidents' differing levels of moral development, both generally and with respect to slavery and black people, were significant factors in their public behavior.

But, as noted above, moral thought is not the same as moral behavior. For many years, psychologists have noted the discrepancy between attitudes and behavior. Often people do not do what they know is right and engage in behaviors that they feel are wrong. Some individuals connect their attitudes and values more clearly to behavior than others;[17] their capacity for self-regulation seems more developed and more consistent.[18] We will see significant variation among presidents in their capacity to do what they know is right.

The inconsistencies that do occur raise their own fascinating questions about how people feel, think, and ultimately act. Most relevant here is Leon Festinger's theory of cognitive dissonance, a social psychological theory that has become increasingly influential outside its discipline.[19] Dissonance theory argues that the inconsistency of thoughts, or "cognitions," creates uncomfortable psychological arousal—cognitive dissonance is the name for that negative or aversive psychological state—which pushes the person experiencing such dissonance to make it go away, to reduce it in some way. Those ways include changing one of the inconsistent thoughts, diminishing their importance, or simply forgetting them.[20] These routes to dissonance reduction are similar in many ways to the ego-defense mechanisms described by Sigmund Freud at the end of his long career.[21] Repression, denial, and, in particular, rationalization are hallmarks of dissonance reduction. We will see that presidents differ in their dissonance reduction strategies. In general, those who were not very good at reducing dissonance ended up doing what their moral commitments dictated more than those possessing what e. e. cummings described as "comfortable minds." A number of historians place Thomas Jefferson in the latter category, suggesting that he was comfortable overlooking how his behavior contradicted his eloquently articulated arguments against slavery. While his case is more complicated than a simple instance of good dissonance reduction, it does illustrate the concept.

Even though presidential leadership affecting African Americans has been consequential—sometimes more so, sometimes less so—throughout American history, the lives and administrations of only some of its chief executives are considered in detail here. What basis can there possibly be for selecting them? A number of criteria seem relevant. One is to consider widely known and highly significant presidents who took action, or failed to take action, with great consequence for African Americans. Abraham Lincoln and his role in ending slavery during the Civil War is an obvious example. Another is Woodrow Wilson, who allowed segregation of federal departments during his eight-year presidency. A second criterion is to study presidents who made, or failed to make, great efforts on behalf of African Americans, even though this aspect of their presidencies is less well-known. Ulysses S. Grant is one who made such efforts. Theodore Roosevelt is one who might have done much more. A third approach is to consider presidents of major importance to American history whose actions outside their presidencies were consequential for African Americans. Both George Washington and Thomas Jefferson are relevant here.

Another consideration is the 2009 C-SPAN survey of presidential leadership. Like the previous C-SPAN survey done in 2000, it asked a large group of historians to rank the presidents and also to rate them on "individual leadership characteristics." One of those dimensions was "Pursued Equal Justice for All."[22] The names near the top and bottom of this list help map the territory. For the most part they are unsurprising. The top three are Abraham Lincoln, Lyndon Johnson, and Harry Truman. They are followed by Bill Clinton, Jimmy Carter, and John F. Kennedy. Their ratings, and those of most others near the top, are almost identical to the year 2000 ratings. An interesting new entrant to the 2009 Top Ten is the ninth ranked, Ulysses S. Grant, who was eighteenth in the 2000 survey. No one moved up on this dimension more than Grant. In light of the criteria above and these rankings, Lincoln, Johnson, Truman, and Grant will be studied in some depth here.

In direct contrast to Grant, Woodrow Wilson fell from twentieth to twenty-seventh between the two surveys. The fact that presidents are reassessed over time and move in various rankings is not particularly surprising. New scholarship, particularly on the Founders and on Lincoln, appears regularly. However, factors other than new scholarship may account for the rating changes of Grant and Wilson. They may reflect changes in the knowledge, values, and political perspectives of the historians in the two surveys. Or, it may be, with the election of Barack Obama, a new awareness of and focus on what presidents have done with respect to racial and equal justice issues.

All these considerations, as well as my own personal interests and perspectives, have led to the inclusion in detail of George Washington, Thomas Jefferson, Abraham Lincoln, Ulysses S. Grant, Theodore Roosevelt, Woodrow Wilson, Harry S. Truman, and Lyndon B. Johnson. These presidents served at crucial turning points, and their lives and administrations arguably had the biggest impact. Other presidents will be discussed in less but varying levels of depth. Almost all will be mentioned, although some very briefly.

In considering these presidents, several criteria for evaluating them as well as describing their actions are important. Most central is simply whether their leadership advanced or set back the freedoms, rights, and welfare of African Americans. Did they move the needle forward or let it slip backward? In assessing that question, the familiar issues of whether they were simply men of their times becomes important. Appraisals of all presidents' leadership with respect to African Americans must address that issue. Were some presidents notably ahead of the curve? Did they lead beyond where the country or their party or the prevailing governmental regime stood at the time? Did individual presidents simply "go with the flow," paddle upstream against it, or race to move the country more rapidly in the direction it was tentatively heading? In a word, could they have done more?

It is also important to consider whether different presidents' moral development progressed in response to the circumstances and experiences they faced. Were they prodded to move forward psychologically, and did they actually do so? Then, did they act on their moral principles, and if so, were they successful? Finally, what can be said about the nature of their struggles with the external and internal conflicts they confronted? What of their own sense of the rightness and wrongness of their actions? What did they do with the cognitive dissonance that may have resulted from actions inconsistent with their evolving beliefs?

We begin with George Washington, for the obvious reason that he was the first president and that everything he did set a precedent. He made decisions early in his presidency that failed to challenge slavery. Those choices reflected both his priorities—establishing and maintaining the new constitutional government—and his sense of what was possible. They set a direction for presidential action from which there was never really a departure until Abraham Lincoln took office. Privately, Washington freed his slaves in his will, a culmination of over fifteen years of struggling with what to do in general with regard to this "species of property" and then more specifically with the human beings whom he held in bondage. In doing so, Washington set a direction, but, unfortunately, none of his slave owning successors followed. Nevertheless, the story begins with him.

Notes

1 Harold H. Kelley, Attribution Theory in Social Psychology. In D. Levine (ed.), *Nebraska Symposium on Motivation, 15,* 1967, pp. 192–238.
2 James M. McPherson, *Tried by War: Abraham Lincoln as Commander-in-Chief* (New York: The Penguin Press, 2008), p. 239.
3 Eric Foner, *The Fiery Trial: Abraham Lincoln and American Slavery* (New York: Norton, 2010), p. 307.
4 Abraham Lincoln, Gettysburg Address, November 19, 1863. In D. Fehrenbacher (ed.), *Lincoln: Speeches and Writings, 1859–1865* (New York: The Library of America, 1989), p. 536.
5 Lincoln, Letter to James C. Conkling, August 26, 1863. In Fehrenbacher, pp. 495–99.
6 Lincoln, Second Inaugural Address, March 4, 1865. In Fehrenbacher, pp. 686–87.
7 See http://www.nytimes.com/1864/09/05/news/fall-atlanta-official-report-majgen-sherman-his-strategy-battles-brilliant.html.
8 Fred Greenstein, *The Presidential Difference: Leadership Style from FDR to Barack Obama (Third Edition)* (Princeton, NJ: Princeton University Press, 2009).
9 Lincoln, Letter to Albert G. Hodges, April 4, 1864. In Fehrenbacher, pp. 583–86.
10 Lee Ross, The Intuitive Psychologist and His Shortcomings: Distortions in the Attribution Process. In L. Berkowitz (ed.), *Advances in Experimental Social Psychology, 10* (New York: Academic Press, 1977).
11 Daniel T. Gilbert & Edward E. Jones, Perceiver-Induced Constraint: Interpretations of Self-Generated Reality. *Journal of Personality and Social Psychology, 50,* 1986, pp. 269–80.
12 James R. Meindl & S.B. Ehrlich, The Romance of Leadership and the Evaluation of Organizational Performance. *The Academy of Management Journal, 30,* 1987, pp. 91–109.
13 Cynthia G. Emrich, Context Effects in Leadership Perception. *Personality and Social Psychology Bulletin, 25,* 1999, pp. 91–106.
14 Roger Brown, *Social Psychology* (New York: Free Press, 1965).
15 Lawrence Kohlberg, Stage and Sequence: The Cognitive-Developmental Approach to Socialization. In D. S. Goslin (ed.), *Handbook of Socialization: Theory and Research.* (Boston: Houghton Mifflin, 1969).
16 Joseph J. Ellis, *His Excellency: George Washington* (New York: Knopf, 2004).
17 James M. Olson & Grahame A. Haynes, Persuasion and Leadership. In C. L. Hoyt, G. R. Goethals, & D. R. Forsyth (eds.), *Leadership at the Crossroads: Volume 1, Leadership and Psychology* (Westport, CT: Praeger, 2008).
18 Roy F. Baumeister, Kim D. Vohs, & Diane M. Tice, The Strength Model of Self-Control. *Current Directions in Psychological Science, 16,* 2007, pp. 351–55.
19 Leon Festinger, *A Theory of Cognitive Dissonance* (Palo Alto, CA: Stanford University Press, 1957).

20 Leon Festinger, Henry Riecken, & Stanley Schachter, *When Prophecy Fails* (New York: Harper Torch Books, 1956).

21 Anna Freud, *The Ego and the Mechanisms of Defense* (Madison, CT: International Universities Press, 1936, 1991 edition).

22 See http://legacy.c-span.org/PresidentialSurvey/Pursued-Equal-Justice-For-All.aspx.

1

GEORGE WASHINGTON

In the year 1728, William Byrd II, founder of Richmond, Virginia, participated in the mapping of the Virginia/North Carolina border. Based on his experience, he wrote the well-known *History of the Dividing Line betwixt Virginia and North Carolina* and then the *Secret History of the Line*.[1] The latter offers a witty account of the mapping experience, as well as amusing and somewhat caustic views of North Carolinians. One anecdote recounts the fact that the surveyors ate corn pone, as that was the only food available. But when they offered some to a rather poor white Carolina native, the man "rode away without saying a word." The problem, you see, is that corn pone was considered food for slaves. The man was insulted that his superior status was disregarded.

Over a quarter-millennium later, not much had changed. In 1968, a graduate student from Massachusetts at a North Carolina university asked his rural landlady if he could have some of the beet greens that she had discarded into the trash. She cheerfully agreed but walked away chortling that this Yankee rube was "fixin'" to eat "colored food." However, while there are continuities across the centuries, by the late-1960s, race relations in the South and the United States as a whole had at least started to change. And they have arguably changed more in the past forty years than in the previous 300.

In 2008, Americans elected an African American president. It's hard to imagine when such a possibility first seemed more than fantasy. Certainly not in 1789, when George Washington was inaugurated as the first president of the United States. Not in the 1870s, when Ulysses S. Grant tried with limited success to combat the white South's resistance to post-Civil War reconstruction. And not in the second decade of the twentieth century, when Woodrow Wilson segregated federal offices. And not in 1968. How did the country finally turn the page? There are many threads in this important tapestry of social change. One of them is the attitudes and actions of American presidents regarding African Americans. Some presidents pulled the thread forward. Others tried to unravel it. The story spans the entire history of the country and of the presidency. In fact, it begins well before the American presidency was invented in Philadelphia in 1787. Still, the attitudes and actions of the first president, George Washington, offer a good place to start.

11

In October of 1781, more than six years after he had assumed the role of commander in chief of the Continental Army of the united British colonies, George Washington faced one of the most climactic leadership moments of his life. The large British army, led by Lord Cornwallis, was trapped on the Yorktown Peninsula in Virginia. A siege operation was tightening the noose around Cornwallis's forces. However, a British fleet from New York was reportedly sailing to the rescue. Washington knew that two strongholds in the British line of defense, Redoubts 9 and 10 at Yorktown, had to be captured by assault before the ships arrived. Otherwise, a near stalemate would aid Cornwallis. Washington selected the best troops in the army to make a clandestine nighttime attack on the two redoubts. Redoubt 9 would be assaulted, silently, by French regiments. Redoubt 10 would be attacked by the best American units, under the command of Colonel Alexander Hamilton. One of the units in the vanguard of Hamilton's forces was the First Rhode Island Regiment. A French officer called that regiment "the most neatly dressed, the best under arms, and the most precise in its maneuvers."[2]

The attack on the redoubts was not only important; it was also dangerous. Before the battle, General Washington spoke to the attacking forces, who had been separated from the rest of the army, and underlined what hung in the balance. The revolution could succeed if the assaults that evening succeeded. But surprise was essential, and Washington ordered that no muskets were to be loaded, in case one should fire by accident and alert the defenders. The men were to attack with bayonets and engage in hand-to-hand combat. Strict silence must be observed. Orders were to be followed meticulously.

Washington's gamble worked. On the evening of October 14, the French and American attackers surprised the British enough, and fought well enough, to prevail. The next day, Washington could hardly contain his elation. He visited the captured redoubts, even though he was in danger from English snipers. Two days later, Cornwallis signaled that he would surrender his army. At the formal surrender ceremony that followed, as its flags were furled, the British army bands played "The World Turned Upside Down." For both sides, it truly had.

But, one more detail. The French officer who noted that the First Rhode Island Regiment was "the best under arms, and the most precise in its maneuvers" also noted that "three quarters of the Rhode Island regiment consists of negroes."[3] In some ways, this was unremarkable. By the end of the war, the Continental army was estimated to be about one quarter black. That blacks were a significant part of the army was simply taken for granted. However, this was far from true at the beginning of the war. When George Washington arrived in Cambridge, Massachusetts, to take command of the army in July 1775—just days after the Battle of Bunker Hill but a year before the Declaration of Independence—he was shocked to see black soldiers. However, in the ensuing six years leading up to Yorktown, much had changed in the army and in George Washington's thinking. The change for Washington during that period was in fact just one part of a much greater evolution in Washington's outlook that started well before the war and ended well after it.

Figure 1.1 George Washington chose the mostly black First Rhode Island Regiment to carry out a crucial combat mission in the Battle of Yorktown.
David R. Wagner, "Desperate Valor, August 26, 1778, the 1st Rhode Island Regiment." By permission of the artist.

The world into which George Washington was born during the winter of 1732 had been taking shape for over a century but had only stabilized a few decades before. England's Jamestown colony in Virginia was begun in 1607, exactly a century and a quarter before Washington's birth. Initially, the labor that kept the colony alive, though just barely, had been supplied by indentured servants. These were individuals, generally from the poorer classes in England's highly stratified social structure, who agreed to work for a period of years, typically seven, before they were free to try to establish their own lives. They were white.

The characteristics of Virginia's, and America's, labor force and overall demographics began to change dramatically in 1619. In August of that year, a Dutch ship brought twenty captured Africans to Jamestown. It is likely that the Dutch crew took these captives by force from a Portuguese ship off the coast of southern Africa near what is now Angola. Arriving in Jamestown, the crew exchanged the twenty Africans with the English settlers for food. This was the start of the practice of bringing enslaved Africans to what is now the United States. By the time Congress outlawed the slave trade in 1808, somewhere between

400,000 and 500,000 African slaves had been brought to North American shores. However, this number represents only a small fraction of the number of Africans forced into slavery in the New World. Historian Eric Foner estimates that roughly 10 million of the 12.5 million people who came to the Western Hemisphere between 1500 and 1820 were African slaves.[4] More than 90% of those slaves were taken to the Caribbean or South America, especially Brazil. Life expectancies for slaves working in the mines of Brazil and the sugar plantations of the Caribbean were much lower than life expectancies for slaves in the English colonies in North America. There were more women among the slaves in North America, the work was less brutal than in the sugar plantations, and slaves married and had children. As a result of natural increase, the population of enslaved African Americans in North America had reached roughly 600,000 by the time of Yorktown, with by far the greatest numbers in Virginia.

When Washington was born, approximately half of the population of Virginia were slaves. There were also significant numbers of free blacks. In the 1660s and 1670s, perhaps as many as one third of blacks in Virginia were free. They had gained their freedom in a number of different ways. Some of the first Africans brought to Virginia were treated the same as white indentured servants. They were given their independence after working for a number of years. Religious considerations also played a role. Some of the Africans brought to Jamestown by Dutch sailors had been baptized, probably by the Spanish. Settlers in Virginia initially did not feel that baptized Christians should be slaves. Laws passed in the late 1660s changed that. By then, economic considerations—the need for slave labor—trumped religion. But for a time, nonwhite Christians were excluded from slavery. In addition, some white Virginians freed their slaves or allowed them to buy their freedom.

One of the factors that added to the number of free blacks—or, more accurately, free mixed-race peoples—is that blacks and whites often intermarried. This was particularly true when white and black indentured servants worked side by side. In the mid- and late-1600s, the concept that people of different races should be categorically treated differently simply on the basis of color had not yet taken hold. At the same time that significant numbers of nonwhites gained freedom, the importation of African slaves declined. In the late 1600s, England was happy to ship poor white people to the Americas. There was no shortage of labor in the colonies.

In about 1700, the mother country began reversing its policy. It worried about a shrinking supply of cheap labor. As a result, fewer white indentured servants were available for planters in Virginia. Virginians made up the difference with African slaves.[5] By the time George Washington was born, Virginia was steadily importing slaves. At the same time, views concerning both the mixing of races and the freeing of black slaves were hardening. Perhaps in the late 1600s, Virginians could imagine a society in which free blacks and whites participated collaboratively. By the time George Washington reached adulthood, that view had disappeared.

The increase in the number of slaves in Virginia during the eighteenth century is startling. There were roughly 10,000 in 1700, 30,000 in 1730, and 105,000 in 1750.[6] The first United States Census, conducted in 1790, showed 293,000 slaves in Virginia, representing 39% of the total population of 748,000.[7] At that time, Virginia was by far the most populous of the fifteen states (the thirteen original colonies plus Vermont and Kentucky), and it had by far the largest number of slaves. South Carolina was second in number of slaves with 107,000. While Virginia's slave population was growing, it was actually declining as a percent of the population. For example, in 1760, thirty years before the first census, Virginia's 120,000 slaves were 41% of the population, more than the 39% in the first US census. Like other North American British colonies, Virginia's white population was also growing dramatically throughout the 1700s. In short, the British North America into which George Washington was born was a dynamic, fast-growing set of colonies with significant slave populations from Maryland to Georgia.

George Washington was born on February 22, 1732. His family enjoyed moderate wealth and status in colonial Virginia. His birthplace was on the shores of the Potomac River, about fifty miles south of present-day Washington, DC. George's father, Augustine (Gus) Washington, owned some 10,000 acres of land and fifty slaves.[8] Gus and his first wife had two sons, Lawrence and Austin. After their mother died in 1729, Gus married Mary Ball, who in turn became the mother of George and four younger siblings. The family moved several times around the area near Fredericksburg, Virginia, but life was otherwise stable and comfortable. George greatly admired his two half-brothers, older by fourteen and twelve years, respectively. Lawrence in particular was a dashing role model: Educated in England, he served in the British Army in North America and was elected to Virginia's House of Burgesses.

Life changed drastically in 1743; George was eleven years old. His father, Augustine Washington, died at the age of forty-nine. In ten years' time, when he reached twenty-one, George would inherit significant property, including ten slaves. But starting immediately, he only inherited heavy family responsibilities. His mother insisted that George help her with the property at their home called Ferry Farm, near Fredericksburg, and also serve as conscientious older brother. He was charged with being mindful of a sister one year his junior and brothers two, four, and six years younger. It amounted to George being captain of a rambunctious team. The young Washington always had a difficult relationship with his mother. She lived until he became president of the United States and frequently complained that he never did enough to take care of her, financially and emotionally. The burdensome eldest son role into which young George was thrust at age eleven was one that he never outgrew.

One reason George had to assume so much family responsibility was that his two older half-brothers, Lawrence and Austin, were grown men, both in their twenties, and had left home. Still, Lawrence watched over George from a distance as much as George cared for his younger siblings up close. It was through

Lawrence that George became acquainted with the wealthy and powerful Fairfax clan at Belvoir, a large estate on the Potomac a day's ride from Ferry Farm. Three months after Augustine Washington's death, Lawrence had married Ann Fairfax, a daughter of Lord William Fairfax, owner of large tracts of land in the Virginia colony. As a young boy, George became attracted to his brother's in-laws, and they to him. Lord Fairfax admired George's casual masculinity and his exceptional riding ability. Fairfax was an ardent fox hunter, and George was able to impress through his way with horses and his talent in the chase. In his early teenage years, George also became a close friend of Lord Fairfax's son George William Fairfax, seven years George's senior. When Washington was sixteen, George William married the beautiful eighteen-year-old Sally Cary. Young George was smitten, and Sally at times reciprocated his discrete flirtations. Thus Washington began an intense but proper relationship with Sally Cary Fairfax that transfixed him for the rest of his life.

Due to his favored position in the Fairfax family, in 1748 sixteen-year-old George was included in a party to venture into the Shenandoah Valley to survey some of the vast Fairfax landholdings. He mastered the art of surveying with the intention of earning part of his living from that skill. He enjoyed his surveying experiences, and they defined him as much as his emotional relationships with his mother and Sally Fairfax. Distinguished biographer James Thomas Flexner wrote that on the expedition, Washington "swam horses across a river swollen by snow melting in the mountains; met a party of Indians carrying one scalp; . . . got lost in the Blue Ridge Mountains, where he encountered a rattlesnake. He found it all exhilarating. During thirty-one days of March and April weather, he gave to the American West a part of his heart he was never to regain."[9]

George's surveying skills allowed him to grow financially comfortable. Surveying assignments kept flowing his way through Lord Fairfax; as the Virginia colony expanded westward, so did George Washington's bank account. When he was seventeen, he helped survey the new port of Alexandria, Virginia, and then secured the position of surveyor of Culpeper County. Most of his surveying work could be completed expeditiously, and most of the work he took on could be done only in the autumn and spring seasons, when sight lines would not be obscured by leaves on trees. He had time for other endeavors.

As George's fortunes improved, those of his beloved older brother Lawrence declined. Lawrence contracted tuberculosis in 1749 and desperately sought a cure. First, he consulted physicians in England and then had George accompany him to the healing springs of what is now West Virginia. Nothing worked. In 1751, he sailed to Barbados with George once again accompanying him. The warm weather did not help. While George came home, Lawrence sought a cure in Bermuda with little success and eventually returned to Virginia. He died the next year. George was twenty.

Soon after Lawrence's death, George applied for a position in the Virginia militia. The British governor appointed him and in short order ordered him to command a dangerous mission across the Appalachian Mountains into the

Ohio Valley toward what is now Pittsburgh, Pennsylvania. The objective was to demand that the French leave the area and return to Lake Erie. Washington's small party started out in October 1753, successfully reached their destination, but failed to achieve their goal. They returned diplomatically empty-handed. Nevertheless, Washington's bravery during the expedition formed the foundation for a heroic reputation back home. The next year, the Governor appointed the twenty-two-year-old major to lead a force of several hundred men toward Fort Duquesne (now Pittsburgh) to force the French out. The result this time was a humiliating rout, and Washington was forced to surrender. Still, his steadiness under fire dominated the narrative in Virginia.

Soon after, in 1755, Washington served as second-in-command of a force of about two thousand men under the command of British General Edward Braddock. Again, their mission was to drive the French away from Fort Duquesne. Washington had impressed Braddock, who took him on as one who possessed knowledge of the region and a reputation for bravery. This time the results were equally disastrous. Washington tried to persuade Braddock not to employ classic English set maneuvers, well suited for open fields in Europe but not the forests and streams of the Ohio Valley. Braddock wouldn't listen to the Colonial, resulting in an ambush that destroyed his force and ended his life. George Washington again emerged as a valiant fighter and a heroic leader. He rallied the remnants of Braddock's force and returned to Virginia to great acclaim. The narrative was that the British, not George Washington, had bungled the operation.

Starting about the time of the Braddock expedition, Washington actively sought a commission in the regular British Army. He traveled to Boston in 1756 and then Philadelphia in 1757—no small achievement in those days—but failed to secure the much coveted position. He did succeed in leading yet another Virginia militia force toward Fort Duquesne in 1758. By this time, the French had abandoned the post, and Washington took possession of it for the British. But his involvement in military affairs then ended for the time being. He would never again fight on behalf of an English king.

During his years in the Virginia militia, Washington was also overseeing business back home. When his brother Lawrence died in 1752, George began to rent Lawrence's estate from his widow, Ann. Lawrence had renamed the property Mount Vernon. It lay on the Potomac River just a few miles upstream from Belvoir, home of the Fairfax clan. Both places had long occupied a central place in George Washington's emotional life: Mount Vernon where he spent time with his adored brother Lawrence, and Belvoir where he befriended George William Fairfax and exchanged flirtations with Sally. As tenant at Mount Vernon, Washington oversaw nineteen slaves and the various activities connected with managing a large agricultural expanse. He viewed himself as a planter and a businessman. He also threw himself into acquiring land, an interest that grew out of his days as a young surveyor.

But something was missing—a wife. George had been spurned by a number of young women during his youth. The rejections had been traumatic. He was impressive enough to the opposite sex physically, and maybe even intimidating, but he was shy and, while a magnificent dancer, not interpersonally adroit. He was rough, not smooth. However, his increasing maturity and growing fame made him a good catch. Or at least so thought a rich young widow several months older than George. She was Martha Dandridge Custis, who at age eighteen had married the much older Daniel Parke Custis. In her marriage to Custis, Martha had four children, the first two dying in childhood. When Martha married George in early 1759, just before Washington turned twenty-seven years old, her two surviving children—Jacky, age four and Patsy, age two—gained a new stepfather. In addition to two children, Martha brought into the marriage roughly six thousand acres and one hundred slaves. By virtue of his alliance with Martha, George became a much wealthier man.

Besides being what Joseph Ellis called a "Strenuous Squire," Washington became increasingly involved in local and then colonial affairs.[10] He ran for a seat in the Virginia House of Burgesses in 1759, the same year he married Martha, and won. While he did not stump in person, he did incur campaign expenses associated with running for office, including the cost of food, alcoholic beverages, and dances for potential voters. In his earlier years in the legislature, Washington spent more time on local affairs and attended irregularly. However, his concerns and those of other Virginia planters began to focus increasingly on issues affecting the whole colony and its relation with the mother country, Great Britain. For one, Washington and others became increasingly indebted to British financiers. Running plantations on a profitable basis became more and more difficult, and dependence on English cash and English manufactured goods became more and more burdensome. The squeeze only got worse after 1763.

Early that year, the Seven Years War between England and France (it's usually called the French and Indian War in the United States) was ended by treaty. The British had run up enormous debts in prosecuting the war; they felt that it had been fought in the interest of North American colonists, so the British turned to the colonists for revenue. In a departure from past practice, by which colonial legislatures raised taxes to pay for colonial needs, taxes on the American colonies were imposed directly by the British Parliament with no participation from the colonies themselves. In a back-and-forth struggle starting with the Sugar Act of 1764 and the Stamp Act of 1765, Americans tried to reach some accommodation with the British. George Washington became increasingly engaged in the struggle. In 1769, with his friend George Mason, he proposed a nonimportation plan by which Americans would make their own goods and thereby pressure the British for relief. Washington himself wore "homespun" clothing made in Virginia. The nonimportation plan failed to resolve the conflict, and it seemed to more and more colonists that some kind of armed conflict with the mother country loomed ahead.

At about this time, Washington had the first of many portraits of himself painted, this one by Charles Willson Peale. The year was 1772, and Washington wore his French and Indian War uniform, which had been retired for nearly fifteen years. Perhaps he thought it prudent, should war be in the future, to remind people of his military experience.

In 1772, Washington was forty years old. From what we know, he was an extremely active, ambitious, and acquisitive young man.[11] He was emotionally high-strung and somewhat impetuous in both love and war. He craved recognition and respect. He had surveyed and purchased land, acquired more land as payment for his military service, and absorbed even more into his holdings through the deaths of his father, his older half-brother, and his marriage to Martha. He had a sense of responsibility to others, most notably his demanding mother, his younger siblings, and his two stepchildren. He had become an active manager of the estate at Mount Vernon, having recently inherited it from Lawrence's widow, overseeing innovative agricultural techniques, planting new crops, and firmly directing a large enslaved labor force. The biography by James MacGregor Burns and Susan Dunn describes him as "a brave, disciplined, and tenacious military leader . . .; an acquisitive planter, harsh slave owner, and profit-oriented business man; . . . an ambitious, self-made man hungry for notice; a class-conscious member of the gentry who enjoyed dancing, cards and fox hunting."[12]

What of his attitudes and actions as a slave holder in a slave-holding society? Can we expand on the "harsh slave owner" attribution? Here are some details. The number of slaves Washington owned increased steadily in the fifteen years between his marriage in 1759 and his leaving for the First Continental Congress in 1774. For example, he acquired an additional 42 slaves between 1761 and 1773.[13] He owned 87 slaves in 1770 and 135 in 1775. There were complex relationships between slaves he owned himself and those owned by Martha. One interesting example comes from a slave named Ann Dandridge, most likely the daughter of Martha's father and a mixed-race African/Native American woman. She was, then, Martha's half-sister. Such children were common in Virginia slave society. Ann was much younger than Martha, probably just a few years older than Martha's own children. The Washingtons did not free Ann but kept her close to their white family. Some historians argue that that was the more humane way to treat her, given her prospects as a free black woman at that time in Virginia. True or false, her case is just one interesting instance of complex interracial relations that were a significant part of George Washington's life.

Washington himself had become an exacting, detail-oriented businessman following his career as a firm military leader. He exerted power through respect rather than affection. He would both reward and punish as he thought appropriate, but he sought to avoid the harshest punishment. As a slave owner, he was relatively kind. He used flogging as little as possible. He knew slaves individually and wrote in his diaries about his concern with their health. That concern seems to reflect natural human empathy as well as a wish to keep his "property" in good working order. He became more averse than many owners to selling slaves, especially in ways that would break up families. Slave families enjoyed no legal status, but Washington respected slave marriages and their family units.

His slaves had some freedom to travel independently and to hunt, fish, and raise crops for their own subsistence and commercial use. He eventually had black overseers on at least three of the five farms he owned.

Although there are benign aspects to Washington as slave owner, and although he grew increasingly disturbed by the glaring inhumanity and immorality of slavery, he was thoroughly immersed in the slave system. He would sell slaves deemed recalcitrant. He often wrote about them as he wrote about crop harvests and livestock, as economic entities only, and neither he nor Martha could understand why slaves whom they treated well did not reciprocate their kindness with loyalty. Both regarded slaves who escaped or attempted to escape as moral failures. Even though Washington never accepted the view that became more prominent in the decades leading up to the Civil War, that slaves were better off than free laborers in the North and better off than their brothers and sisters left behind in pagan Africa, he seemed blind to many of the horrors of slavery. Washington, like other owners, allowed most of his slaves to live in squalid conditions; slaves were given only annual allocations of clothing and food that was enough to keep them able to work from sunup to sundown six days a week, but not much more.

Historian Henry Wiencek argues that Washington reached his "moral nadir" regarding slaves in 1769 when he helped to organize a lottery to sell off the property of an estate that was indebted to Martha's family.[14] The property included fifty-five slaves. Gamblers could take a chance on winning one or more. Among those slaves, some would be sold in intact families, but others would be separated from family members. For whites, such lotteries were light-hearted events taking place at local taverns.[15] Like others, Washington was willing to sport with human lives and human families in order to settle debts. Although Washington may have been kinder than some, his actions were very much in the mainstream for Virginia slave holders.

In the early 1770s, like other delegates in the House of Burgesses, Washington grew increasingly restive with arbitrary English rule. He knew that conflict with England had led to such events as the Boston Massacre in 1770 and the Boston Tea Party in 1773. He worried that peaceful resolution with Great Britain was becoming more and more remote. Though not fully engaged in Burgesses discussions, he was a significant enough figure to gather the third most votes among the seven delegates selected for the First Continental Congress that met in Philadelphia during the fall of 1774. His military experience was not lost on other participants.

The spring of the next year, 1775, changed world history. Again from Massachusetts came alarming news. On April 19, British troops left Boston, where they had been quartered for months, and marched to Lexington and Concord to capture rebel arms. The "shot heard 'round the world" was fired on Lexington Green that morning; skirmishes took place all day until the British finally returned to Boston, much bloodied by American minutemen. The Second Continental Congress met, as previously scheduled, on May 10. George Washington was again a delegate. Within a month, Congress voted to create a Continental Army. John Adams from Massachusetts maneuvered to have Washington named commander in chief. He was elected unanimously. At that moment, he was the only member of that army. He would have to go to Boston to create it out of the several New England militias.

When George Washington reached Cambridge, Massachusetts, to take command of the Continental Army in early July of 1775, a second battle, much larger than the fighting on April 19, had just taken place. It has since been known as the Battle of Bunker Hill. It was almost certainly a surprise to Washington that African Americans fought in both Massachusetts battles. At Lexington, a slave, serving as a minuteman, was wounded in the initial exchange of gunfire. He was Prince Estabrook, simply noted in the accounts of the action as "A Negro man."[16] Estabrook recovered from his wounds and served with the Continental Army throughout the war. He was then freed by his owner. A better-known African American, Peter Salem, fought at Bunker Hill. He is often credited with killing a high-ranking British officer, Major Pitcairn, and appears prominently in artist John Trumbull's famous painting of that battle.[17]

Finding black fighting men integrated into several militia was only one of the surprises facing Washington when he arrived to take command. Perhaps most unexpected was the general attitude and fitness of the New England militias. Washington complained that "they are an exceedingly dirty & nasty people"[18] and disparaged "an unaccountable kind of stupidity."[19] The camps were awash in filth, and independent Yankees showed little respect for authority. Washington's experience and force of personality corrected many of the problems of disorganization and lax discipline, but the question of black fighters was beyond anything in his worldview. One way to get a handle on this new challenge was to distinguish slaves from free blacks. Addressing the question of slaves in the army was relatively easy. There was widespread belief, even in Massachusetts, that having slaves fighting for independence was dishonorable and brought disgrace to the fighting men. Slaves were banned from service. Free blacks presented a different problem.

Initially, Washington believed that any blacks—free or slave—should be banned from service, indeed mustered out of militias in which they had already fought. Washington convened a Council of War in November, which unanimously banned the enlistment of slaves and, overwhelmingly, the service of free blacks. But that did not resolve the issue. Affected African Americans simply did not go away. As happened throughout US history, black men and women asserted themselves. Many found ways to express their strong wish to fight for American independence. Washington seemed touched by their efforts. The next month he changed course in part and allowed free blacks who had previously been in the militia to return.

Washington's thinking about blacks was probably deeply affected by a poem and letter he received about the same time from a young enslaved woman, Phillis Wheatley. Wheatley had been purchased in a slave market in Boston in 1761 by Susanna Wheatley, the wife of a wealthy merchant. At the time, she was probably six or seven years old. *Phillis* was the name of the slaver that brought her to America, probably from Gambia. Wheatley clearly had unusual abilities; as a house slave, she was given the opportunity to read, study, and develop her literary skills. In 1775, she sent her poem to Washington, praising his leadership. It concluded "Proceed, great chief, with virtue on thy side, Thy ev'ry action let the goddess guide. A crown, a mansion, and a throne that shine, With gold unfading, WASHINGTON! be thine."[20] Washington was affected enough to write an exceptionally warm letter in return, inviting Wheatley to visit him in Cambridge: "I shall be happy to see a person so favored by the Muses, and to whom Nature has been so liberal and beneficent in her dispensations."[21]

In short, as a result of largely unforeseeable events, Washington was encountering and responding openly to African Americans who supported the Revolutionary cause. By the time the Continental Army left Boston for New York in mid-1776, it was racially integrated. Historians have noted that it was the last fully integrated United States Army until Korea or possibly Vietnam.[22]

Events and experience moved Washington further. By 1777, the third year of the war, enlistment was an acute problem. It was difficult to recruit and retain soldiers for a stable, trained Continental Army. Enlistment prospects were not helped by a series of defeats in New York and around Philadelphia, punctuated by just enough success at places such as Trenton and Princeton to keep the prospect of victory alive, but barely. In his inaugural address in 2009, President Obama quoted a public statement Washington wrote during those difficult times: "Let it be told to the future world . . . that in the depth of winter, when nothing but hope and virtue could survive . . . that the city and the country, alarmed at our common danger, came to forth to meet [it]."[23] When the army went into winter camp the next year at Valley Forge, Pennsylvania, in 1777–78, the army was desperately short of manpower. A solution was proposed by General James Varnum of Rhode Island. With Washington's assent, the state would recruit a battalion of black soldiers, some who were slaves. Washington quickly agreed. Thus the First Rhode Island Regiment was formed with large numbers of African American recruits.

The success of the Rhode Island plan spurred an idealistic South Carolinian, John Laurens, son of former Continental Congress President Henry Laurens, a close friend of Washington, to propose in 1779 that black troops also be raised in his home state. Henry Laurens subsequently asked Washington for his support and was shocked when Washington refused. Historian Henry Wiencek speculates that Washington worried that the plan would work all too well.[24] If slaves joined the army with the promise of emancipation, the whole slave system might come unraveled. Among other things, this would cost Washington a good deal of money. His holdings in slaves were substantial. This episode indicates how conflicted and inconsistent Washington could be regarding slaves and African Americans. His jumbled thoughts and priorities

are revealed even further in correspondence with Lund Washington, a distant cousin who managed Mount Vernon in Washington's absence during the
war. Based on financial considerations, George Washington directed Lund to
sell some slaves but insisted that such sales not break up families. As noted,
Washington recognized slave marriages, even though the Commonwealth of
Virginia did not. Lund Washington expressed his exasperation with George's
constraints. Meeting George's financial objectives through slave sales would be
accomplished much more simply if slaves' family ties could be ignored, as they
generally were.

While Washington may have been ambivalent about authorizing slaves to
fight, the South was not. Its views became crystal clear when, in March of 1779,
the Continental Congress unanimously passed a resolution providing for the
emancipation of slaves who fought for the duration of the war and compensation for their owners. The resolution went nowhere because it could not pass
muster with the state legislatures in either South Carolina or Georgia. This was
true even though both states would soon be overwhelmed by British sieges.
While those states wanted independence, they seemed to prefer British rule to
freedom for themselves accompanied by freedom for slaves. Their economic
system based on slavery might have been more important than independent
nationhood.

Despite Southern opposition to having blacks fight for freedom—for the
country or for themselves—the military reality was that African American soldiers were needed. Only a minority of the white population supported the
revolution during the best of times, and it is highly unlikely that George Washington could have won the war without black troops. His reliance on African American soldiers was illustrated, as we noted earlier, in the attacks led by
Alexander Hamilton, and also the aforementioned Colonel John Laurens, at
Yorktown. Black soldiers played central roles in that combat. Perhaps less was
made of it at the time because black fighting men were taken for granted. As
Henry Wiencek argues, by the summer of 1776, when the Continental Congress declared independence from Great Britain, the Continental Army had
spontaneously integrated itself.[25] Conventional wisdom generally overlooks the
role of African American fighters in the Revolutionary War; their role at Yorktown is a surprise to many people today. It wasn't a surprise to the rank and file
of the army in 1781.

The battle at Yorktown is commonly regarded as the end of the Revolutionary War. In fact, the war did not end for almost two more years, although
there was no more major combat. A preliminary peace agreement was negotiated in late 1782, but the final Treaty of Paris granting American independence was not signed until September of 1783. Washington did not resign his
military commission until December of that year, when the final treaty was
signed, sealed, and delivered. During that final year of the war, cross-pressures
regarding African Americans worked on Washington. His responses suggest the
mixed, indeed confused, thoughts he was juggling during that crucial year. One

pressure resulted from the terms of the settlement itself. The Treaty of Paris stipulated that enslaved Americans who had been freed by the British, as part of the English effort to undermine the revolution, must be returned to their owners. Under the pressure of slave owners come to reclaim their property, Washington commenced a series of negotiations with British Commander Sir Guy Carleton in New York. Carleton refused to honor the agreement regarding slaves, claiming that the British had promised them freedom and he would abide by that promise, no matter how the treaty read. Washington was furious, but he was powerless to get the slaves back. His actions suggest that at this time Washington still regarded slaves as simply "a species of property." He may have been open to a more nuanced view of the humanity of both slaves and free African Americans, but his view that slaves were a species of property seemed stubbornly resistant to change.

A different side of Washington's thinking is revealed in correspondence with the Marquis de Lafayette. Lafayette was an idealistic Frenchman, similar in many ways to John Laurens. Reaching America in 1777 at age twenty, he was one of a number of French soldiers who provided crucial help to the Continental Army during several important Revolutionary War battles. In Lafayette's case, that included Yorktown. Twenty-five years younger than Washington, the two established an intimate father-son-like relationship. Washington was impressed by Lafayette's military skill and bravery as well as his personal generosity and idealism. In early 1783, Lafayette informed Washington of the impending agreement ending the war and took the occasion to address the meaning of America and its revolution in world history. He well understood the contradiction between American ideals, as articulated in the Declaration of Independence, and "the peculiar institution" of slavery. He proposed to Washington a plan to emancipate slaves: if Washington freed his slaves and set them up as tenant farmers, it would serve as a powerful example to other slaveholders and the country as a whole. Washington expressed a willingness to join Lafayette "in so laudable a work" but declined to get into specifics.[26] They agreed to meet personally to discuss how to proceed.

Before the two could meet, Washington finally resigned his commission from the Continental Army, in December 1783, and returned to Mount Vernon. Returning military power to civilian authority was an historical anomaly, but civilian control of the military and opposition to a standing army were fundamental principles of the revolution. Among those who found this stance baffling was King George III of England. The story goes that he asked the expatriate American painter Benjamin West what Washington would do after the war. When West replied that Washington would simply go back to his farms, the King sputtered, "If he does that, he will be the greatest man in the world."[27]

Lafayette and Washington did meet the next year at Mount Vernon. They discussed Lafayette's ideas but did not agree on a plan that Washington might implement. Lafayette himself established a plantation for freed slaves in French Guiana. In a later letter, Washington praised "the benevolence of your heart" and agreed that emancipation "assuredly ought to be effected" but thought it best done by legislative authority.[28]

In light of these various deliberations, what can we say about Washington's attitudes toward slavery and blacks as he started what historian Joseph Ellis characterized as his postwar "Introspective Interlude" in 1784?[29] How does our understanding of him at age fifty-two differ from the description Burns and Dunn offered of him at age forty—"a harsh slave owner" and a man "principally concerned with his own self-interest and advancement?"[30] Perhaps he was less harsh and more willing to show respect for the humanity of slaves and the integrity of their families. This change in behavior might seem like a minor adjustment in the overall world that historian David Brion Davis calls "Inhuman Bondage."[31] As small as it might be, it reflects significantly larger changes in Washington's moral thought and moral feeling. During the war, he experienced blacks who were brave, dedicated, intelligent, talented, and effective. He also saw that black men and white men could work together in groups in such a way that differences in color faded in significance. What mattered was what one could do, not the color of one's skin.

Beyond his military experiences, Washington was exposed during the war to powerful philosophical Enlightenment ideas. Concepts such as natural rights and equality entered the revolutionary vocabulary and pressed against the prevailing belief system that was part of Washington's intellectual heritage. In the Declaration of Independence, Washington's fellow Virginian Thomas Jefferson eloquently expressed the core beliefs and commitments of the American Revolution just a year after Washington took command of the Continental Army in Cambridge: "We hold these truths to be self-evident that all men are created equal, that they are endowed by their Creator with certain unalienable Rights, that among these are Life, Liberty and the pursuit of Happiness."[32] Washington was obviously aware of these convictions. They had been part of the revolutionary discourse starting in the 1760s. It was certainly clear to Washington that Lafayette's opposition to slavery was influenced by such principles. The contradiction between revolutionary ideology and slavery was obvious. Samuel Johnson in London said it best in 1775: "How is it that we hear the loudest yelps for liberty among the drivers of negroes."[33] Washington was not immune to these contradictions. In short, while Washington's public actions regarding slaves changed little during the course of the war, his thinking clearly had. Time would tell how this change in his private beliefs and attitudes would affect his public behavior as he was once again drawn away from Mount Vernon to the political sphere.

George Washington had been away from Mount Vernon for more than eight years when he returned at the end of 1783. Except for a brief visit during the Yorktown campaign of 1781, he had left the management of his estates to others. He treasured the role of America's great man who could live out his final years at his beloved home. He had achieved greater fame than any person in the Western world, and he would have been content to stay retired. The role of American

Cincinnatus appealed to him. However, his "Introspective Interlude" would last just over three years. The government that the states formed during the revolution was failing. Under the Articles of Confederation and Perpetual Union, ratified in 1781, the country had difficulty raising revenue and paying debts or taking on a range of interstate projects. It had no executive or judiciary. Its capacity to wage war effectively, given the experience during the revolution, was worrisome. A number of political leaders believed that a radical overhaul was needed.

Virginia and Virginians took the lead. James Madison was a driving force. The state of Virginia invited representatives of all the states to meet in Annapolis, Maryland, in 1786 to discuss revisions to the Articles. Only five states sent delegates, but the meeting concluded with a call to have another such meeting in Philadelphia the next year, 1787. The meeting was of dubious legality; it was not initially authorized by the Confederation government. Madison and others knew that such a convention would have legitimacy if, and only if, the most famous and admired man in the country could be persuaded to attend.

While Washington was enjoying playing the Cincinnatus role, he was also in active correspondence with a number of former military officers, including Alexander Hamilton and Henry Knox, and important political figures, including Madison. He was well aware of the difficulties with which the government struggled and the disgust and distrust with which many of the Americans he most highly respected viewed it. Thomas Jefferson (from Paris) and Madison pressured Washington to attend the Philadelphia meeting. Washington spent much of the winter of 1786–87 deliberating whether or not to go. He risked putting his well-earned reputation, perhaps his dearest psychological possession, at risk in a project of uncertain success or legitimacy. But events had changed his thinking, especially the so-called Shays' Rebellion in western Massachusetts in 1786. Daniel Shays had been an officer in the Continental Army, one of many who had not been paid for service during the war. There was little prospect that he would be paid. Many such veterans were forced to sell back-pay certificates issued years before at far below their face value. As the states raised taxes, trying to pay their own debts, farmers such as Shays were pressed for money they did not have. Shays led an armed rebellion to protest both national and state government actions, or inactions. Washington feared that the ineptitude of the Confederation government would create more disturbances like Shays', and that it would not be able to take appropriate action to resolve them. With some reluctance, he agreed to go to Philadelphia.

It was no surprise when Washington was unanimously elected president of the Constitutional Convention. He actually presided over deliberations fairly infrequently since the delegates generally met as a Committee of Whole so that debates could be less formal and members could be free to explore ideas and change their minds. Washington seldom spoke during meetings but talked actively to key figures in after-hour dinners and informal conversations. His presence encouraged moderation and amity as well as thorough exploration of central issues.

One of the most divisive of those issues was slavery. It became apparent that concessions to slavery would have to be made in order for there to be a union of all states. South Carolina and Georgia insisted on keeping the slave trade open. It was allowed until 1808. The most important concession, perhaps, was the three-fifths clause in Article I, Section 2, near the very beginning of the Constitution. It apportioned representatives to Congress, and electoral votes in presidential elections, according to population. The populations counted would include "the whole number of free persons" and "three-fifths of all other persons."[34] "Other persons" meant slaves. Even though they were deemed property and obviously could not vote, their numbers, or three-fifths of their numbers, gave slave-holding states greater sway in Congress and more weight in choosing the president. This was not a trivial matter. For example, in the election of 1800, the swollen number of Southern electoral votes, based on the three-fifths clause, allowed Virginian Thomas Jefferson to defeat incumbent President John Adams from Massachusetts.

There is no definite way to know what George Washington thought of these compromises. Although in private he was increasingly uncomfortable with slavery, he likely understood that such accords were necessary to achieve what he believed was the most important goal of the convention: establishing a viable federal government. He was clearly aware that agreeing on a constitution, getting it ratified by the states, and having the states remain in the union once they had joined was no sure thing. He likely believed that the compromises were necessary.

Many scholars believe that the North gave too many concessions to the South, even though the South acceded to such stipulations as control of trade by majorities in Congress rather than two-thirds. And it is possible that Washington felt the same. But producing any agreement at all was a monumental task, and there were few who would sacrifice the union in an effort—probably futile—to try, for example, to terminate the slave trade earlier. Many recognized the contradiction between revolutionary principles and the institution of slavery but were willing to live with that contradiction.

Research in social psychology shows that the "cognitive dissonance" produced by such conflicting thoughts creates real discomfort, both physical and psychological. For many, one means of reducing such dissonance is simply to push it out of consciousness. This happens much more often than we realize because it occurs unconsciously.[35] It allows for a positive image of ourselves and tidy minds. Richard Brookhiser writes that people, including Washington and ourselves, "encompass their contradictions by not thinking about them."[36] But Washington used denial less often than other founding fathers, and, as we shall see, his not doing so produced important results before his death.

A final note on the Constitutional Convention. David Brion Davis speculates that Georgia and South Carolina might have refused to join the union if they did not prevail on slavery issues in Philadelphia. In that case, he suggests, they might have united with the other British slave-holding colonies in the West

Indies and "might possibly have saved the United States from a Civil War."[37] If there were no Civil War, one wonders whether slavery in North America would ever have ended.

The Constitutional Convention produced a strong executive. The president of the United States was not given the total veto power that some wanted, but the office would be occupied by a single individual rather than an executive group and would not be constrained by any executive council, such as was specified in several state governments. The executive was given substantial power and was described in much less specific terms than the legislature because the delegates knew that George Washington would be the first president, and they trusted him to set the right precedents. In keeping with his selection as commander in chief of the Continental Army and president of the Constitutional Convention, he was elected president unanimously in 1789.

Washington's task was clear, but the means for accomplishing it would be exceedingly difficult and delicate. He had to establish a working government. It was by no means a given that he, or anyone, could succeed. Thus Benjamin Franklin's reputed reply to a woman who asked what the Constitutional Convention had produced: "A republic, madam, if you can keep it."[38] Washington knew that the new government was fragile and that sectional controversies would blow it apart in less time that it was put together. Thus during the first Congress in his first term, Washington chose to avoid the subject of slavery. In February 1790, only ten months into his administration, a group of Quakers submitted a petition to Congress advocating the gradual abolition of slavery. The Constitution ruled out congressional action on the slave trade until 1808, but it was silent on emancipation. Perhaps the subject was unthinkable. But the petition was brought to Congress and endorsed by Benjamin Franklin, who, next to Washington, was the most prestigious revolutionary in the new nation. Washington wanted the issue to go away. He believed it would end the Republican experiment before it had a decent chance to succeed. A Georgia congressman threatened as much, saying the South "will resist one tyranny as soon as another."[39] With the help of Congressman James Madison, the issue was shelved.

Responding to the abolition proposal was the one chance in Washington's presidency when he might have publicly supported the idea of emancipation. We can only wonder as to his thoughts at the time. Historian Joseph Ellis writes that there is "no evidence that he struggled with the decision."[40] Washington's focus was clearly on doing what he needed to do to keep the new government afloat. On the other hand, Ron Chernow's 2010 biography asserts that the public could not possibly know "how much he wrestled inwardly with the issue," implying that he struggled a good deal.[41] It is very hard to know. Washington had expressed in correspondence and conversation with Lafayette and others that he found slavery morally problematic, but that view may not have aroused "cognitive dissonance" when he declined to support the Quakers in 1790.

George Washington acted very publicly in another way to strengthen slavery during the middle of his presidency. In response to Southern slave holders,

Congress passed, and Washington signed, a Fugitive Slave Act in 1793. The law strengthened the constitutional provision in Article IV for the return of persons "held to service or labor in one state . . . escaping into another" that stated that they "shall be delivered up . . . to whom such service or labor may be due."[42] The 1793 Act allowed slave holders to cross state lines to recover their "property."

Also conspicuous by its absence is a nonact by Washington at the end of his presidency. In his famous Farewell Address, he raised several important topics—the importance of national unity and avoiding sectionalism, foreign alliances, and political parties—but did not mention slavery. It was the sectional issue that might destroy national unity.

We get another angle on Washington and slavery during his presidential terms. New York City was the capital of the United States when George Washington was inaugurated as the first president there on April 30, 1789. Slavery was not outlawed in New York until 1799, but Washington was well aware of anti-slavery sentiment in the North. All the New England states had passed laws abolishing slavery, either immediately or gradually, by 1784. So while Washington brought some of his slaves to New York, he made efforts to keep their profile as low as possible. When the capital, and the president's residence, was moved to Philadelphia in 1790, the year after Washington's inauguration, he faced a different problem. Slavery had been illegal in Pennsylvania for ten years. More troubling for the president, the law stated that slaves brought into the state were free if they resided there for more than six months. Both George and Martha Washington conspired with the president's secretary, Tobias Lear, to shuttle slaves back and forth across state lines so that the six-month clock could be reset every time one left Pennsylvania. For example, Martha took several slaves on an overnight trip to nearby Trenton, New Jersey. Exacerbating the problem was that most of the slaves the Washingtons brought north belonged to Martha, or more properly, the Custis estate. The president would be responsible for them, and if they were freed, he would not only lose their labor but he would owe the Custis estate their value.

Thus both publicly and privately Washington acted in ways to reinforce American slavery during his presidency. Still the sentiments he expressed during the 1780s, which the Quakers had tried to use to gain the president's support for their 1790 emancipation petition, were not simply put aside. They continued to disturb George Washington's mental equilibrium. By late 1793, Washington had begun to devise plans for the eventual freeing of his slaves. He wrote that the whole matter of slavery was something he did "not like to think, much less talk of."[43] But it would not go away. The next year he devised a scheme whereby he would free slaves on large plots of his land, sell those parcels to wealthy farmers and planters who would in return hire the freed slaves. He wrote that the most "powerful" motive "for the accomplishment of these things" was "to liberate a certain species of property which I possess, very repugnantly to my own feelings."[44] The plan was too complicated to succeed. Washington could not get what he regarded as a fair price, and some of the slaves at each location belonged to him, others to the Custis estate. The plans do, however, reveal that as Washington contemplated the end of his presidency and his legacy, he sought some way to free both himself and his slaves from the institution into which they were both born.

Figure 1.2 William Lee served George Washington for many decades. He was the only slave the first president freed by name in his will.

John Trumbull, "George Washington and his servant William Lee," 1780, oil on canvas. The Metropolitan Museum of Art, New York, courtesy of Art Resource, Inc.

George Washington left office in 1797. His two-term vice president, John Adams, succeeded him. In leaving the presidency voluntarily, Washington set an enormously important precedent in American politics. Even someone regarded as the greatest and most admired would not serve as president until he died. This was no monarchy. King George III might again have commented that Washington's giving up the presidency, like retiring to his farm after the war, made him perhaps the greatest man in the world. Adams wrote that at the transitional inauguration, Washington seemed to revel in being released from the cares of office. He wrote to his wife Abigail, "Methought I heard him say, 'Ay! I am fairly out and you fairly in! See which of us will be happiest.'"[45]

George Washington lived less than three years after his eight years as president. In that period of time, he settled on a plan for addressing slavery in the only way he thought might produce a good result. He would, as Lafayette had urged him fifteen years earlier, set a personal example. He would free his slaves in his will. The matter was not simple. Some of the slaves at Mount Vernon were his, but others were Martha's; many slave families combined both. But unlike almost any other plan, it was one he could largely control himself. The result was George Washington's last will and testament, a most remarkable American document.

Written in his own hand, without the help of highly educated advisers such as Alexander Hamilton and James Madison, both of whom had aided in drafting various versions of the Farewell Address, here was Washington's final pronouncement on slavery. He would do what none of the other prominent slave-owning revolutionary leaders would do: he would free his slaves. As Lafayette had urged him sixteen years earlier, he would set an example. The language of the "item" in the will about slavery and its placement are both remarkable. The document, written over a period of weeks and signed on July 9, 1799, five months before Washington's death, is twenty-three pages long. Washington initialed each page. There would be no ambiguity about whose words these were.

Slavery is taken up near the very beginning. Second only to a brief paragraph leaving his "Estate, real and personal. . . . To my dearly beloved wife Martha Washington," the will reads "Upon the decease of my wife, it is my Will and desire, that all the slaves which I hold in my own right, shall receive their freedom." Again, there is no ambiguity. But the will goes further:

> And whereas among those who will receive freedom according to this device, there may be some, who from old age or bodily infirmities, and others who on account of their infancy, that will be unable to support themselves; it is my Will and desire that all who come under the first and second description shall be comfortably clothed and fed by my heirs while they live.

Washington would not simply leave former slaves on their own in a hostile world.

Beyond providing for their care as dependents, Washington wanted to prepare them for independence. In an even more extraordinary departure from local norms regarding slavery, the document directed that orphan slaves, who would be supported until they were twenty-five years old, would "(by their Masters or Mistresses), . . . be taught to read and write, & brought up to some useful occupation." Not only does teaching slaves to read and write go against custom and law, it reflected Washington's belief that former slaves could be educated to live fruitfully in a mixed race society. From his experience in the Revolutionary War, he had discarded any racist belief he may have entertained about the innate inferiority of African Americans. If given a chance, they could succeed.

Washington continued, reflecting his life-long concern with detail and his long-standing opposition to breaking up slave families and selling them without their assent: "And I do hereby expressly forbid the sale, or transportation out of the said Commonwealth [Virginia] of any Slave I may die possessed of, under any pretence whatsoever." One can feel the language getting more emphatic, leaving little room for interpretation or equivocation. And then even more forcefully: "And I do moreover most pointedly, and most solemnly enjoin it upon my Executors hereafter named, or the survivors of them, to see that this clause respecting Slaves, and every part thereof be religiously fulfilled . . . without evasion, neglect or delay." Returning to the subject of care for slaves after his death, he charges his executors with "Seeing that a regular & permanent fund be established for their support so long as there are subjects requiring it; not trusting to the uncertain provision to be made by individuals."[46] As it turned out, some former slaves were supported by Washington's estate until 1833. Washington clearly realized that these provisions of his will would not make those left behind, including perhaps Martha, very happy. He dictated them as unequivocally and strongly as possible.

For the most part, George Washington's struggles with the institution of slavery were internal ones. He avoided public action on the issue with little apparent regret or psychological distress, either before or after his decisions. During the Revolutionary War, he initially banned black troops, but when manpower needs arose and the appeals of free blacks who genuinely wanted to fight were heard, he changed course. His thinking about what African Americans could do was partly affected by his correspondence with Phillis Wheatley. Later in the war, he was pleased to have Rhode Island raise regiments that were mostly black. During the debates in the Constitutional Convention, Washington was content to listen both to arguments against slavery and the threats by Southerners demanding to extend the slave trade, having some representation based on nonvoting enslaved populations, and provisions for returning runaway slaves without intervening. As a detail person who followed the deliberations closely, and would have read the final document produced by the Committee of Style and Arrangement, he no doubt noticed that the words "slave" and "slavery" never blemished the final product. While George Washington did nothing to address the contradictions of slavery while he was president, he did write a remarkable personal document, his last will and testament, that made clear his belief that somehow the nation should emancipate slaves and invite them to participate in American society.

Notes

1 William Byrd, II, The Westover Manuscripts: Containing the History of the Dividing Line betwixt Virginia and North Carolina; A Journey to the Land of Eden, A.D. 1733; and A Progress to the Mines (Petersburg: Edmund and Julian C. Ruffin, 1841); Henry Wiencek, *An Imperfect God: George Washington, His Slaves, and the Creation of America* (New York: Farrar, Straus and Giroux, 2003), p. 45.

2 Douglas R. Egerton, *Death or Liberty: African Americans and Revolutionary America* (New York, Oxford University Press, 2009), p. 90.

3 See http://ancientlights.org/firstri.html.

4 Eric Foner, *Forever Free: The Story of Emancipation and Reconstruction* (New York: Knopf, 2005).

5 Wiencek, p.45.

6 *Ibid.*

7 See https://www.census.gov/history/www/through_the_decades/overview/1790.html.

8 James M. Burns and Susan Dunn, *George Washington* (New York: Times Books, 2004), p. 7.

9 James Thomas Flexner, *Washington, The Indispensable Man* (Boston: Back Bay Books edition, 1994), p. 5.

10 Joseph J. Ellis, *His Excellency, George Washington* (New York: Random House, 2004).

11 James M. Burns and Susan Dunn, *George Washington* (New York: Times Books, 2004), p. 18.

12 *Ibid.*

13 Ron Chernow, *Washington: A Life* (New York: The Penguin Press, 2010), p. 111.

14 Wiencek, p. 188.

15 Chernow, p. 118.

16 Walter R. Borneman, *American Spring: Lexington, Concord, and the Road to Revolution* (New York: Little, Brown, 2014), p. 21.

17 See http://www.celebrateboston.com/biography/peter-salem.htm.

18 Edward M. Taylor, *George Washington, the Ideal Patriot* (New York: Eaton & Mains, 1897), p. 189.

19 See http://founders.archives.gov/documents/Washington/03-01-02-0270.

20 Robin Santos Doak, *Phillis Wheatley: Slave and Poet* (Minneapolis: Compass Point Books, 2006), p. 74.

21 Kathryn Kilby Borland, *Phillis Wheatley: Young Revolutionary Poet* (Carmel, IN: Patria Press, 2005), p. 105.

22 Joseph J. Ellis, *American Creation: Triumphs and Tragedies at the Founding of the Republic* (New York: Knopf, 2007), p. 35.

23 Barack Obama, First Inaugural Address, January 20, 2009. http://www.whitehouse.gov/blog/inaugural-address.

24 Wiencek, p. 188.

25 *Ibid.*

26 See http://www.mountvernon.org/educational-resources/encyclopedia/lafayettes-plan-slavery.

27 See http://www.cato.org/publications/commentary/man-who-would-not-be-king.

28 See http://www.mountvernon.org/educational-resources/encyclopedia/lafayettes-plan-slavery.

29 Ellis, *His Excellency*, p. 147.

30 Burns and Dunn, p. 18.

31 David Brion Davis, *Inhuman Bondage: The Rise and Fall of Slavery in the New World* (New York: Oxford University Press, 2006).

32 See http://www.archives.gov/exhibits/charters/declaration_transcript.html.

33 See http://www.samueljohnson.com/slavery.html.

34 See http://www.archives.gov/exhibits/charters/constitution_transcript.html.

35 George R. Goethals and Richard F. Reckman, The Perception of Consistency in Attitudes. *Journal of Experimental Social Psychology, 9,* 1973, pp. 491–501.

36 Richard Brookhiser, *Founding Father: Rediscovering George Washington* (New York: Simon & Schuster, 2006), p. 179.

37 Davis, p. 155.

38 See http://www.aljazeera.com/indepth/opinion/2013/12/republic-if-can-keep-it-2013122762222162319.html.

39 Chernow, p. 623.

40 Ellis, p. 202.

41 Chernow, p. 624.

42 See http://www.archives.gov/exhibits/charters/constitution_transcript.html.

43 Peter R. Henriques, *Realistic Visionary: A Portrait of George Washington* (Charlottesville: University of Virginia Press, 2006), p. 145.

44 Henriques, p. 161.

45 Chernow, p. 767.

46 George Washington, Last Will and Testament. http://founders.archives.gov/documents/Washington/06-04-02-0404-0001.

2

THOMAS JEFFERSON

Figure 2.1 Thomas Jefferson, the Founders' most eloquent proponent of equality, became increasingly sympathetic to the politics of Southern slaveholders after his eight years as president.

Charles Willson Peale, "Thomas Jefferson," 1791, oil on canvas. Independence National Historical Park, Philadelphia, Pennsylvania. Public domain, via Wikimedia Commons.

In June 1776, not long after he arrived in Philadelphia to rejoin the Continental Congress, Thomas Jefferson was appointed to a committee charged with drafting a "declaration of independence." Congress believed that the reasons for separating the American colonies from Great Britain should be explained not only to people in their home states but also the entire world. The war against the British had lasted for well over a year, and most of the delegates in Philadelphia had abandoned hope for reconciliation with the mother country. Jefferson was joined by John Adams, the congressman who had been pushing hardest for independence, and Benjamin Franklin, the very highly respected scientist, inventor, writer, and philanthropist. Two other well-regarded members, Roger Sherman and Robert Livingston, were also appointed.

Jefferson, at age thirty-three, was the youngest of the group, but he was widely admired for earlier writings explaining the American point of view. He was eloquent, incisive, and well versed in the principles of Enlightenment philosophy that gripped many Americans. His words effectively expounded revolutionary ideas such as natural rights. Based on his talents and accomplishments, he was the obvious choice to write a first draft of the Declaration. The opening passages were tweaked by the committee just a bit, and they are now the most famous. In the first sentence, Jefferson wrote that "a decent respect to the opinions of mankind requires" an explanation of the "causes which impel . . . separation." The eloquent second sentence is familiar not only to most Americans, but to peoples it has inspired the world over. In final form it read: "We hold these truths to be self-evident, that all men are created equal, that they are endowed by their Creator with certain unalienable Rights, that among these are Life, Liberty and the pursuit of Happiness."[1] The lasting importance of these words is reflected in Abraham Lincoln's most famous speech, his Gettysburg Address. There Lincoln began, "Four score and seven years ago, our fathers brought forth on this continent, a new nation, conceived in liberty and dedicated to the proposition that all men are created equal."[2] If one does the math, four score and seven years ago, counting back from 1863, was 1776. It was the ringing words of the Declaration that Lincoln asserted as the defining principles of the American nation. Jefferson's words have what Malcolm Gladwell calls "stickiness."[3] They are extremely memorable, not only for the ideas they express, but for the elegance with which they are formulated.

But not all of Jefferson's initial draft was left as much intact. One section took on the institution that made the draft's statement of high-minded principles appear to be a low-minded form of hypocrisy. How could slavery be excused in a new nation based on principles of liberty and equality? Once again, we recall Samuel Johnson asking the year before the Declaration, "How is it that we hear the loudest *yelps* for liberty among the drivers of Negroes?"[4] Though a slave owner himself, Jefferson was well aware of the evil of "inhuman bondage."[5] In his draft, he described that evil forcefully, though he blamed it on King George: "He has waged cruel war against humanity itself, violating its most sacred rights of life and liberty in the persons of a distant people who never offended him, captivating and carrying them to slavery in another hemisphere, or to incur death in their transportation thither." He continued in that vein, writing of an "execrable commerce" and an "assemblage of horrors."[6]

To Jefferson's great consternation, this section was deleted by Congress. He was highly attached to and very proud of every word of his draft and reacted sullenly and caustically—but only in private—to each revision. In his own notes, he attributed the removal of his passage about the slave trade to the political interests of planters in South Carolina and Georgia. There he seems to cast himself as morally opposed to both the slave trade and slavery itself, despite the fact that he enslaved more than one hundred of his fellow human beings and had brought a number to take care of his personal needs in Philadelphia. Jefferson implies that others in Congress were less morally advanced and less bold. The truth is much more complicated.

Jefferson consistently wrote about the immorality of slavery. He raised questions about the slave trade in one of his first writings in 1774. Then, in a famous letter of 1820, when Jefferson was seventy-seven years old, he wrote despairingly of slavery, saying "we have the wolf by the ear" and that "justice" implied letting the wolf go, and effecting "a general emancipation."[7] He wanted very much to be remembered for his opposition to the institution of slavery. From these bits of evidence, we might conclude that Jefferson was one of the leaders in eliminating or at least containing slavery, in accord with the natural rights principles about which he wrote so movingly in 1776. However, Jefferson's contribution to the unfolding events that led to the belated abolition of slavery in 1865 is highly ambiguous, at best. In the same "wolf by the ear" letter of 1820, he wrote "we can neither hold him or safely let him go." He worried that emancipated slaves were likely to turn on their former masters. Thus, "self-preservation" leaned against "justice." As this letter suggests, Jefferson's entire political and personal life was marked by an internal contradiction between his lyrical expressions of morality regarding liberty and slavery and his inability to find a way to move forward toward emancipation, publicly or privately. The contradictions and their immobilizing implications challenge our understanding of Thomas Jefferson.

According to Jefferson biographer R. B. Bernstein, family folklore held that Thomas Jefferson's first memory, when he was a two-year-old, was of "a trusted slave carrying him . . . on a pillow" on horseback as his family moved down the James River toward Richmond from the family home, Shadwell, near Charlottesville, Virginia.[8] At the end, when he died on July 4, 1826, the fiftieth anniversary of the Declaration of Independence, another trusted slave was the only person who could understand how the former president wanted his pillow placed for comfort. Slaves and slavery were around him his whole life.

That life began on April 13, 1743, at Shadwell, a plantation on the Rivana River in Albemarle County, Virginia. He was the third child and first son of Peter Jefferson, a respected farmer, surveyor, and mapmaker, and Jane Randolph, a daughter of one of Virginia's wealthiest and most prestigious families. He was educated primarily by private tutors and was an excellent student, especially in languages and music. He became an accomplished violin player; by age nine, he enjoyed singing with his much-beloved older sister, Jane. He was known to hum

Figure 2.2 Jefferson and other owners of slaves convinced themselves both that slaves were content with their lot while simultaneously believing that slave uprisings, such as that led by Denmark Vesey in 1822 in South Carolina, were a constant danger to Southern society.

Charles Wilbert White, "Denmark Vesey," 1943, charcoal and white gouache on illustration board. Gibbes Museum of Art/Carolina Art Association, 2005.004, Charleston, South Carolina. Museum purchase with funds provided by gifts from Mrs. Rodney Williams, Mr. Charles Woodward, and Mrs. Jean R. Yawkey.

and sing, especially in private moments, as long as he lived. Peter Jefferson died in 1757, when Thomas was fourteen. By then the family included Thomas's brother, Randolph, and four younger sisters.

In 1760, at age seventeen, having outgrown what the local tutors could offer, Jefferson enrolled at the College of William and Mary, about sixty miles downstream from Richmond on the James River. He was an exceptional student. Some of his peers thought him obsessive. He managed to graduate in two years. At nineteen, Thomas Jefferson was a tall, impressive-looking young man. He was an accomplished writer but painfully shy. His intellect was nearly always expressed in writing, almost never in oratory.

Reflecting perhaps the delicate combination of shyness and ambition, wishes to engage but not confront, Jefferson's private and public lives began a fascinating divergence. On the private side, in college he endured a rejection from the beautiful Rebecca Burwell, who later married one of Jefferson's friends.

Then in the late 1760s, he pursued a clandestine affair with the wife of a married neighbor. His overtures were not reciprocated. One wonders whether his shyness and awkwardness contributed to unrealistic and unsuccessful romantic pursuits. While unsuccessful in love to this point, in 1764 Jefferson inherited nearly 5,000 acres of land and twenty-two slaves from his father's estate. He was becoming one of the wealthiest men in Virginia.

In the public sphere, he enjoyed less-tarnished success. Starting upon his graduation from William & Mary, Jefferson began a five-year apprenticeship with the accomplished lawyer, George Wythe, who years later was a signer of the Declaration of Independence. Under Wythe's tutelage, Jefferson was admitted to the bar in 1767. Although not a courtroom showman, his brilliance and hard work made him an effective and much sought-after attorney. Ironically, his accomplishments led to his being engaged to oppose his former mentor Wythe in a case involving a contested will in 1770. Though not certain, it appears that Jefferson won. His growing legal career, and his wealth, led to his election to Virginia's colonial legislature, the House of Burgesses, in 1768, when he was twenty-five years old.

Central to Jefferson's life, and subsequently to the history of the United States, was Jefferson's intellectual development, informing his moral, political, and religious outlook. Always a curious student and a voracious reader, many of his early writings reflect ideas from the Enlightenment that most shaped his thinking. Political theorist John Locke's influence is well known. Locke's assertions of equality and natural rights existing in the state of nature find their way into Jefferson's first draft of the Declaration of Independence, where he writes of "sacred and undeniable" truths and "inherent and inalienable rights." Although Jefferson specified the right of "pursuit of happiness" rather than Locke's right to property, the Locke influence is clear. Also, affecting Jefferson's thinking was the work of Sir Henry St. John Bolingbroke, an English philosopher himself influenced by Locke. Bolingbroke was a deist, who challenged many of the traditions of Christianity. Jefferson consistently endorsed the free expression of religion and more generally was, at least privately, open to unconventional ideas.

We see Jefferson's openness in one of his first cases as private attorney. A three-quarters white servant had been indentured for thirty years because his mother, in indentured service from birth, was of mixed race. The man, Thomas Howell, wanted to be freed from the tangled indentured servant and race laws. Jefferson felt the situation was intolerable and took the case to Virginia's highest court. Before the justices he argued, "Under the law of nature, all men are born free, every one comes into the world with a right to his own person, which includes the liberty of moving and using it as his own will. This is what is called personal liberty, and is given him by the author of nature, because necessary for his own sustenance."[9] This view of personal liberty found its way into one of Jefferson's first acts in the House of Burgesses: In 1769, he drafted and then seconded a proposal moved by the respected Colonel Richard Bland to allow owners the right to free slaves. Bland was excoriated by his slave-owning colleagues. The bill was defeated. Jefferson quickly perceived how counterproductive and even dangerous it was to attempt to disturb the institution of slavery in even the smallest way in Southern colonies.

There were, in particular, two aspects of potential emancipation that resisted resolution for Jefferson. One was what would happen when slaves were freed. In contrast to George Washington, Jefferson firmly believed that America could not become a multiracial society. Freed slaves would have to be deported and colonized elsewhere, but the difficulties of doing that defeated both him and many others who favored emancipation combined with colonization. Second, Jefferson was becoming more and more economically dependent on the value of his property in enslaved African Americans. Like many other Virginia planters, he was sinking deeper and deeper into debt; over time, simply giving away valuable property became less thinkable. One of the stark contradictions between Jefferson's private and public life was that his expansive and expensive personal tastes in architecture, books, and wine ran up increasing debt, while as a public official he regarded debt as enslaving and to be minimized or avoided completely.

As Jefferson's professional and political career took shape, his somewhat messy private life came into focus as well. In 1769, he left Shadwell and began his own home on the top of a hill outside Charlottesville on land he had inherited from his father. This was to become Monticello, the buildings and grounds of which Jefferson was to work and love the rest of his life. He had the top of the hill flattened, designed a large main house strongly influenced by the Italian architect Palladio, and began construction. Of course, most of the work was done by enslaved laborers. These workers varied greatly in their level of skill and the parts of the project on which they worked. Jefferson personally supervised the overall construction very closely.

Leaving Shadwell may have been partly influenced by Jefferson's difficult relationship with his mother. Like George Washington, Thomas Jefferson lost his father at a young age, fourteen, and had a strained relationship with his mother. Psychologist Howard Gardner suggests that many significant world leaders have either lost a parent, had poor relationships with at least one of their parents, or both.[10] There may be something about these family configurations that fosters independence, at least in some individuals.

At about this time, Jefferson's personal life stabilized in another way as well. He had met the wealthy widow Martha Wayles Skelton. Martha and Thomas Jefferson were married on January 1, 1772. She was twenty-three and he twenty-eight. Their marriage was a devoted love match that produced five daughters. However, only two lived past infancy. Martha died following her final pregnancy, in 1782, after only slightly more than ten years of marriage to Jefferson. Of significance to Thomas Jefferson's later life, another death in the family occurred during Martha and Thomas's second year of marriage. That year Martha's father died at age fifty-eight. He had outlived three wives. In his final year, 1773, he fathered a daughter with a half-white slave named Betty Hemmings.

The daughter's name was Sally Hemmings. Like her mother, she was enslaved. Thirty years younger than Thomas Jefferson and twenty-five years younger than Martha, the slave Sally was Martha Jefferson's three-quarters white half-sister.

Increasingly in the 1770s, Jefferson became a prominent figure in Virginia politics. He continued his legal work until 1774, but then retired to Monticello to become a gentleman planter, running several farms that he had acquired from Peter Jefferson and Martha's father's estate. Though he preferred the more withdrawn life of a farmer to the legal profession, he continued serving in the House of Burgesses.

While Jefferson retired, not for the last time, to private endeavors atop Monticello, events in the thirteen colonies did not retire. Nor did Jefferson's political career come to an end. After nearly ten years of quarrel and struggle with the British Parliament over taxes imposed to cover, in part, the expenses of the French and Indian War (1754–1763), leaders in the House of Burgesses, including Patrick Henry, George Washington, and Thomas Jefferson, initiated "committees of correspondence" so that leaders in the thirteen British colonies would apprise each other of local events and British actions that carried implications for them all. The next year, when the colonies agreed to convene a "Continental Congress" in Philadelphia, Jefferson drafted instructions for the Virginia delegation. Although they were not followed, his political, philosophical, and legal talent made the young Albemarle representative an important figure in state political circles.

The First Continental Congress was deemed so successful that the delegates pledged to meet again the next spring, in May of 1775. They would continue their explorations of ways to resist parliamentary violations of their rights as Englishmen and how they might appeal to King George III for help in restraining Parliament. But again, events on the ground outran personal planning and painstaking political deliberation. On the night of April 18, in the Massachusetts colony, Paul Revere watched for warning lanterns to be hung in Boston's Old North Church, signaling plans for a British incursion into the countryside. In Longfellow's famous poem, Revere waited silently: "One if by land, and two if by sea; and I on the opposite shore will be, ready to ride and spread the alarm through every Middlesex village and farm."[11] The next day, shots were fired in Lexington and Concord. The Revolutionary War had started.

Thomas Jefferson had been elected to the Second Continental Congress in 1775, somewhat as an afterthought, when a more senior member of the Virginia assembly was unable to attend. He played an important role in drafting the document "Causes and Necessity of Their Taking Up Arms,"[12] based in large part on his "Summary View of the Rights of British America" written the previous year.[13] These two documents enunciated the colonies' grievances against Parliament and Jefferson's developing ideas regarding political power and governing structures. In December of 1775, he returned to Virginia, very much preoccupied with devising a new Virginia Constitution, further developing Monticello, and caring for Martha, who was ill, probably with a difficult pregnancy.

Jefferson returned to Philadelphia on May 14, 1776. He was delayed in part by the death of his mother at the end of March. When he did return, he joined the five-man committee formulating a declaration of independence and authored its first draft. As noted earlier, fellow committee members Adams, Franklin, Livingston, and Sherman made only minor revisions, and the draft was presented to the full Congress on June 28. It was debated vigorously, and although Jefferson felt that it had been badly mangled by the revisions made over the next week, including the elimination of Jefferson's powerful condemnation of slavery, the original draft survived mostly intact. On July 2, Congress passed a resolution proposed on June 7 by Virginia's Richard Henry stating "that these united colonies are, and of right ought to be, free and independent states." Two days later, on July 4, the Declaration of Independence, stating the rationale for the colonies being free and independent states, was passed unanimously. The famous document concluded: "And for the support of this Declaration, with a firm reliance on the protection of divine Providence, we mutually pledge to each other our Lives, our Fortunes and our sacred Honor."

Thomas Jefferson remained in Philadelphia long enough to sign the Declaration in early August of 1776; he returned to Virginia the next month. He rejoined the Virginia legislature, since independence called the House of Delegates rather than House of Burgesses. Now that Virginia was an independent state (Jefferson thought of it as his country), he took great interest in reforming the state's laws. He was appointed to a Committee of Revisors that considered a range of statutes, including those pertaining to religious liberty. Jefferson's work on the latter was one of his most consistent and persistent endeavors. The committee also took up questions related to slavery. While Jefferson had in the past supported some kind of manumission, or freeing of slaves, the committee actually proposed increased restrictions on slaves and free blacks, including making it unlawful for "free blacks to testify in court against whites."[14] Though Jefferson privately wrote that slavery was wrong and that in some way or another slaves should be freed, he was unable to openly support emancipation or to think through the details and difficulties of accomplishing it. Nothing happened in the flush of revolutionary excitement to address the contradictions between Enlightenment principles of liberty and equality and the institution of slavery.[15]

While Virginians strove to govern themselves and contribute to the ongoing war effort, George Washington's forces won small but crucial battles at Trenton and Princeton in the last days of 1776 and the first days of 1777. In the fall of 1777, American forces under General Horatio Gates at Saratoga, New York, defeated and captured a British army under the command of General John Burgoyne. Then Washington managed, just barely, to hold the Continental Army together during the winter of 1777–78 at Valley Forge, Pennsylvania. The war seemed stalled in the North. In 1779, the British adopted a "Southern strategy" devised to subdue Georgia and the Carolinas by capturing Savannah and Charleston, then invading Virginia. That same year, Thomas Jefferson was elected Governor of Virginia. The following year, English and Hessian forces under the command of the traitor Benedict Arnold invaded Virginia; in 1781, while Jefferson was still governor, additional enemy troops under Lord Cornwallis advanced as far west as Charlottesville and captured Monticello. During the invasion, Jefferson had the government move several times, finally as far inland as Staunton. During the British raids, some of Jefferson's slaves escaped.

At a crucial point, Jefferson made a costly political mistake. His term as governor expired on June 2, 1781, but his successor had not been named. On June 4, after the government had moved to Staunton, Jefferson took his family to his farm called Poplar Forest, near Lynchburg. He left the state without a governor for eight days, until the new governor arrived in Staunton on June 12. There was an outcry at what seemed like the captain of a ship deserting in a time of peril. Jefferson reasoned that he had done his duty. Many legislators disagreed and conducted an investigation into his actions. Although he was cleared, the experience left him embittered and determined to leave public life for good.

Jefferson's decision to avoid public service seemed unshakeable. He declined several offers of posts from Congress. Life on the top of his little mountain seemed idyllic. Jefferson seemingly avoided any discomfort that might have been caused by the contradiction between his professed abhorrence of slavery and his increasing dependence on slave labor and ownership of slave capital. Monticello was designed so that slave dwellings, though near to the main house, were out of sight and therefore perhaps out of mind. Another detail of the building was a dumbwaiter system that would allow slaves to provide meals and dishes to the dining room without actually being there.

However, the integral importance of slaves in the Jefferson family came into stark focus during the next crisis in their personal lives. In August of 1782, Martha gave birth to their sixth child with Thomas Jefferson. She never recovered from the ordeal. Though she lived several more weeks, it was clear to both husband and wife that she would not survive. Nine-year-old Sally Hemmings, Martha's enslaved half-sister, was one of those attending Martha on her deathbed. Jefferson himself was distraught and unable to function. At the end, his older sister had several slaves escort him to his own room.

After recovering from the death of his beloved Martha, a lonely life on Monticello was not so compelling. Jefferson found himself drawn back into public life and a long absence from his hilltop retreat. The last major battle of the Revolutionary War had been fought at Yorktown nearly a year before Martha's death, and the treaty that officially ended it was negotiated in Paris the year after. Early in that next year, 1783, Jefferson was called on to lead the Virginia delegation to the Confederation Congress, serving under the Articles of Confederation and Perpetual Union that the Continental Congress had devised in 1781. His expansive ideas about the shape of a future American "Empire of Liberty" were highly influential. They included the principle that new territories would organize themselves as states, equal in status to the existing states, rather than as colonies of the original thirteen. Jefferson also played a crucial role in the Territorial Ordinance of 1784, less well known than the famous Northwest

Ordinance of 1787, which outlawed slavery in any states entering the Union north of the Ohio River. As part of the Territorial Ordinance, he moved that slavery be excluded from all new states. The proposal was barely defeated when one New Jersey congressman fell ill and could not provide the vote that would have carried his state—and the nation.

Later in 1784, Jefferson was appointed as an American minister to France. He remained there for five years. His years in Paris were crucial in shaping his public political commitments and his private indulgences. He reached France in August, two years after Martha's death, with his slaves, including his talented cook, James Hemmings. He was captivated by many aspects of French life, writing "I enjoy their architecture, sculpture, painting, music. . . . It is in these arts they shine."[16] He so "coveted" these aspects of French culture that he bought numerous books and musical instruments.

During his first year in Paris, he worked closely with Benjamin Franklin, who retired as minister to France in 1785, and John Adams, who later became the first American minister to Great Britain. Having some leisure time, Jefferson returned to a project he had started at home in 1781. A French diplomat had asked the governor of each of the thirteen states to answer a series of questions about their laws, culture, and environment. Jefferson resumed his work on replies to these "queries" and circulated private drafts. He never intended his writings to be distributed in America. However, they were completed during his first year in Paris and published as *Notes on the State of Virginia*.[17] In this famous work, we encounter the full range of Jefferson's often contradictory views on slavery and race.

In his section on Manners, Jefferson is eloquent about the evils of slavery. He only hopes that the problems of slavery "will force their way into every one's mind" and lead to "a total emancipation . . . that . . . is disposed . . . with the consent of the masters." He describes the institution as marked by "the most unremitting despotism" of the master and "degrading submissions" of the slave. He worries that white children will be "nursed, educated, and daily exercised in tyranny." And the consequences of this "commerce between master and slave?" He speculates on the wrath of God: "Indeed I tremble for my country when I reflect that God is just: that his justice cannot sleep forever" and that "The Almighty has no attribute which can take side with us" in a contest between slave and master. It is clear that to Jefferson, slavery violates "those liberties [that] are of the gift of God," the ones about which he wrote so eloquently in 1776.

Yet in an earlier section on Laws, Jefferson discourses on the inferiority of blacks to whites in pseudoscientific terms that could easily suggest to readers that blacks are well fit for slavery. Jefferson proposes that blacks be colonized in a place to be named later and that whites be imported to take their place. He explains that this unusual and expensive step is necessary because, among other reasons, of "deep rooted prejudices entertained by the whites." Then Jefferson strikingly illustrates his own prejudices by outlining "physical and moral" differences between the races that would make incorporating blacks as free American citizens impossible. A brief sampling of his arguments suffices to illustrate his views. He discusses the divergent "share of beauty" of the races, including for whites "flowing hair, a more elegant symmetry of form" leading to blacks' "own judgment in favor of whites, declared by their preference for them," that preference being similar to "the preferences of the orangutan for the black woman over those of their own species." This suggestion that blacks are different species than whites is followed by the observation that blacks "secrete less by the kidneys, and more by the glands of the skin, which gives them a very strong and disagreeable odor." The discourse becomes contradictory as well as disgusting to most modern eyes and ears, as Jefferson on the one hand claims that "they seem to require less sleep" while later explaining "their disposition to sleep when abstracted from their diversions."

Subsequent discussions of blacks' "much inferior" reason and "incoherent and eccentric" thought are followed by his observation that blacks' "improvement . . . in body and mind, in the first instance of their mixture with the whites . . . proves that their inferiority is not the effect merely of their condition of life." In a later section, he decides to:

> [A]dvance it therefore as a suspicion only, that the blacks, whether originally a distinct race, or made distinct by time and circumstances, are inferior to the whites in the endowments both of body and mind. It is not against experience to suppose, that different species of the same genus, or varieties of the same species, may possess different qualifications.

These thoughts were written when Jefferson was near forty years old. They are the musings of a mature and serious mind. His greatest unease was that his pronouncements about the evils of slavery would upset the Virginia gentry. He did not seem to have the same concern about his speculations on race.

In 1787, after Jefferson had been in Europe for three years, his younger surviving daughter, eight-year-old Polly, arrived to join her father. She was accompanied by the slave Sally Hemmings, now fourteen. Sally had cared for Polly for several years, and the two were close. There has been a great deal of speculation that a sexual relationship between Jefferson and Sally began in Paris. When Jefferson left France in 1789 to return to the United States, under French law Sally could have claimed her freedom and remained behind. Her descendants (maybe Jefferson's as well) maintained that at that time, Sally agreed to return with Jefferson to America on the condition that he would free any children they had together.

What manner of man was the forty-six-year-old Thomas Jefferson when he prepared to cross the Atlantic for a return to the United States in 1789? By then he had been a witness to the French Revolution. He supported it wholeheartedly. He had grown to detest the French monarchy, the privileges granted to the nobility and aristocracy, and the large role of the church in French politics. He had long opposed any church-state connection and was delighted that the revolution diminished the church's role. He also grew to hate cities and developed a vision of a large America populated by individual yeoman farmers, overseen by local and state governing bodies. He believed that a central government must be strong enough to conduct international diplomacy and pay the nation's bills, but he was deeply suspicious of centralized or consolidated power of any kind that might infringe on the rights and liberties of the people. His views can be traced with a straight line from John Locke and were essentially those written into the Declaration of Independence. His time in Europe had only strengthened his views about the natural rights of man expressed, for example, in his appeal to the Virginia courts on behalf of the mixed race indentured servant, Thomas Howell.

Jefferson expected his 1789 return to the United States to be brief, but during his absence, and with his encouragement from overseas, delegates at a convention in Philadelphia had drafted a Constitution for the new nation. By 1788, it had been ratified by enough states to put it into force; under its provisions, George Washington had been unanimously elected the first president of the United States. Washington took the oath of office on April 30, 1789, in New York City. One of his first acts was to appoint Thomas Jefferson as secretary of state. The Senate ratified the nomination and, like it or not, Jefferson became a member of Washington's cabinet.

For most of the next twenty years, Jefferson was in public service. However, during his time in Washington's cabinet, he grew increasingly unhappy as he fought Secretary of the Treasury Alexander Hamilton on almost every issue. The two fundamentally disagreed over what kind of United States the new country should be. Jefferson championed an America with limited central government composed largely of small farms. It would be governed by elected officials as close to the voters as possible. Hamilton favored a strong central government, a strong central banking system, and a strong military. Overlaying and to some extent defining these differences was their different attachment to European countries and their governments. Jefferson strongly favored the French. He defended their revolution and its bloody excesses far longer and more vigorously than almost any of his contemporaries of similar mind. In his last year in Paris, he had helped draft the French "Declaration of the Rights of Man and of the Citizen" and was proud of his contribution. In contrast, Hamilton was an Anglophile. He admired the British form of government and worried that the French form was barely better than anarchy. Jefferson felt that Hamilton was a closet monarchist who longed to play the role of Julius Caesar in taking over the American Republic. Their personalities were also entirely different. Jefferson shunned personal conflict and confrontation; Hamilton seemed to thrive on it. Neither enjoyed being in the same cabinet. As he had earlier (in 1774 and 1781), Jefferson sought to retire from public life.

One thing on which Jefferson and Hamilton agreed was the importance of George Washington running for a second term as president in 1792. Both believed, probably rightly, that the American experiment would fail without

Washington's magnetic and cohesive presence. Once Washington was unanimously re-elected, Jefferson pleaded to be released from public duties. The president persuaded him to remain as secretary of state until early 1794.

Jefferson was ecstatic when he returned to Monticello, congratulating himself that he had escaped the strains and controversies of government and returned to his family, his farm, and his books. He threw himself into renovations and alterations at Monticello. Inside the house, Sally Hemmings exerted a great deal of authority, with direct responsibility for "Jefferson's bedchamber and clothing."[18] However, Jefferson was increasingly asked to lead an emerging coalition opposing George Washington's administration. That group included his close Virginia colleagues James Madison and James Monroe, who had become extremely critical of the president's policies, feeling that they were overly influenced by Alexander Hamilton, and consequently too pro-British.

Not surprisingly, then, when Washington made it crystal clear that he would not be a candidate for re-election to a third term in 1796, John Adams and Jefferson became the candidates for what were becoming known as the Federalist Party in Adams's case and the Republican Party in Jefferson's. Joseph Ellis wrote that Adams and Jefferson were the two men who clearly had the most credible Revolutionary credentials and that the election resembled a contest between the heart (Jefferson) and head (Adams) of the Spirit of 1776.[19] That is, while Adams had been the initial advocate of independence in 1776, Jefferson expressed its ideals in some of America's most lyrical phrases. The election was one of the closest in American history. John Adams edged Jefferson by three electoral votes. However, the Constitution at that time provided that the candidate with the second most electoral votes would become vice president. The Federalists' intention was that Charles Pinckney would be the vice president, but in this first contested election, the Federalist electors had not mastered the system well enough to secure Pinckney rather than Jefferson the second spot. Thus for the only time in US history, the two competing candidates from different parties became the president and vice president.

Thomas Jefferson was happy enough to be vice president rather than the chief executive. He feared that the new president would have to clean up what he regarded as the mess created at the end of George Washington's second term, especially the growing tensions with France. Those duties would not fall to him. Also, the vice presidency would not be a demanding position. Jefferson actually looked forward to presiding over the US Senate, the only constitutionally-defined responsibility of his office. In fact, much like his time in the Virginia legislature in the late 1770s, Jefferson involved himself deeply and minutely in devising rules for the Senate, some of which are still in operation today.

Beyond his official duties, Jefferson continued unofficially to lead the Republican Party, keeping in close contact with his colleagues James Madison and James Monroe. He grew ever more distressed by Federalist policies that he worried were bringing the country ever closer to monarchy, even though the only plausible king, George Washington, had just retired from public life, and to an overpowering central government controlled by banks and creditors. His vision of the independent yeoman farmer being the backbone of the United States seemed to be slipping away. In 1798, the Federalists' Alien and Sedition Acts convinced Jefferson that small government republican virtue was doomed under the Federalists. Throughout his term as vice president, Jefferson orchestrated press and pamphlet attacks against John Adams. The Federalists responded in kind. It seemed inevitable that Jefferson and Adams would face each other again in the election of 1800.

During Jefferson's years as secretary of state and his term as vice president, his concerns about slavery, so evidently alive during his time in France, took second place to his philosophical and political conflicts—first with Hamilton and then with Adams. Maintaining Republican unity against the Federalists, especially in the South, dictated that the troublesome issue of slavery simply go away. Once again the very shape of the American government and the legacy of the American Revolution took precedence over the fate of enslaved African Americans. In this respect, Jefferson's behavior was similar to George Washington ignoring the Quaker petitions of 1790 advocating the end of the slave trade and the emancipation of slaves already in the United States. Throughout his life, Jefferson consistently wrote of the evils and dangers of slavery, but doing anything about it was never practicable or timely. And increasingly, anti-slavery sentiment became associated with Northerners and Federalists. Jefferson disagreed with them on too many other important things to ally himself with them in taking any action against slavery.

In this context the election of 1800 unfolded. Although slavery was not an explicit election issue, the outcome turned on the large numbers of slaves in Southern states. Slaves of course were not generally thought of as citizens and could not vote. However, concessions made to Southern states during the Constitutional Convention in 1787 allowed them to count three-fifths of their slave population in figuring the number of their representatives to Congress, and thus their electoral votes. In the election of 1800, the three-fifths provision in the Constitution made the difference. The math is a little complicated, but the difference between Adams's home state, Massachusetts, and Jefferson's home state, Virginia, illustrates the impact of the three-fifths rule. The federal census of 1800 shows Massachusetts having a free population of about 575,000. It had sixteen electoral votes, all of which went to Adams. Virginia had a smaller free population, roughly 535,000, but it had twenty-one electoral votes, all of which went to Jefferson.[20] Virginia's 346,000 slaves gave it at least five extra electoral votes. Large slave populations in the Carolinas also added electoral votes to Jefferson's column. Jefferson defeated Adams, 73 electoral votes to 65.

Nevertheless, the Constitution was clear, and the election was not disputed on those grounds. There was, however, another problem. The parties were wary of the ticking time bomb that lay in the way electoral votes were cast, and they did not want to get the wrong vice president as they had in 1796. Unfortunately, their machinations resulted in a tie for first place between the supposed candidates for president, Thomas Jefferson, and vice president, Aaron Burr. The idea that Burr would quietly step aside turned out to be fiction. The election would be decided by the House of Representatives, which was still controlled by the Federalists elected in 1798. Many of them would have preferred Burr. The House was deadlocked for thirty-five ballots. Finally, Alexander Hamilton, the controlling figure in the Federalist Party, decided that he really hated and feared fellow New Yorker Aaron Burr more than his longtime rival Thomas Jefferson. Jefferson was elected on the thirty-sixth ballot.[21] Hamilton's action added to the ill will between him and Burr. Their mutual antipathy boiled over four years later, and on a warm morning in July 1804, the two rowed across the Hudson River to duel in New Jersey. Vice President Aaron Burr killed Alexander Hamilton that day.

Once Jefferson took office on March 4, 1801, his major concerns were paying off the national debt and more generally leading a "second American revolution" that would revive the Republican principles he perceived to have been perverted by John Adams's Federalists. Slavery was not on the agenda. Already Southern anti-slavery voices, such as they were, were being muted. Southern Republican unity against the North and the Federalists was more important than moral claims regarding slavery. During one telling moment in 1806, Jefferson's wish to remain silent regarding slavery led to the demise of a proposal in Congress to ban slavery in Washington, DC, the nation's new capital. At the time, Jefferson likely had the moral and political authority to bring the ban to fruition.

Race and slavery played a complex role in Jefferson's major presidential achievement, the Louisiana Purchase of 1803. It is, of course, highly ironic that Jefferson lacked the constitutional authority to strike such a deal and that he would have been apoplectic about similar exercises of executive power by the Federalists. The overriding issue, however, was America's future and the doubling in size of Jefferson's "empire of liberty." For President Jefferson, that opportunity trumped political philosophy.

Another important part of the context for the Louisiana Purchase was the ongoing slave rebellion on the French island colony of Saint-Dominique, now the country of Haiti. In 1791, slaves there rose up against their white masters. They wanted to secure for themselves the "Rights of Man" that Thomas Jefferson helped author in Paris in 1789. The struggle had been ongoing for ten years when Jefferson became president. The possibility of a free nation ruled by blacks was terrifying to Southern slave owners. It would serve as an example to American slaves, and it might inspire a similar rebellion in Charleston, South Carolina, and other slave-dominated regions. Also, many Federalists supported Toussaint L'Ouverture, the leader of the rebellion. It was easy for Jefferson's Republicans to think of the Federalists' stand as part of a plot with England to defeat France and establish British supremacy in the Caribbean. For this reason, President Jefferson indicated to Napoleon that he would support the latter's efforts to subdue the rebels in Saint-Dominique.

However, the president's support withered as it became clear that subduing the slave rebellion was part of Napoleon's larger design to strengthen a French empire in America, much of which lay just west of the United States in the Louisiana territory. Such an empire was even more frightening than a black Haiti. As Jefferson shifted ground, the French efforts to subdue the rebellion failed. Napoleon realized that French holdings throughout North America were vulnerable; he decided then to sell all of Louisiana while the selling was good. When the new territory was acquired, Jefferson did ban the importation of slaves into Louisiana, but nothing was done to change the existing conditions of slavery that had been well established in that colony.[22]

Another opportunity to limit slavery came across Jefferson's desk in 1803 when then governor of the Indiana Territory William Henry Harrison lobbied Congress to repeal the provision in the 1787 Northwest Ordinance to ban slavery in territories north of the Ohio River. Congress went along with Harrison for a period of ten years. Harrison also introduced a form of indenturing workers that was, in most respects, very similar to slavery. Jefferson did nothing to stop this *de facto* expansion of enslaved labor.

On the other hand, Jefferson did take significant action regarding slavery during his second term. In 1787, Article I, Section 9 of the Constitution ruled "The Migration or Importation of such Persons as any of the States now existing shall think proper to admit, shall not be prohibited by Congress prior to the Year one thousand eight hundred and eight."[23] This language is fascinating. It refers to the slave trade, but the words "slave" or "slave trade" never appear in the nation's constitution. Most Founders hoped slavery would go away, and most of those thought that it would. Therefore, there was no need to make the institution explicit in the new country's charter. The idea that "such Persons" would arrive on our shores through "Migration" seems laughable today, but the Committee of Style responsible for the document's final language perhaps wanted to dilute the implications of the word "Importation."[24]

During Jefferson's second term (1805–1809), the date on which the slave trade could be prohibited was fast approaching. In his annual message to Congress at the end of 1806, the president took up the issue:

> I congratulate you, fellow citizens on the approach of the period at which you may interpose your authority constitutionally, to withdraw the citizens of the United States from all further participation in those violations of human rights which have been so long continued on the unoffending inhabitants of Africa, and which the morality, the reputation, and the best interests of our country, have long been eager to proscribe.[25]

With Jefferson's urging, during the next year Congress voted to stop the slave trade, effective on the earliest possible date, January 1, 1808. While most states, with the notable exception of South Carolina, had already banned the slave trade, the 1807 legislation was closely fought in Congress and was approved rather narrowly in the House of Representatives by a vote of 63 to 49.

The eloquence of Jefferson's writing on slavery shines through in this annual message, as it did in many other documents composed both earlier and later. The message clearly reflects his moral opposition to slavery. At the time, Jefferson was certain that the end of the slave trade act would hasten the demise of the institution. Yet, the situation is predictably more complicated than it might first appear. As always, Jefferson had his ears tuned to frequencies emanating from the Commonwealth of Virginia. By the early 1800s, that state had a surplus of slaves. Growing tobacco with slave labor was increasingly unprofitable. At the same time, with the 1793 invention of Eli Whitney's cotton gin, the expansion of plantation agriculture into the "black belt" of present-day Alabama and Mississippi, and slavery firmly established in parts of Louisiana, abolition of the slave trade would only make Virginia's surplus more valuable. Thus Congress and the president were doing well for Virginia while also doing good for the nation. Also, the fabulous increase of highly profitable cotton production in the lower South clearly demonstrated that slavery was not withering away. The trend lines were in exactly the opposite direction. Still, until much later in his life, Jefferson clung to the Spirit of 1776 belief that slavery, especially with his signing the law abolishing the slave trade, was on its way to extinction.

Thomas Jefferson returned to Monticello in March 1809, having completed his two terms as president. His close friend and Secretary of State James Madison succeeded him. By this time, the Federalist Party was effectively dead. Jefferson had been re-elected easily in 1804, and Madison faced weak opposition in 1808. Following the close Adams/Jefferson contest of 1800, decided in favor of Jefferson because of the three-fifths rule, the Republican Party candidates faced little opposition until the party splintered in the election of 1824. Only in 1812, when Madison ran for re-election was there much opposition, mostly due to Northern unhappiness over the War of 1812. With so much power in the hands of Republicans, especially Southern Republicans, American politics generally ignored slavery. Jefferson's silence on the issue was typical, not unusual.

Nevertheless, there were those in the South, even Virginia, who attempted to push slavery down the path to extinction on which most of the surviving members of the Revolutionary generation believed it was headed. One of the most interesting was one of Jefferson's neighbors, Edward Coles, who had also served as private secretary to Jefferson's successor, James Madison. Coles decided that he would act. He would sell his land in Virginia and take his slaves into Illinois, part of the Northwest Territory where slavery was illegal, and set them up as independent farmers. He asked for help from Jefferson and also Madison. Both turned him down. Jefferson said that he was too old to participate, that at his age, seventy-one, prayers were his only weapon. He would not lend his name to Coles's endeavor. He also felt that public opinion would have to get behind such emancipation efforts in order for them to succeed and that pushing against current opinion would only weaken the cause.[26]

Jefferson addressed the problem of slavery in America again during the Missouri crisis of 1820. In many ways, 1820 was a quiet year in American politics. After Andrew Jackson won the Battle of New Orleans in early 1815 (it actually took place after a treaty had been signed in Ghent ending the War of 1812, but that was not known in the United States at the time of the battle), Americans largely had an optimistic and prideful sense of themselves. President James Monroe, successor to James Madison in 1817, benefited from what became known as the Era of Good Feelings. Monroe's presidency was effective enough and inclusive enough so that when he ran for re-election in 1820, only one electoral vote was cast against him, for his secretary of state, John Quincy Adams.

Still the issue of sectional dominance was in the wings. While the matter was largely dormant, Southern slaveholding states, despite their emphasis on states' rights, were ever watchful of their supremacy within the federal government. The three-fifths rule and the demise of the Federalists helped, but the United States Senate was vulnerable to Northern domination. In the Senate, each state had two votes. The three-fifths rule would not help there as it did in the House of Representatives. It would be dangerous if free states outnumbered slave states. Shortly after the original thirteen colonies formed "a more perfect union" by adopting the 1787 Constitution, three new states—Vermont, Kentucky, and Tennessee—were admitted. Thus in 1800 there were eight slave states and eight free. A balance was obtained. Then Ohio was admitted in 1803 and Louisiana in 1812; now the count was nine to nine. A precarious balance persisted. Starting in 1816, for four years, one new state was admitted annually, one free and one slave: Indiana in 1816, Mississippi in 1817, Illinois in 1818, and Alabama in 1819. Eleven to eleven.

When Missouri applied for statehood in 1820, the balance was threatened. Would the new state be slave or free? A New York congressman, James Tallmadge, a member of Jefferson's Republican Party, proposed that Missouri, which already included approximately ten thousand slaves out of its total territorial population of sixty-six thousand, be admitted as a state with the restriction that slavery there would be abolished gradually. Thomas Jefferson, who had advocated banning slavery in all territories in the Ordinance of 1784 and was pleased with the ban on slavery in the Northwest Ordinance of 1787, strongly opposed the Tallmadge proposal. At this point in his career, states' rights and property rights seemed to have taken an upper hand to the natural rights and self-evident truths about which he wrote so movingly in 1776. Part of the problem was that though Tallmadge was a Republican, he was allied with a Northern branch of the party that was not willing to go along on all issues with the Virginia Republican Party of Jefferson, Madison, and Monroe, the nation's presidents since early 1801. By that time, Jefferson worried that Northern Republicans such as Tallmadge had strayed from party "orthodoxy."[27] Such apostates were as dangerous as Federalists. Whatever allegiance Jefferson had to an effective national government when he was in Paris in the 1780s, and when he purchased Louisiana as president in 1803, was long gone by 1820. Virginia had always been his country; when the government of the United States was no longer exclusively controlled by Virginians, his allegiance to states' rights took precedence. The Tallmadge proposal would allow the national government to dictate what a state, albeit a new one, could and could not do within its borders. To Jefferson at this time, such a proposal was pure party politics, an effort to wrest control from the states and leave the South increasingly vulnerable to Northern influence.

In some ways, the Republican Party had become a victim of its own success. It had vanquished the hated Federalists. But, as political scientist Stephen Skowronek has pointed out, time after time in American history, winning parties that achieve a breakthrough and reconstruct the political landscape, as Jefferson's Republicans did in 1801, suffer divisions under subsequent administrations. Breakthrough is followed by breakup and eventual breakdown.[28] This was beginning to happen as the "era of good feelings" waned.

The eventual solution to the Missouri issue was the Compromise of 1820, also called the Missouri Compromise. Missouri was admitted as a slave state, while Maine was split off from Massachusetts and admitted as a free state, maintaining the parity of slave and free states. In addition, a line running to the Pacific Ocean was established at 36 degrees 30 minutes, with slavery allowed below that latitude but banned above it.

At this late point in Jefferson's life, his thinking about slavery seemed contorted by his commitment to states' rights. While he still believed that slavery should be eradicated, he came to the conclusion that its demise would most likely happen if slaves were dispersed throughout the country, not confined to the Southeast.[29] Thus he opposed the limits that the Missouri Compromise put on the expansion of slavery.

Ultimately, Thomas Jefferson's leadership with respect to African Americans must be judged as tragically disappointing. On the one hand, his eloquent statement in the Declaration of Independence about the "self-evident" truth that "all men are created equal" and his strong support for abolishing the slave trade during his presidency still stand as important contributions to the dignity and welfare of African Americans. However, his inability to confront the contradictions between slave holding and political support for Virginia and the South versus his own rhetoric regarding the immorality of slavery led him to tortured political positions in his final years. He had changed from the man who in 1784 advocated banning slavery in all US territories to one who argued in the 1820s for its diffusion, in hopes that somehow that would lead to its eventual demise. Unlike George Washington, he did little to emancipate his own slaves in his will, freeing only five members of the Hemmings family, but not including Sally Hemmings. He declined several opportunities to speak out against slavery. There was no final eloquence about its evils. Both Washington and Jefferson struggled with the problem of slavery and, more specifically, with their own personal ownership of enslaved human beings. In the end, Washington took steps against the South's "peculiar institution." Jefferson could not.

Notes

1 Declaration of Independence. http://abcnews.go.com/US/fourth_july/full-text-dec laration-independence/story?id=13976396.
2 Abraham Lincoln, Address at Gettysburg, November 19, 1863. In D. Fehrenbacher (ed.), *Abraham Lincoln: Speeches and Writings: 1859–1865* (New York: Library of America, 1989), p. 536.
3 Malcolm Gladwell, *The Tipping Point: How Little Things Can Make a Big Difference* (Boston: Little, Brown, 2000), p. 19.
4 Samuel Johnson, http://www.samueljohnson.com/slavery.html.
5 David Brion Davis, *Inhuman Bondage: The Rise and Fall of Slavery in the New World* (New York: Oxford University Press, 2006).
6 Thomas Jefferson, 1776. http://files.libertyfund.org/pll/quotes/59.html.
7 Jefferson, Letter to John Holmes, April 22, 1820. http://www.monticello.org/site/ jefferson/wolf-ear.
8 R. B. Bernstein, *Thomas Jefferson* (New York: Oxford University Press, 2003), p. 1.
9 Henry Wiencek, *An Imperfect God: George Washington, His Slaves, and the Creation of America* (New York: Farrar, Straus and Giroux, 2003), p. 161.
10 Howard Gardner, in collaboration with Emma Laskin, *Leading Minds: An Anatomy of Leadership* (New York: Basic Books, 1995).
11 Henry Wadsworth Longfellow, "Paul Revere's Ride." http://www.bartleby.com/42/ 789.html
12 See http://avalon.law.yale.edu/18th_century/arms.asp.
13 See http://www.history.org/almanack/life/politics/sumview.cfm.
14 Bernstein, p. 40.
15 Charles Edgerton, *Death or Liberty: African Americans and Revolutionary America* (New York: Oxford University Press, 2009).
16 Bernstein, p. 56.
17 Jefferson, *Notes on the State of Virginia*. http://avalon.law.yale.edu/18th_century/jef fvir.asp
18 Bernstein, p. 110.
19 Joseph J. Ellis, *Founding Brothers: The Revolutionary Generation* (New York: Knopf, 2000).
20 See https://archive.org/details/1800_census.
21 Edward J. Larson, *A Magnificent Catastrophe: The Tumultuous Election of 1800, America's First Presidential Campaign* (New York: Simon & Schuster, 2007).
22 John Chester Miller, *The Wolf by the Ears: Thomas Jefferson and Slavery* (Charlottesville: University of Virginia Press, 1991).
23 See http://www.archives.gov/exhibits/charters/constitution_transcript.html.
24 See Richard Beeman, *Plain Honest Men: The Making of the American Constitution* (New York: Random House, 2009); David O. Stewart, The *Summer of 1787: The Men Who Invented the Constitution* (New York: Simon & Schuster, 2007).
25 See http://millercenter.org/president/jefferson/speeches/speech-3495.
26 Mark McGarvie, "In Perfect Accordance with His Character": Thomas Jefferson, Slavery, and the Law. *Indiana Magazine of History, XCV,* June 1999, 142–77, p. 166.
27 Miller, p. 259.
28 Stephen Skowronek, *The Politics That Presidents Make: Leadership from John Adams to Bill Clinton* (Cambridge, MA: Belknap Press, 1997).
29 Miller, p. 259.

3

ABRAHAM LINCOLN

Figure 3.1 Abraham Lincoln led the North to victory in the Civil War and thereby achieved a result that he rightly called "fundamental and astounding," the preservation of the Union and the abolition of American slavery.

Alexander Gardner, "Abraham Lincoln, Gettysburg Portrait," November 8, 1863, black and white photograph. United States Library of Congress's Prints and Photographs Division, Washington, DC. Public domain, via Wikimedia Commons.

We do not know much about Abraham Lincoln's early life, partly because he wanted it that way. When John Locke Scripps prepared a campaign biography in 1860, Lincoln would only tell him that his youth could be summed up in a few words from Thomas Gray's *Elegy*, "the short and simple annals of the poor."[1] But we do know more than what the future president revealed then. Abraham Lincoln was born in central Kentucky on February 12, 1809. Thomas Jefferson was president, but only three weeks remained of his eight years in office. Jefferson would be succeeded by his protégé, James Madison, the fourth president of the United States, on March 4. The Union of Lincoln's birth consisted of seventeen states plus large, sparsely populated territories not yet organized into states. Kentucky was one of four states (along with Vermont, Tennessee, and Ohio) admitted to the Union after the thirteen original states adopted the Constitution in 1787, which specified procedures for admitting new ones.

As people poured over the Appalachian Mountains in the early years of the republic, setting the scene for conflict with Native Americans and ultimately the War of 1812, Kentucky grew more rapidly than any other state. Data from the first three US Census counts—in 1790, 1800, and 1810—show that the new state tripled in population between the first two surveys and then nearly doubled again by 1810. That year, with approximately 407,000 inhabitants, Kentucky was seventh in total population. Originally part of Virginia, it was a slave state but was actually sixth in its total count of free people, after Virginia, New York, Pennsylvania, North Carolina, and Massachusetts. Twenty percent of Kentucky's population were slaves, a much lower figure than the original slave states of Maryland (39%), Virginia (40%), North Carolina (30%), South Carolina (47%), and Georgia (42%). The total US population was just under seven million. One-sixth of that number was enslaved, almost all from Maryland southward.

Both of Lincoln's parents were part of the wave of people who settled in Kentucky during its early years of statehood; both were from Virginia. His father, Thomas Lincoln, was six years old when he saw his father murdered by an Indian raiding party. Left largely alone, he had no formal education and was not intellectually curious. When Abraham was born, Thomas owned a modest amount of Kentucky farmland. However, he lost much of it in title disputes when Lincoln was still a young boy. Though limited in education and ambition, Thomas Lincoln had qualities that became part of his famous son's character. He was a born storyteller and a mimic who could relate humorous stories with colorful detail. Abraham Lincoln's penchant for spinning yarns was a constant, sometimes to the annoyance of close friends and associates as well as those who thought him backward and simple. He took even more from his mother. Nancy Hanks Lincoln was a warm and extremely smart woman, described by a cousin as intellectual and "naturally Strong minded."[2] She bore her first child, Sarah, when she was twenty-three. Abraham was born two years later. Nancy read the Bible to both children and modeled a passion for learning and reading as well as a patient and compassionate temperament.

Though Kentucky was a slave state, slavery was different west of the mountains than in the states on the Atlantic seaboard. Not concentrated on large plantations as in the tidewater of Virginia and the low country around Charleston, South Carolina, it was rather dispersed among small farms. Slavery was banned north of Kentucky's border, the Ohio River, by the Northwest Ordinance of 1787. Yet there were slaves on both sides of the Ohio, including the southern counties of present-day Indiana and Illinois. Lincoln's boyhood home in Knob Creek lay near a road between Louisville and Nashville that served as a slave trade route. He might have encountered slavery there. We do know that when Lincoln was seven years old, his family moved from Kentucky across the Ohio River to Spencer County in the south part of Indiana. The move was largely precipitated by the difficulties Thomas Lincoln had with titles to his farms in Kentucky. But Abraham Lincoln claimed that slavery was also one term in the equation. Making this claim plausible is the fact that his parents' religious sect, Separate Baptists, opposed slavery.

The Lincolns arrived in Indiana in 1816, the year that it became the nineteenth state. That was also the year that James Monroe was elected fifth president of the United States. Like his two predecessors, Monroe was a landowning Virginian from the Jefferson-Madison Republican Party. Indiana was admitted under a state constitution that banned slavery, but, as noted, slaves still were present, especially along the river. The land was wilder than the disputed farmlands the Lincoln family left behind in Kentucky. Thomas worked hard to clear land for subsistence farming, and already Abraham was engaged in manual labor. However, from the start, possibly with his mother's encouragement, Abraham dreamed of a life less tedious than that of his father.

Within two years, at age nine, Abraham Lincoln suffered the first of many devastating personal losses. Nancy Hanks Lincoln contracted "milk sickness," a disease caused by drinking milk from cows that grazed on white snakeroot. She soon died. For over a year, Thomas Lincoln raised Sarah and Abraham by himself. When he learned that Sarah Bush Johnston, a woman he had previously met, had been widowed, he persuaded her to marry him. She and her three children and a cousin came to live with the Lincolns in a household now supporting eight people. Abraham was ten years old when his stepmother arrived. He became very attached to her. He always called her "Mother." Like Nancy Hanks Lincoln, Sarah warmly encouraged Lincoln's intellectual bent and his growing thirst for reading. The family suffered another severe loss in 1828 when Abraham's sister Sarah died in childbirth. She had become an eleven-year-old surrogate mother to Abraham in the year after Nancy Hanks Lincoln died.

Abraham Lincoln was nineteen years old when Sarah died. At that age, he was still performing manual labor for his father. Although most of Lincoln's work was done at home, under existing laws, until he reached the age of twenty-one, his father could rent him out as a laborer to others. At age sixteen, Lincoln was engaged to run a ferry taking passengers and cargo across the Ohio River. He became a highly skilled operator of such craft and, by age nineteen, had gained enough reputation for handling flatboats that he was hired by James Gentry to take one down to New Orleans with Gentry's son Allen.

What manner of young man was the nineteen-year-old Lincoln that James Gentry hired? He was clearly intellectually gifted. More striking was an extremely high degree of the trait psychologists call "Openness," loosely translated as curiosity and a thirst for knowledge and experience.[3] Lincoln was ambitious in many ways, and part of that quality manifested itself in a drive to improve intellectually. This might have been frustrated by his almost total lack of formal schooling. Lincoln joked that what schooling he had came "by littles." Still, he both wanted to absorb knowledge and also to communicate it clearly and persuasively. His efforts were highly disciplined in both respects. He walked miles to borrow the few books that were available from neighboring families. He read extensively from the Bible, Shakespeare, and Aesop's fables. He trained himself in Euclid's geometry. Partly because of his father's land-title turmoil, he became interested in the law. He read whatever he could get his hands on. Writing presented more of a challenge. Ordinary pen and paper were hard to obtain. Lincoln wrote with cinders on a board; when the board was blackened, he scraped it down to make a thinner but cleaner writing surface. Besides reading and studying, he worked on articulating his ideas and knowledge. In later years, he related his childhood frustration hearing his father talk with other men about business matters that were difficult to comprehend. Listening to the conversation in the loft, he practiced putting the ideas he heard into plain English that could be easily communicated to others. To some extent, Lincoln's reading and studying annoyed his father, who worried that it undermined his manual labor. But the boy persisted.

One result of Lincoln's efforts at self-education and, more broadly, self-improvement was that he was highly respected by all who knew him for his knowledge, intelligence, and wit. He also possessed a contagious sense of humor, an ability to talk, joke, and communicate and connect with people of all levels of education. But it was not only Lincoln's mind and manner that impressed people. He was tall, long-armed, lean, muscular, and athletic. Strong and sure with an ax, he could also best his peers in running and wrestling. He impressed in several ways. Lincoln's mental, physical, and interpersonal competencies made him a natural leader. As the largest, strongest, smartest, warmest, and wittiest of his peers, he attracted many friends and followers. When Lincoln and young Allen Gentry were hired to take cargo down the Mississippi, and then return by steamer, a standard practice at the time, Gentry, the owner's son, was nominally in charge; however, accounts of the trip make it clear that Lincoln was the more experienced boatman and the actual leader.

Gentry and Lincoln had two kinds of unsettling contacts with African Americans. First, they recounted that on the way to New Orleans they were attacked at night by "seven negroes" intent on robbing and killing them, but they fought them off. Second, on arrival, they almost surely encountered slave auctions that were held throughout the bustling, mixed-race city, which often served as a form of diversion and entertainment for whites. How these experiences may have begun to shape Lincoln's attitudes toward African Americans in general and slavery in particular is difficult to discern.

The Lincoln family remained in Indiana until early in 1830, when they left for Illinois. They had been in Indiana for fourteen years. Abraham Lincoln was then twenty-one years old and had grown from a boy to a young man. He was anxious to learn and anxious to carve out a way of life different from that of his father. As Lincoln grew, so did the nation. By 1830, the total US population had nearly doubled since 1810, growing from about seven million to almost thirteen million. The number of slaves increased from just over one million to just under two million, remaining a nearly constant 16% of the total population. With the Missouri Compromise, tensions over slavery simmered on the political back burner and presidential politics severely strained the national fabric. In 1824, the Republican Party, which had been unopposed when James Monroe was re-elected, split into sectional branches; four candidates, all one kind of Republican or another, ran for office. They were Andrew Jackson of Tennessee, John Quincy Adams of Massachusetts, Henry Clay of Kentucky, and William Crawford of Georgia. (Adams was the only non-slave owner among the four.) Even though Andrew Jackson received the most popular and electoral votes, John Quincy Adams was named the sixth president of the United States by the House of Representatives. Jackson and his supporters complained that a "corrupt bargain" had been struck between Adams and Henry Clay, who was appointed secretary of state. That office had been the route to the White House for Jefferson, Madison, Monroe, and Quincy Adams. It seemed inevitable that Jackson would run, and win, against Adams in 1828. That indeed occurred. Jackson was elected the seventh president that year.

Lincoln was legally obligated to work for his father until he was twenty-one years old in 1830, the year the family moved to Illinois. As anxious as he was to set out on his own, he stayed with his family to help see them through that first difficult winter, one of the most severe in Illinois history. But at age twenty-two, in 1831, he left his family's farm and canoed down the Sangamon River to the settlement of New Salem in Menard County, not far from Springfield. There he held various positions, hoping to leave simple farming behind him. He took positions as store clerk and mill manager before securing the position of postmaster. He also assisted in surveying the county. 1831 was also the year he took a second trip to New Orleans. His experiences with slavery on this second trip seemed to have deeply shaped his attitudes toward slavery. On this occasion, Lincoln was hired by the merchant Dennis Offutt again to take a flatboat down the river. Lincoln actually built the boat with one of his Hanks cousins and one of his Johnston stepbrothers. Hanks later wrote that "we saw negroes chained, maltreated, whipped and scourged. [Lincoln's] . . . heart bled."[4] Ten years later, Lincoln visited St. Louis and saw slaves being transported down river. He wrote to a friend that the slaves he saw "were being separated forever from the scenes of their childhood, their friends, their fathers and mothers, and brothers and sisters" and "were going into perpetual slavery where the lash of the master is proverbially more ruthless and unrelenting than any other where."[5] In later years, he wrote that "that sight was a continual torment to me."[6] That slavery made an impression on Lincoln in his early years is reflected in many of his presidential writings, including his famous 1864 letter to Albert Hodges in which he wrote, "If slavery is not wrong, nothing is wrong. I can not remember when I did not so think, and feel."[7] While it is difficult to trace precisely the evolution of what Lincoln did "think, and feel" about slavery, it is likely that early disturbing and repelling experiences with the institution were important.

As the next ten years played out, first in New Salem and then in Springfield, Lincoln's personal and political lives took shape, with significant disappointment in both. Lincoln quickly became a popular and admired figure in New Salem, as a storyteller, wrestler, and natural leader. Within a year he was persuaded to run for a seat in the state legislature, but he lost his first race in 1832. He was largely unknown outside New Salem, and his campaigning was interrupted by three months of military service in the brief Black Hawk War, in which he was elected captain of his company, an event which he claimed in later years gave him "more pleasure than any I have had since."[8] Despite winning almost every New Salem vote, he was defeated in the district as a whole. Not discouraged, he ran again and won in 1834; he was subsequently re-elected to three more terms. In 1835, his political luck was greater than his personal. Still living in New Salem, Lincoln became acquainted with a young woman named Ann Rutledge. Many historians believe that Lincoln fell hard in love and that his affection for Ann was as ardent as any he experienced for the remainder of his life. Ann died at age twenty-two in 1835, contributing to the first of several known bouts of depression for Lincoln.

During his first years in the state legislature, Lincoln identified with the newly formed Whig Party, organized in the 1830s to oppose Andrew Jackson both politically and personally. Whig Party leaders viewed Jackson as a tyrant, feared overreaching executive power, and strongly favored Henry Clay's "American System," which in turn sponsored "internal improvements" and industrial development. Clay had become an early hero for Lincoln, as had Thomas Jefferson. One particular element of Clay's politics attracted Lincoln. Although Clay was a slave owner and represented a slave state, like Thomas Jefferson, he never wavered in his belief that slavery was an evil, immoral system and that somehow American slavery must be abolished. However, like many opponents of slavery, Clay never viewed the ending of slavery as leading to a biracial society. George Washington could envision such a society, but many like Jefferson, Madison, Monroe, and Clay could not. At different times, both Madison and Clay were longtime presidents of the American Colonization Society, founded in 1816 to deport freed slaves and other free blacks to Africa. One of the accomplishments of the Society was the establishment of the African nation of Liberia. Its capital, Monrovia, was named for the fifth US president, James

Monroe. As we shall see, until well into his presidency, Abraham Lincoln also pushed for the deportation and colonization of former slaves.

During his first term as an Illinois state legislator, Lincoln began the very serious study of the law, mastering, among other texts, Blackstone's *Commentaries*. During his second term, he passed the Illinois bar and moved from New Salem to Springfield. Also during that term he put down at least a tentative public marker as a serious opponent of slavery. In 1837, the Illinois legislature passed a resolution opposing the abolition of slavery in the District of Columbia. It passed 77–76 in the state House and unanimously in the Senate. Lincoln was one of six to vote against that and related resolutions. At the end of session, Lincoln and one other of the six nay-saying legislators explained their votes in what has come to be known as Lincoln's "protest."[9] While they joined in condemning abolitionists, whose agitation, the protest claimed, interfered with the morally superior colonization project, they did state that "the institution of slavery is founded on both injustice and bad policy."[10] In this way, Lincoln publicly carved out an independent position that edged away from Illinois' support of rights to slave property "sacred to the slave-holding states."[11]

While Lincoln won re-election in 1838 and 1840, his political future seemed tenuous. His margin of victory in 1840 was lower that year than in his previous victories, and Illinois was one of only seven states to support the Democratic Party candidate for re-election, Andrew Jackson's protégé Martin Van Buren. Lincoln actually served as a Whig presidential elector for the victorious William Henry Harrison, who became, for one month prior to his death, the ninth president of the United States. The tide in Lincoln's new home state was running against the Whigs, and he decided not to run again for re-election to a fifth term.

At the same time, Lincoln's personal life was going through great upheaval. In 1837, he had proposed marriage to Mary Owens, but he was actually relieved when she turned him down. He had begun to feel that he was unsuited for marriage both to Owens in particular and to other women more generally. He wrote a friend that he was permanently out of the marriage business, saying "I can never be satisfied with any one who would be block-head enough to have me."[12] However, he shortly thereafter became entranced by the bright, voluble, and voluptuous Mary Todd, a visitor from a prominent slave-owning family from Kentucky with close ties to Henry Clay. She had moved to live with a sister in Springfield shortly before turning twenty-one and soon met Abraham Lincoln. The two quickly became engaged, even though some in Todd's family felt that she was marrying beneath her. However, as marriage approached, Lincoln got cold feet and called off the engagement. It is not really clear why. It may have been Mary's demanding, needy personality, Lincoln's infatuation with Matilda Edwards, a relative of Mary's, or his own doubts about whether he could support Mary in the way she was accustomed to living. For whatever reason, during the winter of 1840–41, the engagement was suspended. Lincoln went into a severe depression and, according to his close friend Joshua Speed, contemplated suicide. But after a year and a half, Lincoln was able to regain his footing professionally and personally and resumed his engagement to Mary. They were married on November 4, 1842, just as Lincoln's eight years in the Illinois legislature were drawing to a close. He wrote in a letter, "Nothing new here, except my marrying, which to me, is a matter of profound wonder."[13]

Lincoln turned to the practice of law and raising a family. The first of their four sons, Robert Todd Lincoln, was born in 1843, within a year of Lincoln's marriage to Mary Todd. A second, Eddie, was born in 1846. Still, he had high hopes for a political career. He angled for the Whig nomination for Congress in 1842. While he lost, he did succeed in seeing that a rotation system was established among Whig aspirants for Congress, such that he would get his turn. In the meantime, he stayed active in the party by campaigning for his hero Henry Clay in the 1844 presidential election. Clay was defeated by the Democratic candidate, James K. Polk of Tennessee, another Jacksonian protégé, who became the eleventh president of the United States. The election of Polk, a slave owner, meant that nine of the first eleven US presidents had owned enslaved people. Only the two Adams never owned slaves.

Lincoln's turn for a seat in the US Congress came with the election of 1846. He won that year, but his single two-year term was the last elected office he held until he became president in 1861. There were two especially notable aspects of Lincoln's actions in Congress. First, along with other Whigs, he spoke against the war with Mexico that had been declared by Congress in the spring of 1846 at the strong urging of President James K. Polk. Northerners especially opposed the war. They believed that Polk had sacrificed the North for Southern interests by settling diplomatically the border dispute with Great Britain about the Oregon territory and then going to war with Mexico to grab land west of Texas, which would be open to slavery. In the case of Oregon, they felt that when Polk adopted the campaign slogan "Fifty-four Forty or Fight," he should have fought for Northern interests.

Lincoln challenged the legitimacy of Polk's *casus belli* from the previous spring. Polk had said that Mexicans had spilled American blood on American soil. Since much of the dispute with Mexico was about what was and was not American soil, Lincoln proposed the so-called "spot resolution," demanding to know on exactly what spot American blood had been spilled. This move had little effect, except to annoy Democrats and establish Lincoln's solidarity with other Whigs. He also confirmed his party allegiance by supporting the "Wilmot proviso," stipulating that any land gained from war with Mexico would not be open to slavery.

On a second issue, Lincoln's behavior was oddly out of sync with the Whig party line. Several party members had drafted a proposal for the abolition of slavery in the District of Columbia or the banning of the slave trade in the district. Lincoln voted against most other Whigs on these issues. But later he gave a speech outlining his own plan for abolishing slavery in the capital. Consistent with Henry Clay's approach, it called for gradual emancipation and compensation for slave owners. When it became clear that there was little or no support for his plan, Lincoln withdrew it. As in the case of his 1837 "protest," Lincoln's opposition to slavery was expressed in somewhat inconsistent and idiosyncratic fashion.

Despite his opposition to the Mexican War, Lincoln went home after this term in Congress and actively supported General Zachary Taylor, one of the military heroes of the war, as the Whig presidential candidate in 1848. Taylor won and became the twelfth president of the United States. Although he was a slave owner, he was not particularly supportive of slave interests in Congress.

While Lincoln mostly removed himself from politics in 1849 and the early 1850s, the Mexican War, as predicted, led to one of the most contentious and explosive periods in US history. For Lincoln, the year 1850 was marked by the death of his young son Eddie, but also the birth later that year of a third son, Willie. For the country, that year saw rancorous debate about whether slavery would be allowed in the territory acquired from Mexico, constituting most of the present-day Southwest and California. Civil war was a near thing. With Lincoln on the sidelines in Illinois, the aging Henry Clay proposed a comprehensive compromise settlement. While Clay's "omnibus" approach did not prevail, Illinois Democratic Senator Stephen A. Douglas skillfully guided each piece through Congress to achieve Clay's proposed compromise.[14] The major provisions of the Compromise of 1850 called for the admission of California as a free state, a stringent Fugitive Slave Law, and affirmation of the Missouri Compromise line banning slavery north of the 36 degree 30 minutes line of latitude, all the way to the Pacific Ocean. Thanks to Douglas's adroit political maneuvering, disunion and civil war were put aside for another decade. Lincoln must have noticed the acclaim that fell on his fellow Illinoisan and longtime political and personal rival. Not only did Douglas represent an opposing party, he had also been an early suitor of Mary Todd. Though Lincoln won Mary's hand, it seemed at that time that Douglas would forever eclipse him politically.

While Lincoln continued his law practice, Douglas remained a powerful force in the Senate. Then Douglas made a move in 1854 that disrupted the uneasy peace over slavery that had been in place since the compromise he had so skillfully achieved four years earlier. With the support of Democratic President Franklin Pierce, and in return for Southern support for a transcontinental railroad going west from Chicago, benefitting the citizens of Illinois and some of his own land deals, Douglas proposed what became known as the Kansas-Nebraska act. The act repealed the Missouri Compromise line and opened the large Kansas-Nebraska territory to slavery, if approved by the residents. This act rested on the principle of "popular sovereignty," which held that it should be up to the (white) people of those lands whether they wanted to organize as a free or slave state. He held that slavery was neither inherently good nor evil and that he was largely indifferent to whether new states were free or slave. This is exactly what the Southern "slave power" wanted. Perhaps predictably, this act brought Lincoln in from the sidelines. He became a candidate for the Illinois state legislature.

In the fall campaign of 1854, Lincoln expressed astonishment that Douglas could be indifferent to slavery as an institution. On October 16 in Peoria, he gave one of his most eloquent speeches, calling slavery, in his strongest language yet, a "monstrous injustice." While he still held that blacks could not be made equal, he called for their gradual emancipation from slavery. Citing the foundational republican principles of self-government, he argued that for a white man to govern himself was one thing, but to govern another man as a slave was "despotism." In a stirring closing to the speech, Lincoln returned to Thomas Jefferson and the language of the Declaration of Independence. Opposing Douglas's idea of abandoning the Missouri Compromise and opening more territory to slavery, Lincoln called on "all lovers of liberty everywhere" to "join in the great and good work. If we do this, we shall not only have saved the Union; but we shall have so saved it, as to make, and keep it, forever worthy of the saving."

Lincoln's speech had a galvanizing effect on anti-slavery forces in Illinois and around the country. The attention he received prompted him to withdraw as a candidate for the state legislature and enter a race for the open United States Senate seat. He narrowly lost his Senate bid, but he had become a significant figure in the new Republican Party. That party's unifying principle was opposition to Kansas-Nebraska and any expansion of slavery. In 1856, when the party fielded its first presidential candidate, John C. Fremont, Lincoln narrowly lost the nomination for vice president. Fremont lost to the Democrat, James Buchanan of Pennsylvania, who became the fifteenth president of the United States, and his running mate, John C. Breckenridge of Kentucky. Although Buchanan was a Northerner (just barely: he was born only a few miles above the Mason-Dixon Line), he was sympathetic to Southern slavery, as his predecessor Franklin Pierce of New Hampshire had been.

From 1856 forward, Lincoln was actively involved in Republican politics. Like other anti-slavery leaders, he was astounded by the 1857 Dred Scott decision of the US Supreme Court. By a 7–2 vote, Chief Justice Roger Taney, appointed by Andrew Jackson to succeed John Marshall, and other justices argued, among other things, that the black slave Dred Scott had no rights to citizenship. Taney further wrote that blacks had no rights that whites had to respect and that the Missouri Compromise line was unconstitutional since citizens could not be prevented from taking their property into any territory they pleased. Somehow, Taney (and the recently inaugurated President Buchanan) thought this decision would end controversy about slavery and make clear that there were essentially no limits on the rights to take one's property in slaves anywhere. To Republicans, this opened the possibility that soon the Court would rule that there "anywhere" included the free states, with the effect that slavery would spread throughout the country.

Stephen Douglas supported the Dred Scott decision, although it posed some challenges to his first principle of popular sovereignty. (If property owners could take their chattel slaves anywhere, how could people there vote that their territory or state must be free?) As a result, Lincoln began an almost immediate campaign against Douglas's re-election to the Senate in 1858. His initial strategy was to give speeches where Douglas had just spoken and to assail Douglas's moral indifference to slavery. In Springfield on June 16, 1858, Lincoln famously quoted Jesus from Matthew 12:25 in the Bible, saying a house divided against itself cannot stand and claiming that the Union would one day end up all slave (as Dred Scott seemed to portend) or all free (as, Lincoln argued, the founders had envisioned in the 1770s and 1780s).[15] Later that summer, he succeeded in prodding Douglas to agree to a series of seven carefully choreographed debates, one in each congressional district of Illinois. The debates were a spectacle, drawing thousands of people from nearby communities. The candidates spoke for a total of three hours each time, carefully responding to each other's statements. Both the visual and auditory contrast was unforgettable. Douglas was short, rotund, nattily dressed, and spoke rapidly with a "strong, sonorous voice."[16] Lincoln was tall, slender, unkempt, somewhat gawky, and spoke in a high register that carried effectively to the large crowds. As the debates continued, Douglas's voice began to wear out, while Lincoln became stronger and more forceful. Although Lincoln expressed varying degrees of racist opinion in different parts of the state, he became more outspoken about the evil of slavery, calling it a "moral, social, and political evil,"[17] and that the issue was clearly one of "right and wrong." He chided Douglas, claiming that he built his position "upon the basis of caring nothing about the very thing that every body does care the most about."[18] Although Republicans won more votes for open seats in the Illinois legislature, Douglas won the Senate race with the support of legislators not up for election in 1858.

Despite his second narrow defeat for an Illinois Senate seat, by focusing on the nation's most contested issue, the debates thrust Lincoln into the national spotlight as a possible candidate for the Republican Party's second campaign for the White House. Other party figures such as Salmon Chase of Ohio and William Seward of New York had much more prominence than Lincoln, but their visibility included negatives as well as positives. When Lincoln gave a well-received anti-slavery speech at New York City's Cooper Union on February 27, 1860, concluding by saying "Let us have faith that right makes might, and in that faith, let us, to the end, dare to do our duty as we understand it," he was catapulted to even greater fame.[19] In May, Lincoln was helped when the Republican convention was held in Chicago, his home state. Although he trailed William Seward on the first convention ballot, he nearly caught up on the second, and won on the third.

The presidential election of 1860 was among the most contentious and consequential of any in US history. It was also the most sectional in character. With Lincoln holding firm to the principle of no expansion of slavery, the Democratic Party split into Northern and Southern factions. Lincoln's longtime rival Stephen Douglas won the party nomination, but Southerners bolted and nominated their own candidate, the thirty-nine-year-old incumbent Vice President John C. Breckinridge. Disaffected former Whigs who could not support either Democratic or Republican policies nominated John Bell of Tennessee for their newly formed Constitutional Union Party. Lincoln won the election easily, winning the clear majority of electoral votes, all from the North and West, though just under 40% of the popular votes. Douglas finished second in popular votes with 22%, but he won only Missouri. Breckinridge carried eleven slave states, where Lincoln received almost no votes at all, receiving only 14% of the total votes. Bell won only 13% of the popular vote but carried the Upper South states of Virginia, Kentucky, and Tennessee. Lincoln would have easily won the election in the Electoral College even if all of the votes of the three other candidates had gone to one person. He carried the majority of votes in most Northern states but received almost none in most Southern states.

The challenges facing Lincoln immediately became clear. Even though he had always argued that the Constitution protected slavery where it existed in the Southern states, in just over a month, on December 20, 1860, South Carolina voted to secede from the Union, followed quickly by Georgia, Florida, Alabama, Mississippi, Louisiana, and Texas. To most of the South, Lincoln's opposition to the *expansion* of slavery and his belief that it was on the way to ultimate extinction were both morally repugnant and politically threatening. The seven Confederate States of the Union quickly formed their own government in Montgomery, Alabama, and named former US Senator Jefferson Davis of Mississippi the first president of the new nation. Lincoln contemplated these events as he planned his journey to the nation's capital. He would be inaugurated as the sixteenth president of the United States on March 4, 1861. Shortly before leaving, Lincoln went to visit his stepmother, Sarah Johnston Lincoln, and to pay respects at his father's grave. The winter travel was difficult, taking several days, but Lincoln persevered. The meeting was emotional. Carl Sandburg wrote in his biography of Lincoln that Sarah "was all of a mother to him" and that "He was her boy more than any born to her."[20] After he left, she expressed the fear that she would never see him again.[21] She was right. She lived to hear the news of her stepson's assassination, just over four years later.

As Lincoln left Springfield for the nation's capital on February 11, he spoke to the crowd gathered at the train station. He concluded,

> To this place, and the kindness of these people, I owe everything. Here I have lived a quarter of a century, and I have passed from a young man to an old man. Here my children have been born, and one is buried. I now leave, not knowing when, or whether ever, I may return, with a task before me greater than that which rested upon Washington . . . let us confidently hope that all will yet be well. To His care commending you, as I hope in your prayers you commend me, I bid you an affectionate farewell.[22]

That same day, Jefferson Davis left his home in Mississippi to accept the presidency of the seven states of the Confederacy. The role of slavery in driving the Southern states to secede was underlined by the order in which the first seven left the Union. That sequence was almost perfectly predictable from each state's percentage of slaves. South Carolina led the way with a slave population of 57%. Mississippi, the only other state with a majority slave population (55%), was second. The next four—Florida, Alabama, Georgia, and Louisiana—all had 44–47% slaves. The last of the original seven was Texas. It had comparatively few slaves, 30% of its population, and it seceded despite the opposition of its loyal governor, Sam Houston, the man most responsible for winning Texan independence from Mexico in 1836.

The seven states were prompted toward secession in part because Lincoln, while deftly political and tactically flexible, was immovable on the issue of the extension of slavery. As various compromises were proposed, in an effort to avoid secession or war, Lincoln wrote to one of his close allies, "Let there be no compromise on the question of *extending* slavery. If there be, all our labor is lost. . . . The tug has to come, & better now, than any time hereafter."[23] The tug, of course, did come. As noted, within two weeks, South Carolina began the rush to the Union exits. Interestingly, not all slave states followed. In fact, eight of them did not secede. Four of them were the "Upper South" states of Virginia, North Carolina, Tennessee, and Arkansas, which had—on average—28% enslaved African Americans. The other four were the "Border States" of Delaware, Maryland, Kentucky, and Missouri. Those states had much lower slave populations, ranging from only 2% in Delaware to 20% in Kentucky. Overestimating Union sentiment in the slave states, both those that had seceded and those that had not, Lincoln still hoped that as president he could find a way that would both keep the Upper South and Border States from leaving and bring the wayward seven back home.

The sixteenth presidency is clearly marked by what Doris Kearns Goodwin refers to in the subtitle of *Team of Rivals* as "the political genius of Abraham Lincoln."[24] At the same time, Lincoln's perspective on what we might call "contingency" vs. "agency" in successful leadership seems entirely accurate. In an April 1864 letter to Kentucky newspaper editor Albert Hodges, Lincoln wrote "I attempt no compliment to my own sagacity. I claim not to have controlled events, but confess plainly that events have controlled me."[25] Exactly eleven months later, in the opening lines of his second inaugural address, Lincoln mentioned "The progress of our arms, upon which all else chiefly depends."[26] Lincoln knew that crucial events were beyond his control. His actions were only one of many terms in a complex equation of unfolding history. He is so impressive in so much of what he said and did that it is easy to forget his words to Hodges: much was beyond his control.

Nevertheless, we see the new president attempting in his First Inaugural Address to reassure the South and begin to lure them back into the Union. He sought to hold firm to first principles but to otherwise be as flexible and conciliatory as possible. Thus Lincoln was unwavering, as always, on the subject of expanding slavery, but he wove differences about that one issue into an overall message of openness and reassurance. He acknowledged the divisive question. "One section of our country believes slavery is *right*, and ought to be extended, while the other believes it is *wrong*, and ought not to be extended." But then he added that "That is the only substantial dispute." And he placed that assertion in the middle of the address. In contrast, near the very beginning, he quoted from a speech he had given before: "I have no purpose, directly or indirectly, to interfere with the institution of slavery in the States where it exists. I believe I have no lawful right to do so, and I have no inclination to do so." He also stated that "the property, peace and security of no section are to be in anywise endangered" by his administration. Using the word "property" would have been particularly resonant to Southerners, who regarded their slaves as "a species of property." Lincoln also mentioned a proposed amendment to the Constitution passed by Congress only two days before "to the effect that the federal government shall never interfere with the domestic institutions of the States, including that of persons held to service." He added that he had "no objection" to this provision "being made express, and irrevocable." (As in 1787, even the strongest backers of slavery avoided inserting the words "slave" or "slavery" into the Constitution: thus, "persons held to service.") Finally, Lincoln attempted to appeal to the nation's history of patriotic unity.

> Though passion may have strained, it must not break our bonds of affection. The mystic chords of memory, stretching from every battle-field and patriot grave, to every living heart and hearthstone, all over this broad land, will yet swell the chorus of the Union, when again touched, as surely they will be, by the better angels of our nature.[27]

Despite its overall tone of conciliation and reconciliation, the speech did not move the South. Perhaps no matter how much Lincoln was willing to yield on specific issues, his implication that he personally believed slavery was "wrong" was more than people in slave states could accept. Human beings do not take well to their moral judgments and behavior being called into question. Lincoln could dilute his moral conviction about slavery within a great deal of soft, sentimental flexibility, but he could not and would not hide it. Still, he made the effort. And if he could not initially draw the seceding states back into the Union, he would do all in his power to avoid antagonizing the eight remaining slave states that might withdraw at any time. That approach would also reassure conservative Northerners that his object was simply to save the Union, not to emancipate slaves. Such an approach would not satisfy abolitionists or other radical elements in his party, but he judged that it had the best chance of achieving the main objective, preserving the integrity of the United States. As with George Washington, abolishing slavery took second place to maintaining the Union.

In the second month of Lincoln's presidency, the "tug" came again. Fort Sumter, a Union outpost in South Carolina's Charleston Harbor, was running out of provisions. The Confederates demanded that Lincoln surrender it. Most members of Lincoln's cabinet counseled that he do just that. The fort could not be protected or the soldiers in it rescued. Instead, Lincoln made the fateful decision to attempt to resupply Fort Sumter openly and peacefully. He told the governor of South Carolina that he would do so. He did it in such a way that Jefferson Davis would either have to let the provisions reach the fort or attack first, thus generating strong support throughout the North for military action. Davis chose to order an attack, and Fort Sumter quickly fell. The Civil War had started.

Lincoln responded by calling up 75,000 volunteers for ninety days to subdue the rebellion. He was obviously very much mistaken about what would be needed to achieve that goal, but he was under no great illusion that doing so would not be viewed by the Upper South states as "coercion" against fellow slave-holding states. Indeed, within two months, Virginia, Arkansas, North Carolina, and Tennessee (with the smallest percentage of slaves in the Confederacy, 25%) seceded, in that order. Now it would be crucial to hold the Border States of Kentucky, Maryland, Missouri, and Delaware.

Within a month of Fort Sumter, even before Tennessee seceded, a pivotal event took place that altered the course of the war from the very outset. Perhaps such an event was inevitable. It underlines the view that slaves themselves did more than anyone else to achieve their own emancipation. On May 21, 1861, three slaves who had been digging Confederate trenches in Norfolk, Virginia, heard the rumor that they would be moved south, away from their families, to work on fortifications in North Carolina. Rather than waiting to be deported, late one night they rowed across the mouth of the James River to Hampton and ran down the narrow strip of beach connecting Virginia's Middle Peninsula to Fortress Monroe, commanded by Union General Benjamin Butler. Butler at first was not sure what to do with the three men but it became clear to him the next day when a Confederate officer came down the same ribbon of sand under a flag of truce to demand that they be returned to their owner. In response to Butler's queries, the officer asserted that Butler must return the slaves under the provisions of the Fugitive Slave Act, adopted as part of the Compromise of 1850. One can imagine Butler, an experienced lawyer, trying to construe the officer's argument. He pondered that the officer represented a government formed in opposition to the United States, who was at the same time asking that the laws of the United States govern Butler's treatment of the escaped slaves. Butler said no, he would not return them. He also stated that since Southerners had seceded in order to protect a "species of property," in line with well-established principles of warfare, he would not return rebel slave "property." He sent the officer on his way and declared the three slaves "contraband of war," that is, property taken from the enemy. Although it was unclear, and would remain so for some time, whether the slaves were to be given freedom, Butler set the precedent for the Union holding at least some rebel slave property. Much to Lincoln's political advantage, he cast his decision not as one of freeing slaves but as one of confiscating enemy property. The latter argument most all supporters of the Union could applaud. In less than ten days, Lincoln's cabinet approved the "contraband" approach. Even though in July Congress passed the "Crittenden Resolution" stating that the war was being fought to save the Union and not to free slaves, that is, not to be "overthrowing or interfering with the rights or established institutions" of the rebelling states, the contraband precedent was formalized in August 1861 in the form of the Confiscation Act, signed by Lincoln. It held that escaped or captured slaves being used for Confederate military purposes need not be returned to their masters. Thus, three slaves rowing across a river forced a change in policy and, ultimately, history.

Perhaps the ambiguity resulting from federal policy contributed to an imbroglio involving Lincoln and General John C. Fremont, Lincoln's choice to direct the war effort in Missouri. Fremont had some political clout. The noted "Pathfinder" was married to Jessie Benton, the charismatic daughter of longtime US Senator Thomas Hart Benton. Fremont had been the first Republican presidential candidate in 1856. But he was an ineffective military commander and landed Lincoln in a political hotbox when he declared martial law in Missouri on August 30, 1861, and stated that slaves of rebel sympathizers were free. Lincoln, ever mindful of the uncertain loyalty of the Border States and opposition to emancipation among many Northerners, quickly rescinded the emancipation order.

One of Lincoln's closest allies, Orville Browning, protested that Lincoln was undermining the anti-slavery cause. In a famous letter of reply, Lincoln outlined the importance of not inflaming Border State opposition: "I think that to lose Kentucky is nearly the same as to lose the whole game. Kentucky gone, we can not hold Missouri, nor, as I think, Maryland. These all against us, and the job on our hands is too large for us."[28] These words are reminiscent of Lincoln supposedly telling a friend, "I hope to have God on my side, but I must have Kentucky." Lincoln and other Republicans walked a tightrope, holding firm to anti-slavery principles but not pressing for emancipation in a way that would lose the Border States.

For the remainder of 1861, as battles took place at Manassas Junction and elsewhere, there was relatively little progress on the question of slavery. Lincoln's own position on whether the war would seek to undermine slavery is somewhat ambiguous. In his December 1861 message to Congress, he said he hoped that the war would be fought without "violent and remorseless revolutionary conflict," which seemed to imply that he hoped not to disturb existing Southern institutions, but he did caution that "all indispensable means must be employed" to preserve the Union.[29] He seemed evasive about the status of slaves not returned to owners in accord with the Confiscation Act. He said that "the legal claims of certain persons to the labor and service of other persons have become forfeited" and he characterized "the latter" as "thus liberated."[30]

Still the status of "contrabands" was uncertain. Moreover Lincoln, in the tradition of Henry Clay, again pushed the idea of voluntary and gradual compensated emancipation accompanied by colonization.

In March of 1862, after the first major Union victory of the war, Ulysses S. Grant's capture of Fort Donelson on the Cumberland River in Tennessee, Lincoln submitted a message to Congress further advocating support for "any state which may adopt gradual abolishment of slavery," and in April signed an Emancipation Bill freeing slaves in the District of Columbia. That bill included compensation for slave owners and funds for the colonization of the freed slaves. Up to this point, Lincoln's position on slavery and African Americans had been essentially consistent, if at times somewhat ambiguous. It was the classic Whig/Henry Clay position. Slavery is wrong. It must inevitably be abolished, or else the whole country would have slaves and be dominated by slave interests. Emancipation should be gradual, owners should be compensated for the loss of slaves, white and black could not live together as equals, and freed slaves should be colonized outside of the United States.

One can only imagine the stress Lincoln was under during the first winter months of 1862, especially before Grant's February victory at Fort Donelson. That same month, Lincoln's bright, promising eleven-year-old son Willie died from a fever. Still, during that difficult time, Lincoln continued thinking about slavery. While earlier he had been convinced that emancipation would undermine and even defeat the war to preserve the Union, due to Border State and Northern Democratic opposition, he began to think that perhaps emancipation and preservation might work together. In his December message to Congress, he had already introduced the concept of "indispensable means" to preserve the Union. Clearly taking away Southern slaves had made the Confederacy's war effort more difficult. Slaves at home enabled white boys to leave and fight. Emancipating slaves (or, if one preferred, confiscating rebel property) would further degrade rebel fighting capacity. Furthermore, while it would raise other explosive issues, freed slaves need not be sidelined. They could labor for and perhaps even fight for the Union, against their former owners. That is, freeing (and perhaps, arming) slaves might be one of the "indispensable means." In short, Lincoln began thinking that a harder war policy was indispensable to subduing the rebellion. In a letter he wrote to an attorney in New Orleans that year, he ridiculed the notion that the war could be fought "with elder-stalk squirts, charged with rose water." In the same letter, however, Lincoln foreswore a harder approach than that which was indispensable: "I shall do nothing in malice. What I deal with is too vast for malicious dealing."[31]

The evolution of Lincoln's views aside, in the spring of 1862, Union military success ("upon which all else chiefly depends") seemed to presage an end to the war. If that spring and summer's Peninsula Campaign by General George McClellan, a staunch Democrat and implacable foe of emancipation, had succeeded, the war might have ended in 1862 with no change in the South's "peculiar institution." However, Robert E. Lee took over the Army of Northern

Virginia, defeated and demoralized McClellan in what are known as the Seven Days Battles at the end of June, and Confederate success, along with recognition by Great Britain and France, seemed likely. It was a desperate time for the Lincoln administration.

Lincoln often deliberated slowly, but in July of 1862 he moved fast. He began to seriously consider freeing slaves by proclamation in rebel states; he met with Border State representatives in an effort to enlist their support for compensated emancipation and colonization of slaves from their states. As in the past, he found little support for that idea. The next day, for the first time, he first floated the possibility of an emancipation proclamation to two cabinet officers, Secretary of State William Seward and Navy Secretary Gideon Welles. Both were open to the idea. On July 17, he signed the Militia Act, providing for the enlistment of blacks in the war effort. Five days later, on July 22, Lincoln submitted a draft of an emancipation proclamation to the whole cabinet. It would declare slaves in states or parts of states still in rebellion "forever free," and it included language about compensated emancipation to owners in the loyal states, as well as efforts toward colonization of liberated slaves. While the members of the cabinet generally supported Lincoln, Seward suggested that he time the announcement of any such proclamation carefully. Specifically, he argued, it should wait for a Union victory, so that it did not seem to be a desperate measure (which in some measure it clearly seemed to be). For the time being, Lincoln put the draft back in a desk drawer. Several weeks later, on August 14, he met with a delegation of recently freed men to enlist their support for colonization. Though initially intrigued, both black leaders and white abolitionists soon excoriated Lincoln for suggesting that free blacks be deported from their homes to foreign lands.

Though the concepts of compensated emancipation and colonization received little support, Lincoln proceeded with developing the main thrust of an emancipation proclamation, holding that as president and commander in chief of the army and navy, he would free slaves in disloyal states as an "indispensable means" to defeat the rebellion. At the same time, Lincoln knew he would have to prepare the public for the rationale he would give for the kind of "revolutionary" measure he had stated he wished to avoid in his message of the previous December to Congress. Fortuitously, a letter from the influential and mercurial editor of the *New York Tribune*, Horace Greeley, provided Lincoln the opportunity to lay the groundwork.

Greeley wrote that Lincoln's policies of gradual, compensated emancipation bent too much to the wishes of the Border States and that "all attempts to put down the Rebellion and at the same time uphold its inciting cause are preposterous."[32] This gave Lincoln an opportune moment to begin to explain his thinking about the linkage of slave emancipation and union preservation, and his constitutional and personal views on both. In his famous letter to Greeley of August 22, the president was indirect about his view of his constitutional warrants for freeing slaves but very clear about his personal wishes.

The most often quoted section of the letter reads, "If I could save the Union without freeing *any* slave I would do it, and if I could save it by freeing *all* the slaves I would do it; and if I could save it by freeing some slaves and leaving others alone I would also do that." (Of course, the third alternative is the one Lincoln had written into his draft emancipation proclamation.) Many critics of Lincoln have taken that sentence to mean that Lincoln was indifferent to slaves and the issue of slavery. However, Lincoln made clear, as he always had, his aversion to slavery. He set the last sentence in the letter off as a separate paragraph, reading, "I have here stated my purpose according to my view of *official* duty; and I intend no modification of my oft-expressed *personal* wish that all men every where could be free."[33]

The key passage is Lincoln's assertion that his statement about freeing none, some, or all slaves accords with his view of official duty, that is, his constitutional responsibilities. In his First Inaugural Address, Lincoln stated that he had "no lawful right to interfere" with slavery where it existed, but now he suggested that "*official* duty" may require him to free slaves, as a means of saving the Union. He would, he said, free some or all of the slaves if by doing so he could save the Union. And clearly it was his official duty, above all, to save the Union created by the Constitution.

On September 17, 1862, a Union army under the command of George McClellan achieved a dramatic strategic victory by stopping Robert E. Lee's invasion of Northern states. Five days later, a preliminary emancipation proclamation was issued. It first announced that the president would work with Congress to develop a means of compensated emancipation and colonization of slaves in states that "may not then be in rebellion against the United States." Then it announced that as of January 1, 1863, slaves in states still "in rebellion against the United States shall be then, thenceforward, and forever free." No compensation possibility was mentioned for such slaves. Within the Union, those most opposed to slavery were most supportive. Importantly, outside the United States, with the war now joining the objectives of preservation of the Union and emancipation of slaves, England and France gave up any flirtation with the idea of recognizing the Confederate States of America. The United States had unequivocally claimed the moral high ground, and Europe would support them.

With noncompensated emancipation now the declared fate of states still in rebellion as of the new year, Lincoln took up in earnest the idea of compensated emancipation for loyal states yet one more time. In his December 1, 1862, message to Congress, he used some of his most celebrated rhetoric to promote that policy. The policy didn't endure much longer, but Lincoln's words did. He wrote "we must think anew, and act anew . . . then we shall save our country." He concluded,

In *giving* freedom to the *slave*, we *assure* freedom to the *free*—honorable alike to what we give, and what we preserve. We shall nobly save, or meanly lose, the last best, hope of earth. Other means may succeed;

Figure 3.2 Harriet Tubman helped slaves escape to freedom on the Underground Railroad before the Civil War. During the conflict, she urged them to join the United States Colored Troops.

H. B. Lindsley, "Harriet Tubman," between 1860–1875, black and white photograph. Library of Congress, Washington, DC. Public domain, via Wikimedia Commons.

this could not fail. The way is plain, peaceful, generous, just—a way which if followed, the world will forever applaud, and God must forever bless.[34]

Thus, ironically, some of Lincoln's most quoted eloquence advocated a policy that went nowhere and that he very soon abandoned.

One month later, on New Year's Day, 1863, Lincoln signed the Emancipation Proclamation. It quoted the parts of the preliminary announcement pertaining to states (or parts of states) still in rebellion. No mention was made of loyal states or of compensated emancipation. In addition to declaring that slaves in rebellious states "are, and henceforward shall be, free," it proclaimed that "such persons of suitable condition will be received into the armed service of the United States."[35] This last element made the Emancipation Proclamation even more antithetical to the South. It was bad enough to free slaves, but to arm them was truly frightening. Some people doubted whether Lincoln would actually go through with signing the proclamation. In many places in the North, crowds gathered on January 1 to hear by telegram that he actually had. They became anxious as the hours passed. In the White House, Lincoln had spent much of the day greeting visitors, as was common on New Year's Day. When he returned to his office to sign the proclamation, he said he wanted to wait momentarily until his hand was less tired from shaking hands. He wanted to wait until he could write his signature firmly, so that no one could say that he hesitated. As he did, he said, "I never, in my life, felt more certain that I was doing right, than I do in signing this paper . . . If my name ever goes into history it will be for this act, and my whole soul is in it."[36]

Critics have lamented the fact that such a momentous document is devoid of inspirational rhetoric and is instead populated by legalistic terms such as "Whereas, . . ."; "Now, therefore, . . ."; and "And by virtue of the power and for the purpose aforesaid. . . . " This view does not consider the very delicate political and constitutional step Lincoln was taking and the appropriateness of a lawful-sounding document. Nor does it recognize Lincoln once again stating his personal, moral view at the very end of the document: "And upon this act, sincerely believed to be an act of justice, warranted by the Constitution upon military necessity, I invoke the considerate judgment of mankind and the gracious favor of Almighty God."

With emancipation and preservation joined as war aims, Lincoln never wavered from the transformative goal of freeing slaves without compensation, although he had to withstand tremendous pressures to back off. From the beginning, many people said whites would not fight to free blacks, but Lincoln defended his policies carefully in letters likely to be made public. In his 1864 letter to Hodges, mentioned earlier, he used the word "indispensable," as in indispensable means or indispensable necessity, no fewer than five times. That was always the constitutional justification, and the president repeated it as often as was necessary. At times he was moved to speak eloquently of the contributions of African Americans, who began fighting in units of the United States Colored Troops in 1863. Writing to James Conkling, a friend from Illinois in August of 1863, he wrote, "You say you will not fight to free negroes. Some of them seem willing to fight for you; but, no matter." Toward the conclusion of the same letter he added: "Peace does not appear so distant as it did. I hope it will come soon, and come to stay; and so come as to be worth the keeping in all

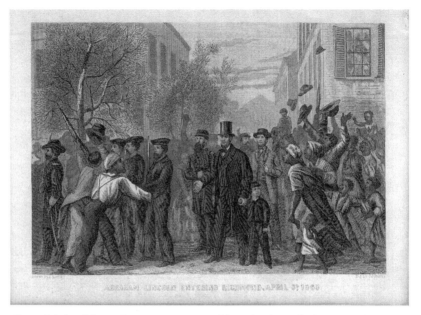

Figure 3.3 An African American woman celebrated when Abraham Lincoln visited Richmond on April 4, 1865. She reportedly said, "I know that I am free, for I have seen Father Abraham and felt him."

Lambert Hollis, engraved by J. C. Buttre, "Abraham Lincoln Entering Richmond, April 3d, 1865," 1865. The Virginia Historical Society, Richmond, Virginia. 1999.161.561.

future time.... And then, there will be some black men who can remember that, with silent tongue, and clenched teeth, and steady eye, and well-poised bayonet, they have helped mankind on to this great consummation."[37]

In early June of 1864, Lincoln was renominated for president with loyal Tennessee Senator Andrew Johnson as his running mate. But that summer, prospects for Union victory reached a new low point. Grant's army in Virginia and William T. Sherman's army in Georgia seemed stalemated at best. The so-called Copperhead Democrats pushed for peace, somehow under the illusion that a truce would bring the South back into the Union. Jefferson Davis knew that if Confederate forces could hold on until the November election, Lincoln would likely be voted out and a new Union government would likely end up letting the Confederacy go. Public debate focused on the Copperhead assertion that if only Lincoln would give up the precondition for talks of "abandonment of slavery," the war would end and the South would come back to the Union. While this view seems absurd—there's no way the South would come back unless compelled by military force—it had enough currency that Lincoln was under tremendous pressure to at least test the waters around that possibility. Even Horace Greeley, who had written two years earlier that it would be "preposterous" to think of putting down the rebellion without also putting down its "inciting cause," now urged Lincoln to give up the emancipation precondition. During the darkest days of August, when the "progress of our arms" seemed completely arrested, Lincoln in fact drafted two letters to intermediaries suggesting that he was willing to agree with Jefferson Davis on the restoration of the Union and then negotiate "all remaining questions," including, presumably, emancipation, "by peaceful modes."[38] In the end, Lincoln sent neither letter, even though he was convinced at that point that he would lose the election and that he must try to win the war before the inauguration of his successor.

In the fall, however, "the progress of our arms" brightened. On September 3 came welcome news from General Sherman in Georgia: "Atlanta is ours, and fairly won." In October, General Philip Sheridan won several spectacular victories in the Shenandoah Valley. Lincoln was re-elected easily over his former general, George McClellan. Although the charismatic "Little Mac" commanded his soldiers' affection early in the war, by the end Lincoln's constancy and his personal contact with men of all ranks at Union encampments had won them over. He prevailed in the election with overwhelming support from troops who went home to vote for him or cast absentee ballots.

Now it was time to look to the future and to plan for reconstruction. In his second inaugural address, on March 4, 1865, Lincoln signaled his vision for the way forward:

> With malice toward none, with charity for all, with firmness in the right as God gives us to see the right, let us strive on to finish the work we are in, to bind up the nations wounds, to care for him who shall have borne the battle and for his widow and his orphan, to do all which may achieve a just, and a lasting peace.[39]

As always, Lincoln was magnanimous. A month later, he did allow himself what today might be called a victory lap. He said, "I want to see Richmond," and arranged to tour the city with a small contingent of sailors just two days after the Confederate government had abandoned the city. Those who welcomed him were predominantly African Americans, some of whom got close enough to touch him. One woman declared, "I know that I am free, for I have seen Father Abraham and felt him."[40] A week later, Lincoln combined his generosity of spirit with humor. Responding to a serenading crowd outside the White House, he declined to speak formally but rather made a request:

> I have always thought "Dixie" one of the best tunes I have ever heard. Our adversaries over the way attempted to appropriate it, but I insisted yesterday that we fairly captured it . . . the Attorney General . . . gave it as his legal opinion that it is our lawful prize. I now request the band to favor me with its performance.[41]

The next night, the president gave a more formal address offering his view of the future. He approvingly mentioned initial progress made by a new government in Louisiana to bring African Americans into the mainstream. He noted that it had "adopted a free-state constitution, giving the benefit of public schools equally to black and white, and empowering the Legislature to confer the elective franchise upon the colored man." In the crowd listening to the speech was John Wilkes Booth. He spat, "That means nigger citizenship. Now, by God, I'll put him through."[42] Three nights later, on Good Friday, April 14, Booth made good on his threat. The war soon ended, but Lincoln was gone.

Abraham Lincoln is often ranked as the greatest American president. He saved the Union and did more than any other president to move the nation toward equality for African Americans. The results of the Civil War, and his presidency, were, as he said in his second inaugural address, "astounding." Slavery was abolished. Giant steps were taken toward resolving the American dilemma. Although Lincoln always regarded slavery as a great wrong, his thinking about African Americans grew tremendously during his years in the White House. He abandoned the view, advanced by Thomas Jefferson, Henry Clay, and others, that blacks and whites could not live together on the North American continent and that African Americans must be colonized somewhere else. He came to believe that black citizens should be educated and given the vote. For that stance, John Wilkes Booth killed him. For the Emancipation Proclamation, Lincoln invoked "the considerate judgment of mankind, and the gracious favor of Almighty God." He earned both.

Notes

1 John Locke Scripps, *1860 Campaign Life of Abraham Lincoln* (Peoria, IL: E. J. Jacob, 1860).

2 Doris Kearns Goodwin, *Team of Rivals: The Political Genius of Abraham Lincoln* (New York: Simon & Schuster, 2005), p. 47.

3 Kendra Cherry, http://psychology.about.com/od/personalitydevelopment/a/big five.htm.

4 Eric Foner, *The Fiery Trial: Abraham Lincoln and American Slavery* (New York: Norton, 2010), p. 10.

5 *Ibid.*, p. 12.

6 *Ibid.*, p. 11.

7 Abraham Lincoln, Letter to Albert Hodges, April 4, 1864. In Don E. Fehrenbacherer (ed.), *Lincoln: Speeches and Writings 1859–1865* (New York: Library of America, 1989), pp. 585–86.

8 Lincoln, http://www.nps.gov/liho/historyculture/1859autobio.htm.

9 Foner, p. 25.

10 *Ibid.*

11 *Ibid.*

12 Goodwin, p. 94.

13 Goodwin, p. 101.

14 Robert Remini, *At the Edge of the Precipice: Henry Clay and the Compromise That Saved the Union* (New York: Basic Books, 2010).

15 Lincoln, House Divided Speech, June 16, 1858. In Don E. Fehrenbacher (ed.), *Lincoln: Speeches and Writings 1832–1858* (New York: Library of America, 1989), pp. 426–34.

16 Henry Villard, "Recollections of Lincoln." http://www.theatlantic.com/past/docs/issues/95nov/lincoln/vilinc.htm.

17 Lincoln, Debate at Knox College, October 7, 1858. In Fehrenbacherer 1832–1858, pp. 701–21.

18 Richard Carwardine, *Lincoln: A Life of Purpose and Power* (New York: Knopf, 2003), p. 84.

19 Lincoln, Cooper Union Address, February 27, 1860. In Fehrenbacher 1859–1865, pp. 111–30.

20 Carl Sandburg, *Abraham Lincoln: The Prairie Years and the War Years* (New York: Stirling Publishing Co, 1954), p. 128.

21 Shelby Foote, *The Civil War: A Narrative: Volume 1: Fort Sumter to Perryville* (New York: Random House, 1958), p. 35.

22 Lincoln, Remarks at Springfield, February 11, 1861. In Fehrenbacherer 1859–1865, p. 199.

23 Lincoln, Letter to Lyman Trumball, December 10, 1860. In Fehrenbacher 1859–1865, p. 190.

24 Goodwin.

25 Lincoln, Letter to Albert Hodges, April 4, 1864. In Fehrenbacherer 1859–1865, pp. 585–86.

26 Lincoln, Second Inaugural Address, March 4, 1865. In Fehrenbacher 1859–1865, pp. 686–87.

27 Lincoln, First Inaugural Address, March 4, 1861. In Fehrenbacher 1859–1865, pp. 215–24.

28 Lincoln, Letter to Orville Browning, September 22, 1861. In Fehrenbacher 1859–1865, pp. 268–70.

29 Lincoln, Message to Congress, December 3, 1861. In Fehrenbacher 1859–1865, pp. 279–97.

30 Lincoln, Message to Congress, December 1861. In Fehrenbacher 1859–1865, pp. 279–97.

31 Lincoln, Letter to Cuthbert Bullitt, July 28, 1862. In Fehrenbacher 1859–1865, pp. 344–46.

32 Horace Greeley, The Prayer of Twenty Millions, August 19, 1862. http://www.civilwarhome.com/lincolngreeley.htm.

33 Lincoln, Letter to Horace Greeley, August 2, 1862. In Fehrenbacher 1859–1865, pp. 357–58.

34 Lincoln, Message to Congress, December 1, 1862. In Fehrenbacher 1859–1865, pp. 393–415.

35 Lincoln, Emancipation Proclamation, January 1, 1863. In Fehrenbacher 1859–1865, pp. 424–25.

36 Goodwin, p. 839n.

37 Lincoln, Letter to James Conkling, August 26, 1863. In Fehrenbacher 1859–1865, pp. 495–99.

38 James M. McPherson, *Tried by War: Abraham Lincoln as Commander in Chief* (New York: The Penguin Press, 2008), p. 241.

39 Lincoln, Second Inaugural Address, March 4, 1865. In Fehrenbacher 1859–1865, pp. 686–87.

40 Foner, p. 329.

41 Lincoln, Address from White House, April 10, 1865. In Fehrenbacher 1859–1865, p. 696.

42 Foner, p. 332.

4

ULYSSES S. GRANT

Figure 4.1 Early in his presidency, Ulysses S. Grant strongly supported the ratification of the Fifteenth Amendment to the Constitution barring discrimination in voting on the basis of race.

Mathew Brady, "US President Ulysses S. Grant," 1870, black and white photograph. Library of Congress, Washington, DC. Public domain, via Wikimedia Commons.

Ulysses S. Grant was the last US president to own a slave. Ten of the first twelve presidents (with the exception of both Adams) owned slaves at some point, and eight of them (Washington, Jefferson, Madison, Monroe, Jackson, Tyler, Polk,

Taylor, but not Van Buren and Harrison) owned them while serving as president. The last presidents to own slaves were Andrew Johnson and Grant.[1] Johnson had freed all his enslaved persons by the time, as military governor in 1864, he declared all slaves in Tennessee free. Grant owned one slave only briefly. The slave, William Jones, was given to him by Grant's father-in-law, Frederick Dent, in 1858, three years before the start of the Civil War. Grant and Jones and two other hired slaves worked Dent's farm, unsuccessfully, that year. One of those Grant hired, "Old Uncle Jason," said that Grant was the kindest master for whom he ever worked and that he paid more than was necessary. Similarly, a white man observing Grant said that he "was fooling away his money paying" way more for the hired slaves' labor than necessary. He also accused Grant of "aspoiling them."[2] Consistent with a lifelong pattern of "fooling away his money," Grant simply freed William Jones in 1859, even though he could have sold Jones for much-needed funds. Biographers of Grant disagree on a great deal, but they concur that his action in freeing his one slave was a principled one. Some of the efforts that Grant made for African Americans during his presidency have been interpreted by some as motivated merely by political opportunism. As we shall see later, the historical record better supports the theory that his presidential actions on behalf of black Americans, as with freeing Jones, were based on principle.

Ulysses S. Grant was the first of six children born to Jesse Root Grant and Hannah Simpson Grant on April 27, 1822. He was called Hiram Ulysses Grant, his classical middle name being given by Hannah's well-educated stepmother. Grant's two brothers and three sisters were born between 1825 and 1839. Grant outlived all but his youngest sibling, Mary. The Grant family lived in a small house with a magnificent view of the Ohio River in Point Pleasant, a small community in southeast Ohio, not far from where thirteen-year-old Abraham Lincoln lived downstream in Indiana. Grant's father owned a tannery. He was ambitious and politically active. His mother cared for her large brood and struck those who knew her as calm, sensible, and somewhat shy.

Grant had an unusual gift in handling horses from his very first years, when he seemed to be able to hang on their tails without disturbing them. By age eight he could drive a team of horses hauling wagon loads of wood. By eleven he was plowing fields with teams of horses. He detested the smell of his father's tannery and shirked work there as much as he could. He and his father finally settled on an arrangement whereby Grant did all the work involving horses. Biographer William McFeely writes that Ulysses, as he was called, saw horses as "wonderfully differentiated individuals," not just a source of leather. "He could size up each animal that he encountered: master this one's truculence and urge that one to a feat of strength in hauling rock."[3] From an early age, his touch with horses was not matched by interpersonal or business savvy. He described in his memoirs how his father agreed that he could buy a colt from a Mr. Ralston and instructed him on negotiations. Instead of following the script, he blurted out to Ralston, "Papa says I may offer you twenty dollars for the colt, but if you won't take that I am to offer twenty-two and a half, and if you won't take that, I am to give you twenty-five."[4]

Grant's work arrangement with his father was operating well enough that he was surprised when, at age seventeen, Jesse, using his political connections, arranged for an appointment to the United States Military Academy at West Point. Grant's initial reaction was that he wouldn't go, but his father said he would, and that was the end of it. In his memoirs, Grant wrote that he doubted that he had what it took to succeed: "I really had no objection to going to West Point, except that I had a very exalted idea of the acquirements to get through. I did not believe I possessed them, and could not bear the idea of failing."[5] But he had long been intrigued by the thought of travel, and going to the academy at age seventeen at least offered that. When he arrived, he quickly acquired a new name, and a new nickname. The congressman who appointed Grant wrote the War Department that the new cadet was Ulysses Simpson Grant, thinking Grant's middle name was his mother's maiden name. Grant quickly discovered that, like it or not, he was to be known at the Academy as U. S. Grant from Ohio. When other cadets saw the initials, a number of nicknames suggested themselves including United States Grant and Uncle Sam Grant. The latter had more resonance, and Grant was known to his classmates, forever, as Sam Grant. One account of Grant's first year reports that during a drill a large cadet repeatedly shoved the slight, 5-foot-1-inch, 117-pound Grant out of line. Grant asked him to stop; when that didn't happen, Grant floored him with one punch. He did not know how to negotiate, but he could stand up for himself.[6]

Although shy, he was well liked, but he was close to only a few. He found himself generally bored with the curriculum and had no abiding interest in the military. He did well enough in mathematics, the subject that required the least effort, and spent as much time as he could reading a range of English and American novels. The one aspect of the curriculum he found compelling was drawing and painting. He spent as much time with the Academy's famous drawing teacher, Robert Weir, as he could, and produced some highly creditable work. Extracurricularly, his energies, predictably, were drawn to horses. When he graduated in 1843, just below the middle of his class, his equestrian talents were a featured attraction at the commencement ceremonies. On a massive horse named York, which only one other cadet could ride, and not as well as Grant, he set a jumping record that stood for twenty-five years. Another cadet remembered the occasion. As horse and rider raced down the riding hall, "The horse increased his pace, and measured his strides for the great leap before him, bounded into the air and cleared the bar, carrying his rider as if man and beast were welded together. The spectators were breathless."[7]

Grant's roommate in his senior year was Frederick Dent, a young man from a well-to-do family in St. Louis. When Grant visited Dent's home in early 1844, from his posting at nearby Jefferson Barracks, he met Dent's sister, Julia. Julia was vivacious and attractive. She and Grant spent many hours together, mostly outdoors, riding horses over her father's extensive holdings. In contrast to Julia,

Grant was reticent. While he likely felt socially inferior, he also clearly viewed himself on a personal basis as tough and capable as anyone else.

In that year, tensions between Mexico and the United States, largely provoked by the Americans, were getting worse and worse. President John Tyler wanted to annex the Republic of Texas, as did most Texans, and Mexico was still smarting from having to grant Texas independence in 1836. It was an explosive mix. In the summer of 1844, Grant's unit was ordered to northwest Louisiana, to be ready to act if troubles with Mexico boiled over. Grant left Jefferson Barracks, and the Dent's home, called White Haven, to visit and say goodbye to his parents. He realized then that he was very much in love with Julia and found that she reciprocated his feelings. In 1845, the two became unofficially engaged, though realizing that it might be some time before they could marry.

In March of 1845, a new president of the United States, the eleventh, was inaugurated. He was James K. Polk of Tennessee, a man clearly interested in a war against a weaker neighbor that could lead to the territorial expansion of the United States. Sparring between the United States and Mexico eventually but inevitably led to an American declaration of war in early 1846. Grant saw plenty of action. Although he was assigned to quartermaster or supply duties, he would go to the front whenever his unit was engaged. In August of 1846, an army under the command of Zachary Taylor entered the Mexican city of Monterey. When house-to-house fighting broke out, Grant's unit found itself in need of more ammunition. Grant was the sole volunteer to ride through the narrow city streets, under enemy fire, to get word to headquarters. On his mount, Nelly, Grant hooked one foot over the saddle and, leaning over the horse's side to shield himself from Mexican bullets, galloped through the streets to carry the news. In his later accounts, Grant seemed to think Nelly was the brave one. He wrote, "It was only at street crossings that my horse came under fire, but these I crossed at such a flying rate that generally I was past and under cover of the next block of houses before the enemy fired."[8] (Grant did not mention the obvious, that he also "came under fire.")

Grant participated in another crucial engagement when General Winfield Scott's army marched from the Gulf Coast town of Vera Cruz to Mexico City. American forces were stalled near the lookout post of San Cosme, near the fortress of Chapultepec. Grant recognized that the belfry of a church offered a commanding view of the area and took the initiative. With a small detachment, he hoisted a light howitzer up to the belfry, fired a few shots, scattering Mexican troops, and cleared the way for bogged down US units to advance. His actions throughout the war drew him favorable notice from superior officers. One of those was a captain from Virginia, Robert E. Lee. Grant played down whatever public attention he might get in a letter to Julia, "There is no great sport in having bullets flying about one in every direction, but I find they have less horror when among them than when in anticipation."[9]

Mexican forces were defeated by the end of 1847, but it was not until February of 1848 that a treaty was signed, and not until late May that it was finally ratified by both sides. During those long months, Grant remained in Mexico City. Fortunately, there was a good deal to see and do, and Grant was quite taken with Mexico. When he finally returned back to a posting in Mississippi, he obtained a leave to reunite with Julia. Wedding arrangements were quickly made, and the two were married in August of 1848, more than three years after their betrothal. Grant was still with the 4th Infantry, and he and Julia were given assignments in Sackets Harbor, New York, and Detroit. For the time being, it looked like Grant would be a career Army officer. Their first son, Fred, was born in Detroit in 1850; by the middle of 1852 Julia was due to have a second child.

Then, rather suddenly, the Grant family's idyllic—if somewhat dull—posting was rudely interrupted. The Gold Rush had begun three years before, and the War Department decided that a greater military presence was required in the new state of California. At that time, there were three ways to get to the West Coast. One could sail around Cape Horn, cross the American continent, or traverse the fifty-mile Isthmus of Panama. Based on faulty extrapolation from the Mexican War, the American military decided that crossing the Isthmus was the best choice. Work on the Panama Railroad had begun, but was nowhere near complete. Nevertheless, the 4th Infantry was ordered west via the Isthmus, and Grant, as quartermaster, was in charge of logistics. However, many of the arrangements made for the regiment created serious obstacles. Grant carefully assembled supplies on Governors Island in New York Harbor, but he discovered that the steamship *Ohio* provided for the trip south was designed for only about a third of the soldiers and the party of civilians on board and that there was insufficient space for equipment and supplies. As a result, many of the regiment had to sleep on deck during the eight-day trip from New York to Colon, located on the Caribbean side of the Isthmus of Panama.

When the tired group arrived at Colon, things went from bad to worse. There was a cholera epidemic in Panama and no medical facilities. It was July, in the midst of the rainy season. Many streets were underwater or no more than mud flats. The transportation that the War Department had supposedly arranged never actually materialized. The thirty-year-old Grant had to improvise. Biographers have noted the "calm determination" and "organizational strength" with which Grant went about finding a way to solve the logistical problems.[10] He also demonstrated the kindness and concern for the welfare of others that were part of his character. The first part of the transit was by the short portion of the Panama Railroad that had been completed. Then the party proceeded by dugout canoe, poled up the Chagres River by naked "natives" who inspired much commentary from both men and women.

Having gone as far as possible by rail and water, roughly halfway, mules would take the party over the continental divide to the primitive Pacific city of Panama. Contracted mules were not forthcoming, and Grant finally made his own arrangements. He remained behind with a group that included most of the sick and the women and children. He was last to leave. It took nine days in all to traverse the fifty miles up the river and through mountainous jungles in intense heat, heavy rains, swamps, and mud. Once on the Pacific side, Grant established a hospital on one of the islands in the Bay of Panama and another for the more seriously ill on a ship anchored in the harbor. The regiment had to wait a month for the cholera outbreak to run its course. During this time, Grant was described by one member of the expedition as "a man of iron, so far as endurance went, seldom sleeping. . . . He was like a ministering angel to us all."[11] Besides caring for the ill, Grant had to contend with a panicky and potentially rebellious group of soldiers. A woman who had met Grant on the journey from New York wrote that Grant "had not only the sick ones to contend with but also the well."[12] Estimates vary as to the loss of life, but roughly one third of the party perished, including most of the children, who were not as resistant to the dehydration caused by cholera.

In late August, Grant and the surviving regiment arrived in San Francisco and made their way overland to Fort Vancouver across the Columbia River from Portland, Oregon. While there, Grant undertook several business ventures with various acquaintances. One was to grow and sell potatoes and oats along the Columbia River. Another was to establish a club for billiards and other games in a seaport hotel near San Francisco. When Grant visited the hotel, he found that the manager had run off with the money he had been given to set up the club. When he returned to the Columbia River, he found that the land he and his fellow captains had cultivated had flooded. Both ventures failed, and Grant lost his meager savings. In addition to the financial setbacks, Grant missed Julia and their two children. Their second son, Ulysses S. Grant, Jr. (known as Buck) was born shortly after Grant had left New York. Grant grew agitated as letters from Julia arrived infrequently. The news he did receive revealed that she was enjoying life in her parents' home in St. Louis much more than he was enjoying Oregon. This further depressed him.

Things only got worse. The young Lieutenant was assigned to duty in Fort Humboldt in Northern California. It was considerably more isolated than Fort Vancouver, and Grant suffered further from loneliness and boredom. For relief, he enjoyed playing cards with friends in nearby Eureka and riding horses around the majestic countryside. Although the accounts are murky, he also enjoyed too much alcohol. For whatever reason, Grant fell out of favor with the fort commander; just when he was promoted to captain, he resigned from the army. Grant was most likely clinically depressed at this point in his life. There is more ambiguity about whether he was forced to resign for reasons of drunkenness. Grant's father, Jesse, tried to forestall the resignation, worrying about Grant's future and the damage to his and his son's reputation if Ulysses failed in the service. However, Grant himself pushed the resignation through and headed back to Julia, by way of Cape Horn and New York City. When he arrived in New York, debt payments he expected had not appeared, and Grant borrowed money from his close West Point friend, Simon Bolivar Buckner. He also delayed travel to St. Louis because he had not heard word from Julia, and he was uncertain whether she would welcome him home. This clearly was one of the low points of Grant's life. However, Julia did finally write a warm letter, and Grant eventually made his way home in August of 1854, a thirty-two-year-old former army officer with uncertain prospects. His father once again attempted to intervene in Grant's life, offering him a position in the family leather goods store in Galena, Illinois, on the condition that Julia and the children stay with him in Kentucky. Grant quietly declined.

While the next six years brought little improvement to Grant's professional life, being reunited with Julia outweighed all other failures. The couple's only daughter Ellen (Nellie) was born in 1855, less than a year after Grant returned from California; their last child, a son named Jesse, was born in 1858. They initially made their home on a sixty-acre parcel of White Haven land given to them by Julia's father. Grant felt that farming suited him, worked industriously to build a two-story house, somewhat jokingly called Hardscrabble, and planted crops. Reflecting the social and racial arrangements of the times, even though Grant had little money, Julia owned several slaves given by her father, and Grant himself therefore was in command of slave labor. As mentioned above, he not only treated his own slaves humanely but intervened to stop a neighbor from whipping his own slaves. Despite strenuous effort, the economy of the time did not support Grant's farming. He was seen by former fellow officers on the streets of St. Louis peddling fire wood and, like the husband Jim in O. Henry's classic story "The Gift of the Magi," he pawned his watch to buy his family Christmas presents.[13]

After farming failed, Grant tried his hand at a number of other jobs, the most unlikely being a collector of past due rents with a real estate business. It is difficult to imagine a position less suited to the shy, gentle, and humane army officer. He had a brief political appointment working in a St. Louis customs house, but a change in administration brought that to an end. Then, in the summer of 1860, he reluctantly turned to his father. Coincidentally, his two younger brothers, Simpson and Orvil, needed help in the Galena leather store. Simpson was in poor health and would die the next year, and Orvil was only twenty-four years old. Grant and his family moved to Galena. By conventional standards he was a failure, but he and his family were for the time being economically secure, and they were together.

What manner of man was Grant at this point in his life? He had a quiet self-confidence despite his professional failures and his marginal social status. As much as possible, he did the lonely, hard physical work at the leather store and hoped that someone else would deal with customers. He was content in his family life. Despite having enjoyed travel in the army, he had clearly settled into a domestic routine that was unlikely to take him very far from Galena. He had little interest in the political issues of the day.

While Grant's life seemed quite settled in 1860, the affairs of the nation were anything but. In May, Abraham Lincoln won the Republican Party's nomination for president. He was elected in November, and the next month South Carolina started the exodus of seven slave states from the Union.

The Civil War started in April 1861, after shots were fired at Fort Sumter. Lincoln called for 75,000 volunteers for ninety days of service. All over the north, regiments were organized to put down the rebellion. As one of the few trained military officers in northwest Illinois, Grant felt he could be helpful. Initially, he did paperwork to support the governor's efforts to raise troops and tried to get a command himself. Just when it looked like he would be overlooked, a Galena neighbor and congressman, Elihu Washburne, got the governor's attention long enough to urge him to give the former Captain Grant command of the troubled and rebellious 21st Illinois Regiment of Volunteers. It was a disorganized and rambunctious lot that had run off its previous colonel. The new Colonel Grant was unprepossessing as he showed up to take command in late June. He was a small man, dressed in sloppy civilian clothes. The way Grant quickly took control of the 21st Illinois is difficult to fully appreciate. He realized that commanding a group of volunteers was different from issuing orders to officers. He often phrased his wishes to the enlisted men as requests. He was very clear as to expectations for essentials such as drilling and guard duty. At the same time, his demands were reasonable and fair. As in the early going at West Point, on one of the first days with the regiment he threw a large, rebellious enlistee to the ground and had him tied up. Later Grant untied the man himself. Very quickly the regiment came to respect and revere Grant and took pride in being one of the best drilled and trained in the state. It wasn't long before Grant was given the first of a series of promotions and ever larger responsibilities.

In less than a month after taking command of the 21st, Grant was ordered to attack a Confederate force under Colonel Thomas Harris in Florida, Missouri. Grant felt terrified as he led his force into their first engagement. He discovered, however, that the rebel force had withdrawn. Grant wrote, "It occurred to me at once that Harris had been as much afraid of me as I had been of him. That was a view of the question I had never taken before; but it was one I never forgot afterwards."[14] Grant was never afraid in battle again. Much later in the war, a private from Wisconsin, watching Grant calmly compose orders with shells exploding all around him, wrote: "Ulysses don't scare worth a damn."[15] There was a downside to this sense of confidence as well. At times Grant thought too much about what he was going to do, and not enough about what the enemy might do. Grant was from then on offensively, strategically oriented and was constantly thinking, planning, and acting.

In August, Grant was ordered to Cairo, Illinois, at the critical confluence of the Ohio and Mississippi Rivers. He quickly brought order to a chaotic, disease-ridden river town reminiscent of the worst of Panama. Grant realized immediately the crucial importance to the war effort of the rivers in the western part of the country. If the Union could control the Mississippi from Cairo to New Orleans, it would cut the states of Texas, Arkansas, and Louisiana off from the rest of the Confederacy. If it could control the Cumberland and Tennessee Rivers flowing into the Ohio River in Kentucky, a few miles upstream from

Cairo, the states of Tennessee and then Georgia, Mississippi, and Alabama would be vulnerable to Union attack.

Events moved quickly. In September, after Confederates first violated Kentucky's neutrality and drove it into the Union side, Grant took the initiative to occupy that state's town of Paducah, where the Tennessee River flows into the Ohio. In November, his men had their first taste of battle. Grant was commanded to drive the Confederates out of the Mississippi River town of Belmont, Missouri, opposite the Kentucky town of Columbus. Grant's forces initially routed the rebels, but Confederate reinforcements from Columbus counterattacked and surrounded Grant. Rather than surrender, as might have been prudent, Grant declared to the effect: "We cut our way in, and we can cut our way out."[16] As in the transit of the mountains in Panama, Grant was the last one onto the flatboat retreating up the river. While the battle was inconclusive, it gave Grant and his troops their first taste of battle and solidified the men's already strong identification with their leader. In Washington, DC, Abraham Lincoln noticed that out west there was a fighting commander.

In the last part of 1861 and into early 1862, Grant repeatedly sought authorization from his much more cautious commanding general, Henry Halleck, to attack Confederate Fort Henry just above Paducah on the Tennessee River and then the more formidable Fort Donelson a few miles east on the Cumberland River, controlling access to Nashville. Eventually in February, Grant got a green light from a nervous Halleck and was on his way.[17] Cooperating with navy gunboats, he forced the abandonment of Fort Henry and then set out for Donelson. Grant was surprised by a Confederate breakout attempt but rallied his disorganized troops and successfully counterattacked. The next day he received the surrender of the Confederate commander, who turned out to be his old and close friend Simon Bolivar Buckner, who had eight years earlier lent Grant money in New York. Roughly six weeks later, Grant won the Battle of Shiloh further upstream from Fort Henry on the Tennessee River. Again, Grant did not anticipate a Confederate attack, but he rallied his troops to victory on the second day of the battle. Shiloh was by far the biggest and bloodiest battle of the war thus far. Grant was criticized for the high number of Union casualties, and the recent hero of Donelson (then dubbed Unconditional Surrender Grant) fell out of favor with many. But not Abraham Lincoln. He was temporarily sidelined by General Halleck and almost resigned from the army. Only his close friend and Shiloh veteran General William T. Sherman convinced him to await events.

By early 1863, Halleck had been transferred to Washington, and Grant was again in charge along the western rivers. For months he attempted various ways of capturing or bypassing the Confederate citadel on the bluffs of the Mississippi in Vicksburg. He finally carried out one of the most daring and complex operations of the war, again working closely with the navy. He ran troops on transports below Vicksburg at night, crossed the river from Louisiana to Mississippi, and, after a series of preliminary battles, finally took Vicksburg by siege on July 4, 1863, the day after the Union won the battle of Gettysburg.

Now the Union controlled the entire Mississippi River and its tributaries. Lincoln wrote, "the father of waters again goes unvexed to the sea." The president also sent Grant an especially warm and personal letter. Referring to Grant's decision to turn into central Mississippi after getting his forces over the river below Vicksburg, he wrote, "I feared it was a mistake. I now wish to make the personal acknowledgment that you were right, and I was wrong. Yours very truly, Abraham Lincoln." Then Lincoln was reputed to have said, "Grant is my man and I am his the rest of the war."[18] Now, just over two years after being appointed colonel of the 21st Illinois Regiment, Grant was given command over all armies west of the Appalachian Mountains. In October and November, Grant conducted perhaps his most impressive and important campaign of the war: lifting the Confederate siege of Chattanooga, Tennessee, and driving rebel forces from the area. In victory, Grant noticed the work of the relentless and especially aggressive Union General Philip Sheridan. Sheridan would later become more and more important to Grant, in war and in peace. After Chattanooga, Lincoln brought Grant to Washington, named him lieutenant general, reviving a rank last held by George Washington in the Revolutionary War, and placed him in charge of the entire Union war effort.

Starting in early May of 1864, Grant began a series of offensive engagements with Robert E. Lee's Army of Northern Virginia. Famous battles were fought at the Wilderness, Spotsylvania, and Cold Harbor. Grant took tremendous casualties, as did Lee. After Grant succeeded in "stealing a march" on Lee by withdrawing from the battlefield at Cold Harbor, bypassing Richmond, and crossing his army over the James River, the war in Virginia settled into a ten-month siege. While this made Union military victory inevitable, as Lee recognized, that summer Lincoln confronted a worn-out Northern electorate hungry for peace. As noted in the previous chapter, in August of 1864, Lincoln faced almost certain defeat for re-election in November. However, Sherman, who had been left to command the Western armies after Grant came east, finally captured Atlanta in September, and Sheridan won stunning triumphs in the Shenandoah Valley in the early fall. These battles here gave Lincoln the victories he needed to revive Northern morale and win a second term.

By early 1865, the end was clearly in sight. On March 28, three weeks after Lincoln was inaugurated for his second term, Lincoln met with Grant, Sherman, and Admiral David Porter aboard Lincoln's steamer *River Queen,* anchored near Grant's headquarters at City Point, Virginia, to discuss strategies for the final days. Grant and Sherman had by then completely signed on to Lincoln's dual war aims of unification and emancipation, along with as generous a peace as was possible. The difficulties of combining a magnanimous reconciliation with protecting the rights of freed slaves had not yet come into focus.

For Grant and Sherman, attitudes about slavery and the rights of African Americans had been shaped, as was the case with George Washington, by their military experience. They knew better than anyone the contributions that black soldiers had made to winning the war. The United States Colored Troops

(USCT) constituted roughly 10% of the Union army by war's end. Almost 180,000 African Americans served at one time or another in the USCT. Lincoln surely had both Grant and Sherman in mind when he wrote to opponents of emancipation in the summer of 1863,

> I know as fully as one can the opinions of others, that some of the commanders of our armies in the field who have given us our most important successes, believe the emancipation policy, and the use of colored troops, constitute the heaviest blow yet dealt to the rebellion. . . . Among the commanders holding these views are some who have never had any affinity with . . . republican party politics; but who hold them purely as military opinions.[19]

Both Grant and Sherman also seemed to understand Lincoln's view that freed slaves, called Freedmen, had to be given some path to integration into full equality as American citizens. While the Fourteenth Amendment to the Constitution, guaranteeing citizenship and equal rights to blacks, was still over a year from being introduced in Congress, provisions for both education and employment for Freedmen were under wide consideration. Consistent with these initiatives in January of 1865, before the meeting on the *River Queen,* Sherman, in Savannah, Georgia, had issued his now-famous Field Order 15, which confiscated land from slave owners along the coasts of South Carolina, Georgia, and Florida, and issued that land in parcels of forty acres to former slaves.[20] Sherman also turned over surplus army mules to the Freedmen, thus originating the Reconstruction concept of "forty acres and a mule" for emancipated slaves.

Lincoln was willing to let Sherman's order stand as a military matter, freeing his army to continue their advances into South Carolina without caring for the thousands of emancipated slaves who followed his forces. But Lincoln made it clear on the *River Queen* to both Grant and Sherman that they were not to negotiate anything other than military surrender. Political matters were the president's concern. However, Grant understood Lincoln's general conciliatory approach as expressed in his second inaugural address and, less formally, to General Godfrey Weitzel when Lincoln visited Richmond on April 4, two days after the Confederate government had abandoned the capital city. When Weitzel asked the president's advice about overseeing the occupation, Lincoln only offered, "If I were in your place I'd let 'em up easy, let 'em up easy."[21]

At that moment, with Lincoln's sentiments in mind, Grant was conducting one of his most skillful campaigns, catching and capturing Lee's army as it tried to escape the Richmond/Petersburg area to join another Confederate army facing Sherman in North Carolina. After making a final attempt to escape on Palm Sunday, April 9, Lee finally asked to meet with Grant to discuss terms of surrender. The night before, Lee had told his staff that he would probably have "to go and see General Grant and I would rather die a thousand deaths." Grant's famous meeting with Lee at the McLean House in Appomattox Court House was crucial in putting into practice Lincoln's "let 'em up easy" approach. In being generous, Grant for the first time crossed a line into political matters. He had generally planned the terms of surrender but had not had time to think through specific wording. Grant's final sentence in the written terms stated that once the soldiers in Lee's army laid down their arms, "each officer and man will be allowed to return to his home, not to be disturbed by United States authority so long as they observe their paroles and the laws in force where they may reside."[22] In effect, Grant accorded Lee and his men amnesty. This statement of Federal postsurrender policy exceeded Grant's military authority, as had been made clear earlier by Lincoln. However, Lee said that it would do a great deal to advance the cause of peace. In fact, Lee and other Confederate officers and men never forgot Grant's magnanimity, and many did their best as a result to achieve a genuine reconciliation. Historians generally agree that Grant, and Lee, acted wisely.

After the surrender at Appomattox, Grant returned to City Point and then to Washington, DC. He and Julia were anxious for a brief reunion with their family in New Jersey and declined the president's invitation to join him and Mrs. Lincoln in seeing the play *Our American Cousin* at Ford's Theatre on Good Friday, April 14. They left the capital on an afternoon train. About midnight, Grant received a War Department telegram in his hotel room in Philadelphia stating that Lincoln had been shot and would not survive. Grant later wrote that "It was the darkest day of my life."[23] Nevertheless the war soon ended as other Confederate forces rapidly surrendered, the largest being General Joseph Johnston's army to Sherman outside of Durham, North Carolina.

In the wake of Lincoln's assassination, Grant was still in command of the military and was clearly the most admired man in the country. While the new president, Andrew Johnson, needed Grant's support as he undertook his own approach to Reconstruction, the two came into conflict almost immediately. Johnson was from Tennessee and, though sympathetic to the South and Southern customs, was vindictive toward many Confederate officers, especially Robert E. Lee. Johnson and some holdovers in Lincoln's cabinet wanted to try Lee, Johnston, and others for treason. Since Grant was still in command of the army, he would have to order the arrests. This he refused to do, telling Johnson that he would resign rather than, in effect, go back on his Appomattox pledge that those paroled there, including Lee, would not be "disturbed by United States authority" as long as they were law-abiding citizens. Johnson knew that he could not sustain politically an open breach with Grant, and he backed off.

More troubling to Grant, who had fully internalized Lincoln's views regarding blacks, including the granting of some degree of suffrage, was Johnson's increasingly apparent disdain for African Americans. Lincoln had selected Johnson as his running mate for what was called the National Union Party in the election of 1864. As a strong supporter of the Union and a so-called War Democrat, Johnson might be able to broaden the appeal of the ticket. The party platform on which he and Lincoln ran strongly supported a constitutional Amendment to abolish slavery. That amendment, with Lincoln's skillful lobbying with the House of Representatives, had won approval of two-thirds of both houses of Congress by January of 1865 and had been submitted to the states for ratification when Johnson succeeded Lincoln in April. But Johnson looked increasingly hostile to the rights and aspirations of former slaves. For example, in the summer of 1865, he rescinded Sherman's Field Order 15 and returned confiscated lands to their former white owners.

Grant well understood the principle of civilian control of the military and that President Johnson was his commander in chief, no matter what he thought of his policies. But Grant also knew that he was himself a leader of political consequence, no matter what he thought of that reality. He worried that Johnson's policies would undo the results of the war and turn the South back over to the political leaders who had started it. Hoping to co-opt Grant, Johnson sent him on a highly visible fact-finding trip to the South to assess conditions. While the area was generally peaceful, it was clear that the war's gains for African Americans were being eroded. Grant recommended to Johnson that military occupation of the South be continued and that the Freedmen's Bureau, established shortly before Lincoln's assassination to help emancipated slaves, be left in place to help establish a peaceful integration of African Americans into the new society. Johnson had hoped to manipulate Grant's support toward his own ends, but Grant's report made it very clear that he could not be so manipulated. Grant was clearly in support of African Americans and wanted to continue the trajectory that Lincoln had established.

Now Grant had to walk a very fine line. It was clear that he was a likely candidate for the Republican presidential nomination in 1868. He must be true to his convictions and commitments to protect what the war had gained, but he must also remain at least outwardly loyal and obedient to Johnson. Working closely with Secretary of War Edwin Stanton, Grant resisted Johnson as much as possible without being outright insubordinate. For example, in January 1866, roughly nine months after the end of the war, Grant issued General Orders, No. 3, authorizing occupying troops in the Southern states to avail themselves of federal courts when state courts were not protecting the rights of blacks. When Johnson tried to nullify the effects of this order in April, Grant worked secretly with Stanton to keep it in force, and in July he issued General Orders, No. 44 in a further effort to continue to protect blacks and consolidate the accomplishments of the recent war. It authorized military commanders to arrest:

> all persons who have been ... charged with the commission of crimes ... against officers, agents, citizens, and inhabitants of the United States, irrespective of color, in cases where the civil authorities have failed ... to arrest ... such parties.[24]

Increasingly, Grant affiliated with the so-called Radical Republicans who were concerned with African American rights. The November elections in 1866 rejected Johnson's approach to Reconstruction—essentially walking away—and returned overwhelming Republican majorities to both houses of Congress. Conflicts with Congress eventually led to the 1868 impeachment trial of Andrew Johnson and his acquittal by one vote. By this time, Grant's identification with Radical Republican goals had been solidified, and his nomination for president later that year seemed assured.

Still, the nature of Grant's allegiance to the legacy of Abraham Lincoln and the aims of Radical Republicans is somewhat complicated. Lincoln clearly favored a more conciliatory approach to the white South than radicals in Congress. In that sense, one could argue that Johnson's policies were more moderate and in line with Lincoln's than were the policies of the Radicals, which Grant supported. However, one must make a distinction between issues of lenient treatment of former rebel leaders and the white South generally versus protecting the rights of African Americans. Lincoln and Grant favored both leniency and supporting the Freedmen. Radicals favored the latter, not the former. As noted earlier, achieving both lenient reconciliation with white Southerners and protection of African Americans may never have been possible, but that is what both Lincoln and Grant attempted.

As expected, Grant was easily nominated for the Republican ticket. The National Union label on which Lincoln and Johnson ran in 1864 disappeared. Grant accepted the nomination with a brief message concluding, "Let Us Have Peace."[25] The Democrats had a difficult time coalescing around a candidate. Andrew Johnson was available, but his clumsy handling of the presidency and his impeachment doomed him. Eventually, former New York Governor Horatio Seymour, an extremely reluctant candidate, was nominated.

In the fall, Grant won an overwhelming Electoral College victory, but the popular vote was much closer than many Republicans expected. Grant won by roughly 300,000 votes, or 53% to 47%, over Seymour. In winning, Grant rolled up a plurality of 400,000 votes from African Americans, mostly in the South. That is, Seymour won the white vote nationally, reflecting the fact that Grant, like Lincoln in 1860, received very few white Southern votes. However, like Lincoln, Grant would have won in the Electoral College without black votes. Still, the closeness of the election signaled that despite Grant's personal popularity, the punitive approach of Radical Republicans in Congress and Republican support for African Americans generated a great deal of opposition among white voters in the North as well as the South.

When Grant was sworn in on March 4, 1869, his inaugural address emphasized the rights of African Americans. First he noted the complex issues the country would face "having just emerged from a great rebellion." He pleaded for the nation to address these matters "calmly, without hate, prejudice, or sectional pride." Just before the conclusion of the address, he focused on voting rights:

> The question of suffrage is one which is likely to agitate the public so long as a portion of the citizens of the nation are excluded from its privileges in any State. It seems desirable that this question should be settled now, and I entertain the hope and express the desire that it may be by the ratification of the fifteenth article of amendment to the Constitution.[26]

Grant's mention of the Fifteenth Amendment to the Constitution is notable, as is his action to assure its ratification. The amendment states simply that citizens shall not be denied the right to vote "on account of race, color, or previous condition of servitude," and that "the Congress shall have the power to enforce this article by appropriate legislation." It was adopted by the overwhelmingly Republican Fortieth Congress, elected to oppose Andrew Johnson's Reconstruction policy in 1866. It was finally passed by Congress on February 26, 1869, less than a week before Grant took office and a new Congress was seated. Two states (West Virginia and Nevada) ratified the amendment before Grant's inauguration and five more did so the next day. However, the pace of ratification slowed down; by early 1870, the amendment still required the approval of eight more states. During his first six months in office, Grant watched the snail-like ratification progress and decided to take action in the fall of 1869. He contacted the governor of Nebraska, David Butler, and asked him to convene a special session of the state legislature to take up the question:

> In view of the fact that the next session of the legislature of Nebraska does not occur until the year 1871, and that it will therefore not have an opportunity of taking action upon the ratification of the fifteenth amendment to the Constitution until that time, I would respectfully suggest that you consider the propriety of convening the legislature in extra session for this purpose, and if the proposition should meet with your views, I request that a proclamation be issued to that effect at as early a period as you may deem expedient. I am induced to write you upon this subject from the earnest desire I have to see a question of such great national importance brought to an early settlement, in order that it may no longer remain an open issue, and a subject of agitation before the people.[27]

Six months later Nebraska did ratify, ironically just a few days after the amendment had been approved by enough other states to be added to the Constitution.

When the amendment was finally ratified, Grant took the unusual step of expressing his great satisfaction in a special message to Congress. In that message, he also expressed the importance of providing for equal educational opportunities for blacks so that they could use their new franchise well. Grant wrote of the "vast importance of the fifteenth amendment" and, referring to the Dred Scott decision of 1857, added that:

> A measure which makes at once 4,000,000 people voters who were heretofore declared by the highest tribunal in the land not citizens of the United States, nor eligible to become so . . . is indeed a measure of grander importance than any other one act of the kind from the foundation of our free government to the present day.

In addressing the challenge of education, he quoted George Washington's Farewell Address of 1797, urging the promotion of "institutions for the general diffusion of knowledge" and urged Congress "to take all the means within their constitutional powers to promote and encourage popular education throughout the country, and upon the people everywhere."[28]

Despite Grant's consistent support for African Americans, his management of Reconstruction is still controversial. For many years, historians argued that Grant did far too much, greatly exceeding his authority, to impose Radical Reconstruction policies on the South. Later historiography takes more or less the opposite view, accusing Grant of failing to do all he could to protect black rights. At present, there is wide agreement that Grant did all that could have been done, as he continued to try to protect African Americans in the South long after most whites stopped caring. In reviewing the changing consensus, recent historians Jean Edward Smith and Frank Scaturro both note that "the tone of American historiography concerning Reconstruction was set by William A. Dunning," a professor of history at Columbia University from 1886–1922. According to Smith, Dunning argued that Reconstruction was dominated by Freedmen committing "hideous crimes against white womanhood" and that "The widespread acceptance of the Dunning School's interpretation of Reconstruction reflected the prejudices of the period and the desire of the most Northerners to conciliate the white South."[29] Thus for much of the twentieth century, Grant was seen as ruthlessly oppressing the South. Dunning wrote that with Grant "there was no peace; with Hayes [Grant's successor as president] peace came."[30] The subsequent opposite view has been expressed by William McFeely, for one, in his 1981 Pulitzer-prize winning *Grant: A Biography*. McFeely famously wrote, "by the summer of 1876 [Grant's last full year in office] there was no one around the White House who gave a damn about the black people."[31] This view has been strongly contested by Scaturro and biographer Brooks Simpson. For example, Simpson wrote that there was at least one man who cared, "the principal occupant of the building."[32] Again, it is only very recently that scholarly consensus seemed to agree that Grant's efforts were about the best that could be managed, given Southern resistance to black rights.[33]

The history of that Southern resistance and Grant's efforts to overcome it is not pretty. Grant took strong action throughout his administration to stop organized, violent persecution of African Americans in the South, and, as best he could, to ensure fair elections. The means at his disposal, sending in federal troops and declaring martial law to restore order and monitor elections, were not well suited to the task. Furthermore, political support for such interventions declined in the nation and in the Republican Party throughout Grant's eight years in office. People were tired of conflict, and Southerners became more skillful at covert intimidation. The long-term result, of course, was increasing subjugation of blacks under Jim Crow laws until the mid-twentieth century. Yet the record of strong and consistent intervention during Grant's years as president is clear.

In the spring of 1871, the actions of the newly formed Ku Klux Klan in South Carolina were of special concern. Grant wrote informally to James G. Blaine, speaker of the House of Representatives, urging legislative action to give Grant the authority to protect black citizens:

> There is a deplorable state of affairs existing in some portions of the South demanding the immediate attention of Congress. If the attention of Congress can be confined to the single subject of providing means for the protection of life and property to those Sections of the Country where the present civil authority fails to secure that end, I feel that we should have such legislation.[34]

Two weeks later, Grant renewed the pressure with a formal request to the House and Senate requesting the necessary action:

> A condition of affairs now exists in some of the States of the Union rendering life and property insecure, and the carrying of the mails, and the collection of revenues dangerous. The proof that such a condition of affairs exists in some localities is now before the Senate. That the power of the Executive of the United States, acting within the limits of existing laws, is sufficient for present emergencies is not clear. Therefore, I urgently recommend such legislation, as in the judgment of Congress, shall effectively secure the life, liberty, and property, and the enforcement of law, in all parts of the United States.[35]

Responding to Grant, the so-called Ku Klux Klan Act was passed. Six weeks later, Grant issued the following proclamation:

> This law of Congress applies to all parts of the United States and will be enforced everywhere to the extent of the powers vested in the

Executive. But inasmuch as the necessity therefor is well known to have been caused chiefly by persistent violations of the rights of citizens of the United States by combinations of lawless and disaffected persons in certain localities lately the theatre of insurrection and military conflict, I do particularly exhort the people of those parts to suppress all such combinations by their own voluntary efforts. . . . I do, nevertheless deem it my duty to make known that I will not hesitate to exhaust the powers thus vested in the Executive whenever and wherever it shall become necessary to do so for the purpose of securing to all citizens . . . the peaceful enjoyment of rights guaranteed to them by the Constitution.[36]

Predictably, local authorities did nothing, and Grant sent troops to crush the Klan in 1872. That same year, he also sent troops to support the recently elected Republican governor of Louisiana against a militia mutiny and rioting mobs.

Though there was increasing restiveness about such interventions, the combination of national support for the perceived Lincoln legacy and Grant's personal popularity assured his re-election in the fall of 1872. This time his opposition came from a group of dissident Republicans calling themselves Liberal Republicans. They nominated newspaperman Horace Greeley for president. The Democratic Party also nominated Greeley. Greeley campaigned against alleged corruption in the Grant administration but also emphasized ending Reconstruction and withdrawing Federal troops from the South. As in 1868, Grant won easily. Greeley carried six states, all of them—not surprisingly—former slave states that wanted to see the end of Reconstruction.

Shortly after the election, Grant not only urged civil rights and equal treatment for African Americans in the United States, he also strongly and consistently denounced continuing slavery in Cuba. In his fourth annual message to Congress near the end of 1872, Grant discussed the long-simmering insurrection there. He argued:

> I can not doubt that the continued maintenance of slavery in Cuba is among the strongest inducements to the continuance of this strife. A terrible wrong is the natural cause of a terrible evil. The abolition of slavery and the introduction of other reforms in the administration of government in Cuba could not fail to advance the restoration of peace and order.[37]

Despite Grant's urgings that African Americans be accorded the same opportunities to build good lives for themselves as any other citizen, opposition in the South kept moving that goal further away. On March 4, 1873, in his second inaugural address, Grant again promoted equal rights and fair treatment:

> The effects of the late civil strife have been to free the slave and make him a citizen. Yet he is not possessed of the civil rights which citizenship

should carry with it. This is wrong, and should be corrected. To this correction I stand committed, as far as Executive influence can avail. Social equality is not a subject to be legislated upon, nor shall I ask that anything be done to advance the social status of the colored man, except to give him a fair chance to develop what is good in him, give him access to the schools, and when he travels let him feel assured that his conduct will regulate the treatment and the fare he will receive.[38]

Grant's resolve to protect the lives and the rights of the Freedmen remained steady in the subsequent years of his administration. He wrote a special report to Congress in January 1875, seeking legislative action to clarify his duties in these matters while at the same time strongly supporting the actions of General Philip Sheridan in forcibly restoring Republican control to the legislature in Louisiana after brutal attacks on blacks and white sympathizers. Speaking into the political wind, he framed a passionate message in terms of his duty to enforce the Fifteenth Amendment and the crying need to redress a recent massacre of blacks in the town of Colfax:

Fierce denunciations ring through the country about office holding in Louisiana, while every one of the Colfax miscreants goes unwhipped of justice, and no way can be found in this boasted land of civilization and Christianity to punish the perpetrators of this bloody and monstrous crime. To say that the murder of a negro or a white Republican is not considered a crime in Louisiana would probably be unjust to a great part of the people, but it is true that a great number of such murders have been committed, and no one has been punished therefor, and manifestly, as to them, the spirit of hatred and violence is stronger than law.[39]

Editorial reaction to Grant's Louisiana intervention is telling. One powerful cartoon showed "Ulysses I" enthroned atop the "murder of Louisiana," with the attorney general perched on his shoulder, a demon spawn.[40] The general policy of sending federal troops south was so unpopular that mass meetings of protest occurred in the North. Grant steadily lost political support. Republicans feared electoral defeat. Even Grant's pro-Reconstruction vice president, Henry Wilson, described him as "the mill-stone around the neck of our party that would sink it out of sight."[41] The Supreme Court increasingly took the view that using troops to defend blacks when their own state governments failed to do so represented an unprecedented and worrisome expansion of federal power. The white public wanted the whole mess to go away.

Jean Edward Smith wrote that "for the last two years of his administration, Grant stood watch over the South almost alone."[42] He would continue seeking congressional authorization to enforce the laws and suppress violence, but he would exercise his own judgment as to when executive action was required. Grant also worked hard to push through an expansive Civil Rights Act, which was passed by Congress in 1875. This bill was not only progressive by the standards of its time, but it was very much like the Civil Rights Act that finally passed in 1964. (Sadly, it was held to be unconstitutional by the Supreme Court in 1883.) In October 1876, in the last months of his presidency, with much less legislative backing than he had in 1871, Grant once again issued a proclamation before he took steps necessary to enforce the laws and protect black citizens, this time in South Carolina. It commanded "all persons engaged in . . . unlawful insurrectionary proceedings to disperse and . . . submit themselves to the laws and constituted authorities" of their state."[43] They did not, and Grant then sent troops to protect black citizens and keep the peace.

The election to succeed Grant in 1876 was one of the most complex in US history. Samuel J. Tilden of New York was the clear popular vote winner. (Tilden is one of only five Democrats to win the majority of popular votes in a presidential election since Franklin Pierce did so in 1852. The other four are Franklin Roosevelt, Lyndon Johnson, Jimmy Carter, and Barack Obama.) But Tilden was one vote short of an electoral vote majority. Three Southern states had disputed results. Eventually Congress formed a commission to settle the contested votes. Democrats believed that they were being cheated. Grant's willingness to use force to keep the peace assured an orderly if highly questionable outcome. The commission awarded all the disputed votes to the Republican candidate, Rutherford B. Hayes, who was named the nineteenth president of the United States two days before his inauguration on March 4, 1877. A deal had been struck not only on the winner of the election, but a promise was also made to the South that all Federal troops would be withdrawn. The South continued its path toward the repressive Jim Crow era. Civil rights and voting rights for African Americans would await another ninety years.

There is a reason Grant never lost the support of famed African American leader Frederick Douglass, whose final assessment held that:

> To Grant more than any other man the Negro owes his enfranchisement. . . . In the matter of the protection of the freedman from violence his moral courage surpassed that of his party; his place at its head was given to timid men, and the country was allowed to drift, instead of stemming the current.[44]

After leaving the White House, Julia and Ulysses spent nearly two years traveling around the world, during which Grant effectively acted as an ambassador for the United States. After returning home, Grant entertained the possibility of running for a third term in 1880, but he lost the Republican nomination to James A. Garfield, who won a narrow victory over Democrat Winfield Hancock and became the twentieth president of the United States on March 4, 1881. Grant went into private business, and an investment firm named Grant and

Figure 4.2 Frederick Douglass was unstinting in his praise of U. S. Grant, writing that "to Grant more than any other man the Negro owes his enfranchisement."
Frederick Douglass," c. 1866, black and white photograph. The New-York Historical Society, New York. Public domain, via Wikimedia Commons.

Ward became the central focus of his efforts. In May 1884, the firm collapsed, due to Ward's malfeasance, leaving Grant essentially penniless. He then began writing articles about the Civil War for modest sums in order to survive financially. By the fall of that year, he knew that he had contracted throat cancer and would soon die. In the last months of his life, at the urging of Samuel Clemens (known as Mark Twain), he undertook writing the *Personal Memoirs of U. S. Grant*, his masterful account of his Civil War campaigns. Enduring great pain breathing and swallowing, Grant completed the final editing a few days before his death in July of 1885. Clemens oversaw the publication of the two-volume work, which won Grant fame as a writer and saved his family from financial disaster.

Personal Memoirs has been acclaimed by many. Gertrude Stein, writing about Grant in her 1947 volume *Four in America*, assessed the *Memoirs* as "one of the finest books ever written by an American."[45] Edmund Wilson commented:

in general the writing of the *Memoirs* is perfect in concision and clearness, in its propriety and purity of language. Every word that Grant writes has its purpose, yet everything is understated. These literary qualities, so unobtrusive, are evidence of a natural fineness of character, mind and taste; and the *Memoirs* also convey the dynamic force and definiteness of his personality . . . the narrative seems to move with the increasing momentum that the soldier must have felt in the field.[46]

Grant's narrative voice in *Personal Memoirs* is simple, direct, modest, and generous. The brief excerpt below conveys his graceful, gentle, but commanding style. Shortly before Grant died, he finished writing about his 1865 meeting with Robert E. Lee at Appomattox. On the day after the surrender, he rode out from his lines and met again with Lee:

> I then suggested to General Lee that there was no one in the Confederacy whose influence . . . was as great as his, and that if he would now advise the surrender of all the armies I had no doubt his advice would be followed with alacrity. But Lee said, he could not do that without consulting the President first. I knew there was no use to urge him to do anything against his ideas of what was right.
>
> I was accompanied by my staff and other officers, some of whom seemed to have a great desire to go inside the Confederate lines. They finally asked permission of Lee to do so for the purpose of seeing some of their old army friends, and the permission was granted. They went over, had a very pleasant time with their old friends, and brought some of them back with them when they returned.
>
> When Lee and I separated he went back to his lines and I returned to the house of Mr. McLean. Here the officers of both armies came in great numbers, and seemed to enjoy the meeting as much as though they had been friends separated for a long time while fighting battles under the same flag. For the time being it looked very much as if all thought of the war had escaped their minds. After an hour pleasantly passed in this way I set out on horseback . . . for Burkesville Junction."[47]

Though Grant's *Personal Memoirs* do not recount much about his presidency, it is his actions during the last eight years of Reconstruction, when Grant was chief executive, that underline the extent to which he made efforts on behalf of African Americans. As noted earlier, Frederick Douglass makes plain his respect for what Grant accomplished. Recent scholarship has praised Grant as well. For example, one recent addition to the literature called *The Unknown Architects of Civil Rights: Thaddeus Stevens, Ulysses S. Grant and Charles Sumner*, emphasizes Grant's strong support for the Fifteenth Amendment to the Constitution and also his backing for the 1875 Civil Rights Act.[48] Though during his years as president, Grant was unable to stem the white supremacist tide of American history—a tide that flowed until the 1960s—his many constructive accomplishments warrant greater attention from students of presidential leadership.

Notes

1   See http://home.nas.com/lopresti/ps.htm.
2   William S. McFeely, *Grant: A Biography* (New York: Norton, 1981), pp. 62–63.
3   McFeely, p. 10.
4   Ulysses S. Grant, *The Personal Memoirs of U. S. Grant* (New York: Charles Webster, 1885), Volume I, p. 30.
5   Grant, I, p. 32.
6   Charles Bracelen Flood, *Grant's Final Victory: Ulysses S. Grant's Heroic Last Year* (Cambridge, MA: Da Capo, 2011), p. 15.
7   Jean Edward Smith, *Grant* (New York: Simon & Schuster, 2001), p. 28.
8   Smith, p. 56.
9   McFeely, p. 32.
10 McFeely, p. 47; Smith, p. 78.
11 Charles Bracelen Flood, *Grant's Final Victory: Ulysses S. Grant's Heroic Last Year* (Cambridge, MA: DaCapo Press, 2011), p. 179.
12 McFeely, p. 47.
13 O. Henry, "The Gift of the Magi," *New York Sunday World,* December 10, 1905.
14 Grant, I, p. 250.
15 John Keegan, *The Mask of Command* (New York: Penguin, 1987), p. 210.
16 Grant, I, p. 276.
17 Smith, p. 141.
18 T. Harry Williams, *Lincoln and His Generals* (New York: Knopf, 1952), p. 272.
19 Abraham Lincoln, Letter to James C. Conkling, August 26, 1863. In Don E. Fehrenbacher (ed.), *Lincoln: Speeches and Writings 1859–1865* (New York: Library of America, 1989), pp. 495–99.
20 See http://www.georgiaencyclopedia.org/articles/history-archaeology/shermans-field-order-no-15.
21 Benjamin P. Thomas, *Abraham Lincoln: A Biography* (New York: Knopf, 1952), p. 512.
22 Grant, *Personal Memoirs of U. S. Grant* (New York: Charles Webster, 1886), Volume II, p. 492.
23 See http://foxessa-foxhome.blogspot.com/2012/04/ulysses-s-grant-learning-presi dent.html.
24 John Y. Simon, *The Papers of Ulysses S. Grant* (Carbondale: Southern Illinois Press), Vol. 16 (1988), p. 228.
25 Grant. http://www.presidentprofiles.com/Grant-Eisenhower/Ulysses-S-Grant-Elect ion-of-1868.html.
26 Ulysses S. Grant, First Inaugural Address, March 4, 1869. http://www.bartleby.com/124/pres33.html.
27 Simon, 20 (1994), pp. 15–16.
28 James D. Richardson (ed.), *Messages and Papers of the Presidents (New York: Bureau of National Literature),* Vol. 8, pp. 55–56.
29 Smith, p. 700.
30 Frank J. Scaturro, *President Grant Reconsidered* (Lanham, MD: Madison Books, 1999), p. 65.
31 McFeely, p. 439.
32 Brooks D. Simpson, "Butcher? Racist? An Examination of William McFeely's *Grant: a Biography" (Civil War History,* 1987), Vol. 33, pp. 63–83.

33 See Douglas R. Egerton, *The Wars of Reconstruction: The Brief, Violent History of America's Most Progressive Era* (New York: Bloomsbury Press, 2014).

34 Simon, 21 (1998), pp. 218–19.

35 *Ibid.*, p. 246.

36 Richardson, p. 134.

37 *Ibid.*, pp. 189–90.

38 *Ibid.*, p. 221.

39 Simon, 26 (2003), pp. 7–8.

40 See http://www.knowla.org/image/1183/&view=summar.

41 Scaturro, p. 94.

42 Smith, p. 571.

43 Simon, 27 (2005), p. 330.

44 Frederick Douglass, *The Papers of Fredrick Douglass* (New Haven, Yale University Press, 1992), Volume 5, p. 202.

45 Smith, *Grant,* 627; Gertrude Stein, *Four in America* (New Haven, Yale University Press, 1947).

46 From Mark Perry, *Grant and Twain: The Story of a Friendship That Changed America* (New York: Random House, 2004), pp. 234–35.

47 Grant, II, pp. 559–60.

48 Barry M. Goldenberg, *The Unknown Architects of Civil Rights: Thaddeus Stevens, Ulysses S. Grant, and Charles Sumner* (Los Angeles: Critical Minds Press, 2011).

5

THEODORE ROOSEVELT

Figure 5.1 Late in his presidency and as a candidate for another term in 1912, Theodore Roosevelt retreated from earlier actions supporting African Americans and racial justice.

Pach Brothers, "Theodore Roosevelt," 1904, black and white photograph. United States Library of Congress's Prints and Photographs Division, Washington, DC. Public domain, via Wikimedia Commons.

By the mid-1870s, black Americans' prospects for a place of equality and respect in the United States had begun a long downward trajectory. That slide did not hit bottom until the mid-twentieth century. The March 4, 1877, inauguration of President Rutherford B. Hayes, made possible by Republican Party pledges to withdraw the last US army troops from the former Confederate states, marked the end of Reconstruction. In fact, during President Ulysses S. Grant's second term, Reconstruction efforts had largely been thwarted by the Democratic Party majority elected to the House of Representatives in the 1874 midterm elections. While President Hayes vetoed a number of congressional bills designed to impede black voting, continuing Democratic domination of Congress blocked any efforts the president made to protect blacks. After Hayes, decades of presidential passivity—or worse—hostile congresses and regressive Supreme Court decisions combined with national indifference to enable the almost complete disenfranchisement of blacks, the emergence of repressive Jim Crow laws, and increasing marginalization of African Americans. There were, however, twice moments of hope with the ascension to the presidency of two dynamic personalities, Theodore Roosevelt in 1901 and Woodrow Wilson in 1913. African Americans had reason to be optimistic about presidential support from both Roosevelt and Wilson. They were sorely disappointed. Nor did the man who served in the White House between them, William Howard Taft, contribute to their struggle.

Roosevelt, Taft, and Wilson were all born shortly before the Civil War in a span of less than two years. They graduated from Harvard, Yale, and Princeton, respectively, during the Hayes administration and grew into adulthood during the years of retrenchment from the goals of Reconstruction. Any one of them might have reversed the South's trend toward disenfranchisement and ever more rigid segregation. That did not happen. The lives of Roosevelt and Wilson are especially instructive.

Theodore Roosevelt was born on October 27, 1858, over a year after William Howard Taft and nearly two years after Woodrow Wilson. Though the youngest of the three, Roosevelt became president first. The newborn arrived to a wealthy New York City home two weeks after the final Lincoln-Douglas debate. When Lincoln was elected president in 1860 and the Civil War began, Theodore Roosevelt was two years old. He was the second child in the family. His sister Anna, or Bamie, was almost four years his senior. The war affected the whole nation, not least the Roosevelt family. In July of the hot summer of 1863, their city of New York was torn apart by riots against the draft of more Union soldiers. The riots were largely precipitated by Irish immigrants, who could not afford to buy substitutes for the draft, as Theodore's father had. Rioters focused their anger on the blacks, who were seen as the cause of all the sectional trouble. Although four-year-old Theodore, or Teddy as he was nicknamed, was away during the riots, vacationing at the shore with his family, the Roosevelts surely felt the tensions.

Theodore's father, Theodore Roosevelt, Sr., known as Thee, was descended from a wealthy New York family of Dutch ancestry. He was Republican and strongly pro-Union. In the early 1850s, he fell in love with Martha (Mittie) Bulloch of Georgia, thought to be one of the most beautiful women in the South. The Bullochs were a leading Georgian family, at one time owning hundreds of slaves. While they enjoyed social prominence, their financial fortunes had declined. When Mittie's father died suddenly in 1849, four years before Mittie married Thee, the family had to curtail their lavish lifestyle. In fact, times were such that the cost of Mittie and Thee's 1853 wedding had to be financed in part by the sale of four slaves, including Bess, one of the family's personal favorites. Bess and her young son fetched $800.[1] After the wedding, Mittie's mother, Mrs. Bulloch, moved in with the newlyweds in Manhattan.

Mittie and her mother sympathized with the draft rioters, in part because of their Southern sympathies. Two of Mittie's brothers fought with the Confederate Navy. They also understood the social class dynamics that fueled the outbursts. Mrs. Bulloch wrote about the system by which her son-in-law had been able to buy his way out of the fighting: "I really do not wonder that the poor mechanics oppose conscription. It certainly favors the rich at the expense of the poor."[2] Both Mittie and Mrs. Bulloch tried to help the Confederate cause in small ways, keeping their efforts from Thee. In later years, Theodore Jr. was ashamed of his father's not fighting in the Civil War, but he likely understood that one reason that Thee bought a substitute was to avoid the family rift that might have resulted in his going to war against Mittie's Confederate brothers.

Although at age four Theodore was unlikely to be aware of these submerged conflicts, there were more obvious challenges facing the family, especially young Theodore. Like his older sister Bamie and his younger brother Elliot, and, finally, his younger sister Corinne, Theodore had serious health problems. His physical and intellectual strengths and weaknesses would combine with those of his siblings to influence every aspect of family life. Added to the vexing mix was Mittie's own irregular but chronic bouts with headaches, intestinal upset, and occasional depressive episodes.

Because of Mittie's health problems, Bamie helped look after the younger three—Theodore, Elliot, and Corinne. However, Bamie herself suffered from a deteriorating bone condition. She was in frequent pain and had to wear an uncomfortable steel and leather harness in a vain attempt to support her back and correct her posture. Despite various treatments, she remained a hunchback for most of her life. Still, she was a source of strength to her parents as well as to her younger brothers and sister. Theodore's problems, at least as a child, were the most difficult and threatening. He was frail, near-sighted, often beset by digestive discomfort, and—most seriously—by debilitating and at times life-threatening asthma. The asthma attacks were irregular, but the severe ones made it nearly impossible for Theodore to breathe. Whenever and wherever the family went, they had to think about Theodore's condition and how they might deal with a severe asthma attack.

In contrast to Theodore's fragile health, Elliot, only sixteen months younger than Theodore, was physically robust and socially charming. He had emotional problems, in some ways similar to Mittie's, and in later years he would become dissolute. (Elliot died at age thirty-four, but not before marrying the beautiful Anna Hall and fathering Eleanor Roosevelt, Theodore's niece, who would marry a distant cousin, Franklin Delano Roosevelt.) As a child, however, Elliot seemed to outshine and dominate Theodore. He, rather than Theodore, occupied the big brother role. Finally, Corinne suffered from bouts of asthma, though they were not as debilitating as Theodore's.

Surely, the challenges of various illnesses stressed the Roosevelts. However, the family's difficulties were cushioned by their wealth and privileged status. A sense of their upper crust position, and of the closeness of the two brothers, Theodore and Elliot, is suggested in a photograph taken during Abraham Lincoln's 1865 funeral procession through New York. The picture shows two small children looking out the window of Grandfather Roosevelt's large Union Square home. The two are thought to be six-year-old Theodore and five-year-old Elliot. Also offsetting Theodore's physical limitations were his prodigious intellectual abilities. He became an avid reader with a steel-trap memory. Like everything else in his life, Theodore threw himself into reading with remarkable intensity. He also took to writing. As a seven- and eight-year-old, he undertook recording notes worthy of a careful naturalist, starting shortly after seeing a dead seal in a New York City market. That event led to a deep fascination with zoology and then taxidermy. While his physical health was limiting, his mind was exercised widely and intensely.

Another marker of the family's wealth was a yearlong trip to England and the European continent from mid-1869 to mid-1870. Theodore was ten when they departed and eleven when they returned. In England, the family's connections to the Civil War again came into focus. Young Theodore met two of his mother's dashing Confederate brothers, James and Irvine Bulloch. Both had fought for the South during the war and were now living in exile in England. James had been a major figure in the conflict, acting as a secret agent for the Confederate Navy, urging British shipyards to build commerce raiders against Union shipping in violation of England's neutrality laws. He achieved a great deal, most notably getting the *C.S.S. Alabama* launched in England and armed in the Azores. The ship had a remarkably successful career wreaking havoc on Northern shipping. Irvine was part of her crew and was the last man to leave the *Alabama* when it was finally sunk by the Union Navy. The contrast between Theodore's father, whose only flaw was that he did not serve in the war, and his two navy veteran uncles was striking. Theodore would later describe James Bulloch "as valiant and simple and upright a soul as ever lived . . . one of the best men I have ever known."[3] Still, his father was heroic for other reasons, and Theodore Jr. did not forget that Theodore Sr. supported the right side during the war. During their time in England, young Theodore encountered Confederate President Jefferson Davis's young son and "sharp words ensued." Despite his uncles' compelling naval exploits, Theodore's loyalties were clear.

The year in Europe did not mean that Theodore missed a year of school. Until he went to college, he was educated at home or while traveling. The family could easily afford private tutors and, given Theodore's fragile health as well as the family's extended trips abroad, that model made good sense. Home schooling took on an additional dimension in Theodore's preteen and teenage years. A gymnasium was built from several rooms in the large Roosevelt residence in New York. Now, with the encouragement and oversight of his father, Theodore could develop his boxing skills, acquire a gun, and begin bodybuilding. With much of the senior Theodore's focus on young Theodore's asthma and overall weakness and frailty, his solution for all the children was to push them toward as much vigorous physical exercise as possible. Their father was himself a large and powerful figure who exuded youthfulness underneath his proper and formal exterior. The children adored him. They responded to his urgings to exert themselves to the utmost, especially Theodore.

Slowly during his teenage years, Theodore's asthma attacks became less frequent and finally all but disappeared. While he was easily beaten in boxing matches at camp in Maine during the summer he was thirteen, within three years his "sporting calendar" showed that he now dominated Elliot and several cousins. His bodybuilding was paying off. During that time, the family had another yearlong trip abroad, including extended stretches in Egypt and Germany. Fourteen-year-old Theodore shot birds, in the naturalist tradition of the time, refined his knowledge of taxidermy, and kept a supply of cyanide to use in his work. A focus on belligerent physical activity marked Theodore's outlook and behavior from then on. That personal orientation carried over to a lifelong political and leadership style marked by intense engagement in conflict.

Theodore's health, though improving, was thought to be insufficiently robust for him to go to boarding school. But when he became old enough for college, his private tutors readied him for Harvard University's entrance exams. He studied diligently and was duly admitted to the class of 1880. He carried with him his interests in natural history and contemplated a career in science. Initially, Harvard was a bit of a struggle. He was not considered brilliant, though he compensated for any lack of native ability with his usual drive and intensity. The world of higher education was changing, and Theodore found the new emphasis on specialized lab work stultifying. He wanted to be outside, preferably shooting specimens. Something other than academia would be his calling. Theodore kept at his exercise regimen, walking and skating in the winter, rowing in the spring, and boxing all year round.

At first, the intense, competitive, and bespectacled young man was considered eccentric by his peers. But two events in the middle of his college career transformed the unusual young man. First, during his sophomore year, his father died from cancer. The family blamed the stresses of politics. The new president, Rutherford B. Hayes, had appointed the senior Roosevelt to be collector of the Port of New York, but the nomination was blocked by a rival New York State Republican faction. Theodore's great love for his father, and his strong identification with him, made the loss devastating. However, he understood that he, along with Bamie, now had to be the strong ones in the family. The fact that Theodore inherited a great deal of money from his father only added to his sense of responsibility. Second, Theodore spent a summer in Maine with the wilderness guide Bill Sewall. Although he did not have all of Sewall's outdoor skills, he had become a very good shot and accomplished hunter and, most importantly, could keep up with Sewall on all-day tramps through the woods, hiking up to thirty miles in a single day. By his junior year, he had become a "self-confident, if still quirky, young adult."[4] He excelled socially as well as academically. He was eventually admitted to the most prestigious clubs and graduated with Phi Beta Kappa honors.

The road to Phi Beta Kappa, and also Magna Cum Laude, took something of a detour during the fall of Theodore's junior year. He fell in love. The object of his affections was Alice Lee, a young beauty nearly three years younger than Theodore. She was seventeen when they were introduced; she lived with her family in the nearby Chestnut Hill area of Boston. He met her in the fall and proposed to her in the spring. While Alice did not say yes, she also did not say no. Theodore pressed his case unrelentingly, as usual, visiting as much as her family would stand and writing often when he was traveling. Eventually, during his senior year, Alice agreed to marriage. The wedding took place on October 27, 1880, Theodore's twenty-second birthday.

After their honeymoon, Theodore and Alice settled into an apartment in New York, where Theodore was attending Columbia Law School. Being newly married and a first-year law student was not enough to consume all of Theodore's energy. He enlisted in a mounted unit of the New York National Guard, continued work on a book about the naval aspects of the War of 1812 that he had started in his senior year at Harvard, and—most consequentially, but somewhat secretly—began attending meetings of local Republican Party politicians.[5] Although Theodore's background and experience did not make him a natural for New York politics, he joined the local Republican leaders nevertheless. This was a surprising turn. Theodore had not previously shown much interest in public affairs. His father's experience with the machinations of the Republican Party during the Hayes presidency had been bitter. But a second presidential assassination in sixteen years somehow engaged his attention.

It happened this way: Just days after Theodore and Alice's wedding, GOP candidate James A. Garfield won the 1880 presidential election, one of the closest in history. Initially during the campaign, Republicans blamed Democrats for the Civil War while the Democrats charged Republicans with stealing the 1876 election. Soon, however, the contest focused on which party was less corrupt. For the first time in forty years, none of the issues in the campaign focused directly on issues pertaining to African Americans.[6] Still, consistent with his background as an abolitionist and his experience as a Union major general during the Civil War, Garfield was concerned with the erosion of African Americans' rights in the South, particularly their limited access to education. Garfield also represented the reform wing of the Republican Party, as had outgoing President Hayes, fondly remembered for his earlier support of Theodore's father. In fact, Garfield would have been Theodore Sr.'s ideal candidate. Not surprisingly, Theodore Jr., casting his first ballot in a presidential election, voted for Garfield, who carried New York State, and thus the election. That outcome was entirely gratifying to Roosevelt. Unfortunately, the good feeling did not last long.

In May of 1881, two months after Garfield's inauguration, Theodore and Alice took an extended second honeymoon trip to Europe. One part of their tour included Theodore's third visit with his Bulloch uncles in England. James helped Theodore with his book project by giving him vast quantities of information about the US Navy's role in the War of 1812.[7] At the same time, Theodore encouraged James to pull together his memoirs of his own service with the Confederate Navy during the Civil War. In July, while still in Europe, Theodore learned that President Garfield had been shot by an assassin at a railroad station in Washington, DC. By the time the couple returned to New York in the fall, Garfield had died, and Chester A. Arthur was president. Arthur belonged to the "Stalwart" anti-reform arm of the Republican Party and, coincidentally, was the man President Hayes had tried to oust by appointing Theodore Sr. as collector of the Port of New York. Although it is risky to speculate about personal motives, it seems likely that the combination of an assassination and the succession to the presidency of a man who had stood in the way of his father's political appointment in 1877 helped propel Theodore Roosevelt into politics.

Whatever role the Garfield assassination and the Arthur accession played in Roosevelt's turn to public affairs, it is clear that his strong identification with his father tilted him toward the reform wing of the GOP. Young Roosevelt adopted two other elements of his father's politics, to varying degrees. First, the senior Roosevelt believed strongly that the federal government should "help the poor and disenfranchised."[8] Second, Theodore Sr. had been an abolitionist before the Civil War and worried during and after Reconstruction that haste for reconciliation between North and South would lead to discrimination against African Americans.[9] Young Theodore wholeheartedly adopted the first principle, actively helping the poor. His attitudes about race and discrimination are a little more complex. While Roosevelt befriended and supported individual African Americans, it is not clear that he believed in racial equality. His book on the naval war of 1812, published in 1882, expressed "a nascent imperialism in his depiction of white settlers filling empty lands and subduing backward races."[10] In his later years, Roosevelt would hold strongly to the view that the "Aryan" race would move steadily westward, across the western hemisphere, across the Pacific Ocean, to dominate the world.[11] Such views would compete with the belief in equality and African American rights that had animated Theodore Roosevelt, Sr.

Still, when young Roosevelt entered politics in late 1880, he became affiliated with the reform wing of his party. Even within that wing, the match was an odd one. Roosevelt came from a much more privileged class than most of his fellow politicians. With his high voice and spectacles, he cut an almost comical figure. As in college, he struck others as eccentric, and eccentricity would have played less well among New York politicians than Harvard students. On the other hand, the Roosevelt name lent luster to the city club of political operatives; within a year, Theodore won the nomination for an Assembly seat over another veteran Republican. He was not yet twenty-three years old. He then won the Assembly seat in the general election, going to Albany early in 1882.

For the most part, Theodore found both the political personnel and the political practice in the capital dismaying. Corrupt deal-making was rampant. However, he did find some allies, especially among upstate Republicans, and an occasional Democrat, who sought to end or at least limit corruption. By this time, Roosevelt had developed a very definite sense of what was right and what was wrong. For him, issues were black or white, with not much gray. For this reason, perhaps, his approach to his Assembly seat was somewhat dilettantish. He was not one with most of his fellow political professionals either in social background or in their engagement in dealing and compromise. He had some success opposing powerful financier Jay Gould's manipulations of trolley taxes and rail rates in Manhattan, but he didn't seem fully immersed. His travels, his family, and his writing, both articles and books, absorbed more focus and energy.

Despite his limited engagement in state politics, Roosevelt's family background, restless drive, and unique persona made him something of a media star. He was good copy for the press, which both covered him and coached him. And he loved being the center of attention. Years later, his daughter Alice, a celebrity herself, said that Theodore wanted "to be the bride at every wedding, the corpse at every funeral, and the baby at every christening."[12] Despite his somewhat tepid level of party engagement, in a few years he was chosen as the Republican candidate for speaker of the Assembly. This honor didn't mean a great deal, since it was clear that a Democrat would be chosen. But the nomination showed his political potential.

Roosevelt was re-elected in 1882 and in 1883 and began his third term in the Assembly in January 1884. Then his world turned upside down. On Valentine's Day 1884, two days after their daughter Alice was born, Theodore's wife, Alice Lee Roosevelt, died from Bright's Disease, apparently hidden by her pregnancy, at the family's Manhattan home. Later that same day, Theodore's mother died. Roosevelt's diary entry that day was a large black X and the words "the light has gone out of my life."[13]

Roosevelt's reaction to this double tragedy was itself twofold. First, he wanted to escape. Leaving his infant daughter with his elder sister Bamie, Theodore headed for the Dakotas. The previous year he had bought land and invested in cattle out West. Now he would go to his ranch. Initially he was regarded as a dandy or a dude by many of the tough local cowboys. But, as with Bill Sewall in Maine, Roosevelt soon showed that he could ride, shoot, and scrap with anybody. The bespectacled "Four eyes" soon became "Mr. Roosevelt." Roosevelt quickly showed that he could deal with Westerners as effectively as he had with senior politicians in Albany. Now, however, he would give up state politics, concentrate on ranching, writing, and, as in New York, making himself known. He arranged to have pictures taken showing him looking tough and focused in western gear. He took pains to tell the story of chasing and capturing three bandits who had stolen his boat. He even photographed a staged recreation of the scene, featuring buckskinned Theodore holding a gun on the three miscreants.

But the other side of TR's reaction to his double loss was to work harder than ever, both as an aspiring politician and as a writer. On the political front, while he did not run for re-election to the state assembly in 1884, he did become active on the national political scene for the first time. Roosevelt and other New Yorkers opposed both leading candidates for the Republican presidential nomination in 1884. One was the incumbent, President Chester A. Arthur, who succeeded the slain James Garfield in 1881. Arthur, of course, was the man who had retained the post of collector of the Port of New York after Theodore's father was nominated for that post by President Hayes. The other contender was James Blaine, a prominent and long-serving congressman from Maine who was severely tainted by various episodes of corruption. Returning to New York from the Dakotas in the spring of 1884, Roosevelt managed to get himself selected as an uncommitted delegate to the GOP convention in Chicago. Though only twenty-five years old, his active support for an independent "reform" candidate garnered national attention. As always, Theodore was happy to be in the spotlight. Despite his efforts, Blaine won the nomination. Returning to the Dakotas after the convention, Roosevelt pondered whether to support Blaine or join the "mugwumps," a band of corruption-weary Republicans who were supporting the Democratic candidate, New York Governor Grover Cleveland. In the end, Roosevelt decided that it would be prudent to support the party nominee, or at least attack the other party's candidate. The issues in the general election pertained once again to corruption but also tariffs and free trade, an issue that had dominated politics for the first part of the nineteenth century but had recently faded. Little was said about African Americans. While Roosevelt's participation in the campaign disappointed many of the reform-minded Republicans with whom he most identified, his active independence was noted and appreciated by loyal party regulars.

At the same time, Roosevelt threw himself into writing. In 1885, he published *Hunting Trips of a Ranchman*.[14] He continued to shuttle back and forth between the Dakotas and New York, doing research and writing back East, ranching out West, and finding ways to stay involved in politics. His political leanings pulled him into a race for mayor of New York in 1886. He ran third, but as a twenty-eight-year-old, his performance was creditable and showed that he had some kind of future in politics. His intelligence, independence, intensity, and carefully cultivated image as a tough western cattleman with roots in the East ensured that he was taken seriously. However, those same qualities had made party regulars somewhat uncomfortable with him. As a result, his journey on the political rail was—for the moment—sidetracked. Then a severe winter in the Dakotas in 1886–87 killed most of his cattle and effectively ended his ranching career. He continued to have an interest in the strenuous life outdoors, not as a rancher, but more as a vacationer in the West.

With ranching and politics closed off for the moment, Roosevelt undertook more serious writing. *Hunting Trips of a Ranchman* was amusing, but it was not written at the same lofty scholarly level as *The Naval War of 1812*. Biographies of Thomas Hart Benton and Gouverneur Morris appeared in 1887 and 1888.[15] These two books re-established Roosevelt as a first-rate historian. Besides his work as rancher, writer, and politician, another element of Roosevelt's life came into focus late in 1885. In the months and years after his beloved Alice's death, his sister Bamie continued to look after Baby Alice, with help from the Lees, Alice's maternal grandparents. Then, about a year and a half after his wife passed away, Theodore became reacquainted with an old flame, his younger sister Corinne's friend, Edith Carow. Edith felt a loss when Theodore married Alice Lee; when he appeared back East the year after Alice died, she was more than happy to step in. Theodore and Edith became secretly engaged and then married in December 1886. Meanwhile, Theodore had abandoned his failed investments in the Dakotas and finished building a new family compound called Sagamore Hill in Oyster Bay, New York, near where he had vacationed as a child. Theodore and Edith became parents of their first of five babies in September of 1887. A boy, he was named Theodore Roosevelt III.

Traveling between Oyster Bay and New York City, the father Theodore worked assiduously on a history called *The Winning of the West*. The first two of an eventual four volumes were published in 1889.[16] That series, along with the biographies of Benton and Morris, solidified Roosevelt's reputation as a serious scholar and distinguished historian. Meanwhile, his family was expanding again. Edith became pregnant and appeared to be doing well. However, she miscarried in July of 1888. Theodore then decided to go hunting in Idaho and British Columbia. As in past trips to the West, he behaved somewhat recklessly. This time there was less chance of being shot by Indians or rustlers or killed by a grizzly bear. The danger was traveling over narrow mountainside trails in the Rockies. His guide once told him that if Roosevelt fell crossing a narrow ridge, he would have to shoot him, as there would be no chance of rescue. Roosevelt, annoyed, led the way across the ridge. Both he and the guide traversed safely.

Theodore returned to New York in time to campaign, with his usual intense vigor, for Benjamin Harrison in the presidential election of 1888. As in 1884, the issues focused on free trade and tariffs, with Republicans favoring protective tariffs for US industries. Race issues were not mentioned. Harrison won, beating the incumbent, Democrat Grover Cleveland. His victory was somewhat spoiled by the fact that while he captured a clear majority of votes in the Electoral College, he lost the popular vote. Thus for the second time in twelve years, the Republicans won the presidency while failing to win the popular vote. However, the Harrison-Cleveland contest was different from the 1876 election of Rutherford B. Hayes in which Hayes was awarded twenty disputed electoral votes by an 8–7 vote of an election commission. In Harrison's case, there was no need for an election commission. It was simply the case that the states Harrison won had more electoral votes than those Cleveland won. (The only other case in which the electoral vote math gave the presidency to the loser of the popular contest was the 2000 election between Republican George W. Bush and Democrat Al Gore. Unlike the 1888 election, however, that contest was not decided on Election Day, but only after a 5–4 Supreme Court decision stopped a recount of disputed ballots in the state of Florida.) Harrison had won fairly by the rules of the game. Now that he had, Theodore Roosevelt hoped to win something in return for his avid support. Oddly, perhaps, for a reformer, Roosevelt wanted a traditional reward for his political efforts.

It wasn't long before he got it. In May of 1889, President Harrison appointed the thirty-year-old Theodore Roosevelt to the Civil Service Commission. His appointment to a significant post was urged by Theodore's friend and mentor, newly elected Massachusetts Congressman Henry Cabot Lodge. Lodge was a fellow historian and Harvard graduate whom Roosevelt had come to know through their writings and mutual upper-class social connections. Theodore's role in his new position was to ensure that appointments to federal office were based on merit, in line with the Pendleton Act, the name of the civil service act of 1883, which was signed into law, ironically, by Chester Arthur. Roosevelt's reputation for independence and opposition to corruption, as well as his campaigning—and of course his relationship to Lodge—recommended him to Harrison.

It wasn't long before Roosevelt was in a fight, his favorite stance, it seems, in and out of politics. His opponent this time was Postmaster General John Wanamaker. Theodore and fellow Civil Service commissioner Hugh Thompson toured post offices around the country and found many of them were not complying with Pendleton principles. Exposing those violations was fine as long as the offenders were Democrats. Wanamaker howled when the commissioners uncovered Republican lapses. Still, Roosevelt persisted. Along with his vigorous approach to his civil service work, Roosevelt found time to continue his writing. His histories of the West continued to celebrate the spread of English-speaking Americans across the North American continent and the subjugation of savage native tribes. H.W. Brands characterizes Roosevelt's prose as "heroically nationalistic" and as revealing "ethnocentrism and moral self-assurance."[17]

Despite his immersion in both government and writing history, during the summer of 1889 Roosevelt had time for another Western trip, shooting as many animals as possible, both for food and his trophy room. Edith was then effectively a single mother, living in New York and raising both her stepdaughter Alice and her own child, Theodore III. Her situation and the family's were eased when Theodore rented a home in Washington, and he could spend more time at home enjoying his children. A second child was added to the mix that fall. Kermit Roosevelt was born in October 1889.

One important development in Theodore's political evolution took place in his Washington years when he became acquainted with the writings of Alfred Thayer Mahan, an expert on sea power and naval warfare. Roosevelt had been fascinated with both subjects since he learned of his Bulloch uncles' Civil War naval exploits. His interest was deepened by his own work on the War of 1812. Roosevelt not only read Mahan but became acquainted with him personally and reviewed some of his books. The two formed a close, mutually supportive relationship. Mahan's work only reinforced Theodore's sense that sea power was essential to the American exercise of influence in world affairs.

While the Civil Service Commission was not a natural springboard to partisan politics, Roosevelt used it as a base for political activism nevertheless. Working with Henry Cabot Lodge, he became something of a "Republican attack dog." When Democrats criticized President Harrison's bellicose warnings to Chile over several dustups with the US Navy, Roosevelt lashed out to support him. The matter was soon smoothed over, but Roosevelt had relished the possibility of a shooting war with ships.

While serving in the Harrison administration, Theodore Roosevelt would also have tracked his friend Lodge's efforts on behalf of African Americans. Those efforts took place in a complex context. From 1877–1885, Presidents Hayes, Garfield, and Arthur had at least tried to protect the gains African Americans had made during Reconstruction. But Grover Cleveland, a Democrat dependent on Southern support, expressed no such interest during his first term, from 1885–89. Also, between the end of Reconstruction in 1877 and the beginning of Harrison's term in 1889, black rights, especially voting rights, had been rolled back in various Southern states.

Conservative Democrats in the north, including Cleveland, had little concern about the issue and were in concert with Southern Democrats on a range of economic issues, especially low tariffs. The Northern wing of the party had no interest in challenging the Southern wing on race. Furthermore, protections for blacks had been further undermined by an 1883 Supreme Court decision, issued during Arthur's presidency, which ruled that the Equal Protection Clause of the 1868 Fourteenth Amendment to the US Constitution, while barring states from discriminating on the basis of race, did not govern the behavior of individuals or groups within states.[18] Those parties were governed by state laws but were not subject to federal government jurisdiction. Therefore, individuals and groups were free to discriminate. This decision held the 1875 Civil Rights Act, signed into law by Ulysses S. Grant, to be unconstitutional. That act, in many ways similar to the 1964 Civil Rights Act passed ninety years later, barred discrimination in public accommodations, such as restaurants, inns, and theatres.

Benjamin Harrison was a Union Civil War general, like Hayes and Garfield, and was concerned with African American rights. As a result, he supported legislation offered by Henry Cabot Lodge in 1890 to protect black voting rights in the South.[19] Despite the 1870 Fifteenth Amendment to the US Constitution barring discrimination in voting, Southerners had devised numerous ways—some violent, others nonviolent—to suppress voting. Lodge wanted to put teeth into the Fifteenth Amendment. Even with Harrison's support, the legislation was defeated by Democrats. Theodore Roosevelt was serving on the Civil Service Commission in Washington at the time and played no direct role in the legislative battles. It is likely that he was not as animated by Lodge's struggle as his father might have been. To many in the Republican Party, that struggle seemed less important.

Roosevelt's political position and future prospects seemed dim when Grover Cleveland beat Benjamin Harrison when the latter ran for re-election in 1892. In avenging his defeat by Harrison in 1888, Cleveland became the only president of the United States to serve two nonconsecutive terms. It would not have escaped Theodore's notice that Democrats had won the popular vote in four of the five presidential elections after Grant's re-election in 1872 and had barely lost that vote against Garfield in 1880. With the Democratic Party's stigma of opposition to Lincoln's Civil War efforts fading, anti-corruption, pro-business Democrats like Cleveland were consistently finding favor with the public. Not only were Roosevelt's prospects clouded by being with the losing party, his intense partisanship, moral certitude, and pugnacious style made him somewhat suspect within the GOP. It was a pleasant surprise, then, when President Cleveland kept Theodore on as a member of the Civil Service Commission. There needed to be at least one Republican on the Commission; since Roosevelt had gone after violations by members of his own party as well as Democrats, he might as well be retained.

With a secure place in Washington, Roosevelt could continue his collaboration with his friend and mentor Henry Cabot Lodge. Despite the defeat of his Voting Rights legislation, Lodge was becoming an increasingly powerful figure in Congress, having won a Senate seat from Massachusetts in the same 1892 election that returned Cleveland to the White House. TR and Lodge would collaborate on a range of issues. Still, the Civil Service Commission was not a position from which Roosevelt could exert much direct influence, and it didn't offer much in the way of advancement opportunities. Theodore became restless. He had an opportunity to return to New York politics when he received overtures from Empire State colleagues to run again for mayor of New York City in 1894. With considerable regret, Roosevelt declined to run. Part of the reason was that Edith liked DC living very much. The family had grown closer in their years there. Indeed, it had grown larger as well. A daughter Ethel was born in the summer of 1891 and a third son, Archie, was born in the spring of 1894. But after Theodore declined the race for mayor that year, and began to believe he might have easily won, he blamed Edith at least in part for the decision not to run. This was one of the low points of their marriage. Typically, Roosevelt went west for vacation. His political career seemed dead-ended, and he needed to get away.

In short order, however, the influence of Henry Cabot Lodge once again influenced Roosevelt's life. Through contacts that Lodge had in New York,

Roosevelt received an invitation to serve as a police commissioner of his home city. He was elected president of the commission and immediately made a highly visible impact. He roamed the streets late at night, uncovering corruption on the beat, such as a conversation between a patrolman and a prostitute that was headed in the wrong direction. He saw that police got bicycles so that they could move faster around the city. He tried his best to close illegally operating Sunday saloons. Through all of this, he was great copy for the New York press. Although Lodge initially helped broker Theodore's appointment, he grew concerned that Roosevelt's immersion in local city affairs would sidetrack TR's promising career. Again Lodge was instrumental in Roosevelt's next big break, perhaps the most decisive. Senator Mark Hanna of Ohio, a wealthy former businessman, had been pushing William McKinley's career in some of the same ways Lodge promoted Roosevelt's. Hanna had paved the way for McKinley's nomination and election as Republican governor of Ohio in 1891. After the failed re-election campaign of Benjamin Harrison in 1892, Hanna maneuvered the presidential nomination for McKinley in 1896. Lodge and Roosevelt hoped that if McKinley won, TR might have a prominent place in a McKinley administration. Roosevelt could win such a position if he paid his political dues by campaigning hard and effectively for the Republican ticket. As the election unfolded, that is exactly what he did. The Democrats turned away from the conservative, pro-business policies of incumbent President Grover Cleveland and nominated a charismatic populist, William Jennings Bryan. Bryan's economic policies, which advocated basing the nation's money supply on silver rather than gold, were deemed too radical by almost all Republicans and substantial numbers of Democrats. The Republicans won a majority of the popular vote for the first time since Grant was elected to his second term in 1872, a generation earlier. Theodore Roosevelt contributed to the Republican margin of victory by campaigning almost viciously against Bryan, claiming that the Republicans actually represented the interests of the ordinary citizen better than Bryan's rhetoric claimed. Once he assumed office, McKinley, at the urging of Lodge, appointed Roosevelt to the post of assistant secretary of the navy. That position put TR at the right place at the right time when the Spanish-American War broke out in the second year of McKinley's presidency.

In fact, the Spanish-American War did not just break out. Lodge and Roosevelt had long had a nationalist, expansionist, and imperial outlook. The seeds of this outlook for Roosevelt lay in his intense, almost hyperactive, pugnacious personality and personal style, with militaristic political views that allowed those traits full expression. Once Roosevelt became assistant secretary of the navy, his passive and sickly superior, Navy Secretary John Long, often authorized TR to run the department. Turned loose in this role, Roosevelt plotted how the United States could go to war, truly believing that a war would be good for the moral fitness of the country. While his first preference might have been to battle with Germany, reinforcing American hegemony in the Western Hemisphere, war with Spain offered riper possibilities. Rebellions on the Spanish colony of

Cuba had been simmering periodically since the Civil War. Roosevelt believed that an American war with Spain would free Cuba and allow it to fall under American influence or even American domination. Such a war could also lead to the American annexation of the Philippines in the Pacific, which had been a Spanish colony for nearly 400 years. Roosevelt pushed President McKinley as hard as he could. He persuaded the president to send the battleship *Maine* to Havana in early 1898, in case war should break out and American interests were threatened. The *Maine* mysteriously exploded three weeks after arriving in Havana. Many in America blamed the Spanish. They shouted "Remember the Maine." At that point, conflict became inevitable. Spain declared war on the United States on April 23, 1898; two days later, the US Congress voted that a state of war now existed between the two countries.

Theodore Roosevelt was beside himself. He not only wanted a war, he wanted to play a leading part in fighting it. Although colleagues such as Lodge and members of his family tried to talk him out of serving himself, there was no dissuading him. Fighting battles would be the ultimate expression of the toughness he had nurtured since his teenage years. It would also allow him to eclipse his father in the one way his father fell short. Theodore Jr. would never hire a substitute as Theodore Sr. did in the Civil War. He would fight himself. As events unfolded, Roosevelt was appointed a lieutenant colonel in the 1st United States Volunteer Cavalry. It was composed mostly of Westerners, including Native Americans, who knew how to handle horses in battle. This diverse collection of fighters became known as the Rough Riders. Their unit trained outside of San Antonio, Texas, and eventually made its way to Tampa, Florida, and then Cuba. In the Battle of San Juan Hill on July 1, 1898, Roosevelt took advantage of confusion and caution by commanding officers to lead a charge, first on horseback and then on foot, that helped capture the high ground. His charismatic leadership clearly rallied and coordinated disparate units and contributed significantly to a victory in some of the bloodiest fighting of the war. Among the troops that fought at San Juan Hill were African American "Buffalo Soldier" units, led, as always at that time, by white officers. Roosevelt did not credit them as fully as he might have, largely because in his telling the story of the battle was largely about him. Members of the press and photographers knew Theodore would make good copy, and Roosevelt made good use of their skills to display himself as a heroic leader. Roosevelt biographer Edmund Morris once said that when a Roosevelt manuscript arrived on a publisher's desk, the company sent out for more capital letter I's and that his 1899 book *The Rough Riders* could have been called "alone in Cuba."[20] Theodore was the star.

When the United States won the war, not surprisingly, political opportunities came Roosevelt's way. In the fall of 1898, Republicans in New York pondered nominating him for governor. Now happily settled in Washington, DC, with Edith and six children (Alice plus Edith's five children; the youngest, Quentin, was born the previous November), TR was initially unsure about running. He might have preferred a position in the federal government, perhaps secretary of

119

war. President McKinley, like many other established political leaders, was wary, however, of giving the pugnacious, seemingly hyperactive Roosevelt too much power. Edith clearly would have preferred avoiding another move of her large family, typically accomplished without much help from Theodore. As possibilities distilled themselves, New York became the most promising option.

By this time, at least, TR was contemplating a run for the presidency, probably in 1904 after a second McKinley term. He would still be quite young then, forty-six. Being a successful governor of New York was one viable step on a path to the White House. But the road to the governor's office was not smooth. New York's Republican boss, US Senator Thomas Platt, was as wary of Roosevelt's independence and power as William McKinley. He would have preferred someone else. But the excitement that the cowboy war hero generated overwhelmed the Republican machine. Roosevelt was nominated. The outgoing GOP governor was having his own corruption issues heading into the 1898 election, and Theodore was probably the only Republican who could have been elected. He was, just barely.

Once he was governor, Roosevelt led in the same aggressive way he charged up San Juan Hill. Always an anti-corruption reformer, he upset some of the cozy arrangements that Platt and others had put in place. It wasn't long before Platt was hoping to find another job for TR so that a more sympathetic and traditional governor might take his place. But where to place the popular Theodore? Fortuitously for Platt, McKinley's vice president, Garret A. Hobart, died less than a year before the 1900 presidential election. Could Roosevelt be McKinley's running mate? The president's political mentor, Senator Mark Hanna, another party boss, thought it far too dangerous to have Roosevelt a heartbeat away from the presidency. But others, including McKinley, felt that the vice presidency would effectively sideline Roosevelt, as it had so many others, and that TR could help McKinley wage a vigorous re-election campaign against William Jennings Bryan. In effect, Senators Platt and Hanna were playing hot potato with Roosevelt. Platt won the battle, in that Roosevelt was nominated for vice president with overwhelming enthusiasm by the 1900 GOP convention. McKinley had his running mate.

The election of 1900 offers an illuminating snapshot of presidential politics as they related to African Americans. Beginning with the election of 1872, when Grant was re-elected, white Democrats in the south had sought to suppress black and white Republican votes. Initially, various forms of intimidation, disruption, and violence were the means of choice. With the end of Reconstruction, the strategy changed somewhat. Now, working through state governments, white supremacists could devise new laws and pass new constitutions that in one way or another took the vote away from African Americans. Across the South, particularly, in the 1890s, the black vote was suppressed through literacy tests, residency requirements, and poll taxes. The results were dramatic, especially in the states with high proportions of black citizens. With blacks excluded, the numbers of votes simply plummeted in those and other Southern states.

For example, in the election of 1880, 170,000 popular votes were cast in South Carolina. That number declined to 80,000 in 1888 and 51,000 in 1900.[21] In Mississippi, the number of popular votes in the 1880 presidential election was 117,000. Twenty years later, in 1900, that number declined to 59,000.[22] At the same time, because those states still had relatively large numbers of electoral votes, based on the total population of whites and blacks, the white voters there exercised disproportionate influence compared to voters in the North. For example, in the 1900 election, Minnesota's 316,000 popular votes decided its nine electoral votes. In contrast, Mississippi's nine electoral votes were decided by the 59,000 popular votes noted above.[23] Almost all of them would be cast by whites.

One factor that facilitated the disenfranchisement of black voters was the position of former slave and African American leader Booker T. Washington, a contemporary of Theodore Roosevelt. Washington, born in what is now West Virginia, had worked tirelessly and effectively to advance the education for African Americans in the South. At age twenty-five, in 1881, the year after TR graduated from Harvard, Washington was named the first president of the Tuskegee Normal and Industrial Institute in Tuskegee, Alabama. Washington raised funds in both the North and South for African American education, pushing for black advancement as quickly as he believed was safe in the white supremacist South. Partly to stave off resistance from powerful white Southerners and partly to focus blacks on education, Washington made a famous speech in Atlanta in 1895 arguing that blacks should not fight Jim Crow laws or disenfranchisement in the former Confederate states but concentrate on education, employment, economics, and entrepreneurship.[24] He believed that achievement in these areas would provide the necessary foundation for eventual political equality and voting rights.

Washington's strategy is controversial today. In the short run, it gave extraordinary power to white voters in the South. One consequence of these dynamics, specifically the effective disappearance of black votes in the South, was that the Republican Party, the party of Lincoln and Grant, began to compete for white votes in the South. While Grant's Republican successors Hayes, Garfield, Arthur, and Harrison had attempted, however ineffectively, to stand up for African Americans, William McKinley, even though he had fought in the Civil War, effectively gave up. In 1898, he did visit Booker T. Washington at the Tuskegee Institute but also spoke to the Georgia legislature, wearing a badge of gray to memorialize the Confederate cause. Perhaps McKinley, as other politicians, was trying to have it all ways. Reconciliation between North and South was still an important political agenda in the 1890s. But as Theodore Roosevelt Sr. worried, black interests were overlooked and set aside in the rush to complete the work of restoring national unity.

In this context, William McKinley ran for re-election in the first contest of the twentieth century, with Theodore Roosevelt as his hard-charging running mate. Roosevelt's popularity and dynamism aided the Republican cause, and

Figure 5.2 Booker T. Washington developed educational opportunities for African Americans in the South but judged that it would be counterproductive to push the region toward political equality for blacks.

Harris and Ewing, "Booker T. Washington," circa 1905–15, black and white photograph. Harris and Ewing Collection, Library of Congress, Washington, DC. Public domain, via Wikimedia Commons.

McKinley beat William Jennings Bryan again, by a larger margin than he had in 1896. (McKinley won no Southern states, despite efforts to appeal to voters there.) But once McKinley had made use of TR in the election, the vice president-elect was no longer of much value to the president. It seemed as if Theodore's political career was at best sidelined. Perhaps he could win the Republican nomination in 1904, but Martin Van Buren in 1836 was the last vice president to be nominated by his party. His prospects were not bright, especially since so many in the party, especially in the dominant business community, feared Roosevelt's reformist and even populist inclinations. Then, as had happened in 1865, an assassin's bullet changed the course of American history. William McKinley was shot by an anarchist on September 6, 1901, in Buffalo,

New York, just six months after his second inauguration. He died on September 14. Mark Hanna reportedly summed up one prevalent point of view: "Now that damned cowboy is president."[25] Theodore Roosevelt had ascended to the highest office in the land.

What could the American people expect of the new forty-two-year-old president? For starters, he was one of the most intellectually brilliant presidents in history. His record as a scholar and writer proved that. He was also one of the most physically and mentally energetic, perhaps the most energetic of all the presidents. His priorities included reforming politics by reining in powerful corporate interests and their cozy relationships with government. But most prominent was his belief in a strong and aggressive America playing a central role on the world stage. He held that the role must be based on a strong military, especially, as Mahan had taught him, on sea power. The continuity between Roosevelt's emphasis on personal strength, combativeness, and masculinity and his belief that the United States should be strong and aggressive is striking. Somewhere in the mix was a concern with justice and advancement for African Americans. But that concern was overshadowed by others.

Nevertheless, the prospects for a better place for blacks were bright as the nation recovered from the shock of McKinley's assassination and turned to their new, dynamic, young president. Like McKinley, Roosevelt had begun to develop a relationship with Booker T. Washington. Or, it might better be said that the politically sophisticated Washington had begun to develop a relationship with Roosevelt. He had invited Vice President Roosevelt to visit the Tuskegee Institute in 1901, as he had President McKinley, and the vice president had accepted. Washington's strategy was to make as many connections as he could with Northerners—especially wealthy, philanthropic Northerners—and powerful politicians, up to the point that white Southerners would be offended or threatened. In large measure, Washington's strategy to educate Southern blacks and prepare them for economic advancement was a success. Roosevelt supported that approach and was planning to see Tuskegee for himself in the fall. When McKinley was shot, those plans had to change. But when Washington was in Washington, DC, on business in October, he was invited to dinner at the White House, just over a month after Roosevelt took office. Both Washington and Roosevelt were pleased with the meeting and agreed on a plan whereby Roosevelt would appoint moderate whites and, occasionally, exceptional African Americans to federal positions in the South.

For once, this time the president had to retreat. Booker T. Washington would not have been as surprised as Roosevelt by the venom that was heaped on the president for this breach of Southern, white supremacist norms. Washington was a sophisticated thinker about navigating the ways of the white South. Theodore Roosevelt having dinner with a black man in the people's house was unthinkable, especially as Mrs. Roosevelt sat at the same table. The president was denounced in the most strident terms. The word "nigger" was used freely in the press for the first time in decades. Allusions were made to Washington and the

First Lady touching thighs under the dining table and to Alice marrying a black man.[26] Roosevelt was dumbfounded by the criticism. As always, he assumed he had done the right thing. He cheerfully identified himself, publicly and privately, as half Southern but thought himself somewhat more enlightened than his mother, Mittie. While perhaps it was sensible that most blacks were denied the vote and kept separate from polite white society—given their natural inferiority, at least at their present state of development—surely it was just to treat a black man who had risen, on the basis of his own exertions, to a high level of education and sophistication, with due respect. While never doubting his moral rightness on this, or any other matter, Roosevelt was chastened. Never again would he dine with Washington publicly.

In the years ahead, race issues and violent Southern reaction to any decent presidential treatment of African Americans continued to be a minefield. Federal appointments were a particularly volatile area. A black woman postal official in the small town of Indianola, Mississippi, had offended local whites by acquiring some degree of wealth in her own right through investing in local businesses. Local citizens voted to expel her from the town. She wisely left. Rather than replace her, Roosevelt then closed the local post office. He thus risked Southern wrath. In fact, he did so with almost any appointment of an African American, especially if that individual was to replace a white official. A second sensitive issue was racial violence and intimidation. Lynching was growing more frequent in the south. Booker T. Washington, among others, drew the president's attention to it. Roosevelt was horrified by lynching, mostly because of its lawlessness. However, he thought it not surprising that whites were sometimes impatient as the wheels of justice turned slowly when black men were accused of crimes, particularly rape. Although he worried that taking on the lynching issue, so toxic in the South, might be counterproductive, he did speak out forcefully against the practice in the summer of 1903. The aspect of lynching that worried him most was the transforming effect it could have on people participating in vicious, mob violence involving torture and burning. He said such a person "can never be the same man."[27] Once again Roosevelt was shocked at the bitterness of whites' reactions. He knew he was right to condemn lynching, but he did not close his mind to the justifications white Southerners often articulated for it.

The summer of 1906 occasioned the most troublesome chapter in Theodore Roosevelt's handling of racial matters. A riot occurred in Brownsville, Texas, where African American soldiers of the 25th United States Infantry (colored) were stationed under white officers. One white man was killed and there were several other injuries. The mayor of Brownsville wrote to the president and accused about twenty black soldiers of shooting the homes of white citizens and terrorizing white women and children. There was considerable doubt about what had happened and to what extent the soldiers had been provoked by white residents. The president ordered an investigation. It was inconclusive. None of the soldiers would offer information about any of the others.

The investigating officer took their silence to be a conspiracy to shield surely guilty parties. The president ordered that if no man came forward to reveal wrongdoing, all 167 soldiers in the unit would be given dishonorable discharges from the army and never be allowed to return to service. Blacks around the country had hoped that the distinguished contributions of African American soldiers in the Spanish-American War, including some who fought bravely with Theodore Roosevelt at San Juan Hill, would foster better race relations. But the Brownsville incident, and Roosevelt's handling of it, constituted a worrisome setback.

Roosevelt weighed both white pressure to act swiftly and harshly and black pressure for a more balanced investigation. Booker T. Washington pleaded with the president to wait for further information. At one point, Roosevelt privately admitted to Secretary of War William Howard Taft that maybe he was acting too hastily. However, when his judgments were publicly criticized by political opponents, most pointedly Senator Joseph Foraker of Ohio, his own sense of righteousness only hardened. Perhaps the fact that Foraker had fought for the Union during the Civil War and pushed strongly for equal civil and political rights for white and black afforded his criticism an extra sting. In any event, Roosevelt became increasingly shrill and belligerent in defending his moral and constitutional right to dismiss all 167 black soldiers. Although the president included further condemnation of lynching in his 1906 message to Congress, his words seemed forced given his increasing condemnation of the black soldiers' refusal to name names.[28] He wrote that their actions made him realize that white Southern suspicions of black silence and solidarity were more credible than he had earlier imagined.[29] His views of black social inferiority only hardened. Biographer H. W. Brands suggests that the Brownsville matter made Roosevelt "rethink . . . his earlier condemnation of lynching."[30]

Racial issues did not much affect President Roosevelt for the remainder of his term. When he ran for election in his own right in 1904, he pledged that he would not run for re-election in 1908. Though he may have regretted that promise, he stuck by it and was duly followed into the White House by Secretary of War Taft in March 1909. Then Colonel Roosevelt, as he preferred to be called, left the country for a long hunting safari in Africa; he returned in early 1910. He soon became disillusioned with his successor and eventually contested Taft for the GOP presidential nomination in 1912. Despite his personal popularity and his hold on the public imagination, party bosses felt much more comfortable with the pliable, pro-business Taft than the rambunctious Roosevelt. In fact, the Republican establishment had always felt uneasy with the reform-minded, anti-business TR. When Roosevelt lost at the convention, he bolted with some of his supporters and became the nominee of what was called the Progressive Party.

Here again racial issues came into play. Roosevelt supported all-white delegations from Southern states to the 1912 Progressive Party Convention. He explained his reasoning in a long letter to Julian LaRose Harris, son of the famous *Uncle Remus* author, Joel Chandler Harris, and a Pulitzer Prize-winning journalist in his own right.[31] Harris, like his father a white man committed to racial equality, worried that in acquiescing to all-white delegations Roosevelt was backing away from any support he had ever given to African Americans. Roosevelt's letter argued that Republican policies since the Civil War, which had supported and protected blacks in the South, had simply caused antagonism and undesirable outcomes for both races. In pointing out how few votes Republicans got in the South, Roosevelt did not mention that much of that happenstance was due to the effective disenfranchisement of Southern African Americans that had taken place over the previous two decades. He went on to assert that Southern blacks could only be helped by Southern whites and that it was best not to inflame racial tensions by having mixed-race Southern delegations at the Progressive Party Convention. Some Roosevelt critics have argued that the former president was willing to sacrifice the interests of blacks so as to compete for white votes in the South. As a result, Booker T. Washington and other black leaders abandoned Roosevelt and supported Taft in the three-person 1912 presidential race between the Progressive Roosevelt, Democrat Woodrow Wilson, and the GOP nominee, Taft.

There are good reasons for Theodore Roosevelt's high rating among presidential historians. He is generally ranked fourth on various "greatness" lists after Washington, Lincoln, and his distant cousin, Franklin D. Roosevelt.[32] Theodore Roosevelt was the most active president since Lincoln. He brought a distinctly progressive stance to the White House, emphasizing curbing corporate power for the public interest and supporting workers through child labor and workman's compensation legislation. He pushed a Pure Food and Drug act in 1906. The economics of the United States had been going through very rapid evolution, and the power of trusts and monopolies was staggering. Roosevelt was the first president to battle their power. Roosevelt also transformed the role of the United States in world affairs. He initiated the building of the Panama Canal, stood firm against European attempts to gain footholds in the Americas, and sent the "Great White Fleet" of large naval vessels around the world to dramatize US power. He was also a skilled diplomat, winning the Nobel Peace Prize for negotiating an end to the war between Russia and Japan in 1905 and steering Germany away from war with Venezuela in early 1903. He also was the first conservationist in the White House, continuing the development of the national park system initiated during the Grant administration and championing protection of the wilderness throughout the United States.

Besides his vigorous and largely successful exercise of power, Roosevelt's greatness also lies in his almost magical personal appeal to the American people. While he scared political and corporate bosses, his exuberant style won the affections of the public. "Teddy" was a hero to many in his generation. His election victory in 1904 was by the largest margin in American history. Despite these achievements, his role in race relations is disappointing. While he had Booker T. Washington to the White House, the inflamed reaction of Southerners ensured that he never did so publicly again. He condemned lynching, but he failed to accord due process to black soldiers after the Brownsville incident, and he supported all-white Southern delegations to the Progressive Party Convention in 1912. He justified the latter decision by claiming a desire to avoid black vs. white conflict that would be to the detriment of both races. But he clearly hoped for some political gain from white Southerners. That meant not antagonizing the South on matters of race. Sadly, he never used his political power or his personal pugnacity to defend blacks or criticize the disenfranchisement of African American voters in the South. His claim that Republican policy since the Civil War resulted in few votes for the GOP in the South ignored the fact that disenfranchisement of blacks accounted for most of that outcome. Black disappointment with Roosevelt, and to some extent with his successor Taft, gave Democrat Woodrow Wilson inroads into the black vote in 1912. As we shall see, however, African American hopes for better treatment by Wilson were badly disappointed.

Notes

1 David McCullough, *Mornings on Horseback: The Story of an Extraordinary Family, a Vanished Way of Life, and the Unique Child Who Became Theodore Roosevelt* (New York: Simon & Schuster, 1981), p. 53.

2 H. W. Brands, *T.R.: The Last Romantic* (New York: Basic Books, 1997), p. 16.

3 Theodore Roosevelt, *Theodore Roosevelt, An Autobiography* (New York: Charles Scribner's Sons, 1913), p. 12.

4 Brands, p. 86.

5 John Milton Cooper, Jr., *The Warrior and the Priest: Woodrow Wilson and Theodore Roosevelt* (Cambridge, MA: Harvard University Press, 1983), p. 13.

6 Candice Millard, *Destiny of the Republic: A Tale of Madness, Medicine and the Murder of a President* (New York: Doubleday, 2011).

7 Theodore Roosevelt, *The Naval War of 1912* (New York: Putnam, 1902).

8 Douglas Brinkley, *Wilderness Warrior: Theodore Roosevelt and the Crusade for America* (New York: Harper Collins, 2009), p. 41.

9 *Ibid.*, pp. 41–42.

10 Cooper, p. 13.

11 James Bradley, *The Imperial Cruise: A Secret History of Empire and War* (New York: Little Brown, 2009), Chapter 2, pp. 11–60.

12 See http://www.theodore-roosevelt.com/alice.html.

13 See http://www.fordlibrarymuseum.gov/museum/exhibits/TR/light.htm.

14 Roosevelt, *Big Game Hunting in the Rockies and on the Great Plains: Comprising "Hunting Trips of a Ranchman" and "The Wilderness Hunter"* (New York: Putnam, 1899).

15 Roosevelt, *Thomas Hart Benton* (Boston: Houghton, Mifflin, 1887); *Gouverneur Morris* (Boston: Houghton, Mifflin, 1888).

16 Roosevelt, *The Winning of the West, Volume 1, From the Alleghenies to the Mississippi, 1769–1776* (New York: Putnam, 1889); Roosevelt, *The Winning of the West, Volume 2, From the Alleghenies to the Mississippi, 1777–1783* (New York: Putnam, 1889).

17 Brands, pp. 232–33.

18 See http://caselaw.lp.findlaw.com/scripts/getcase.pl?navby=case&court=us&vol=1 09&page=3.

19 Kirt H. Wilson, The Problem with Public Memory: Benjamin Harrison Confronts the "Southern Question." In Martin J. Medhurst (ed.), *Before the Rhetorical Presidency* (College Station: Texas A&M University Press, 2008), pp. 267–88.

20 Roosevelt, *The Rough Riders* (New York: Scribner's Sons, 1899); Edmund Morris, Address at National Portrait Gallery, October 1980.

21 See http://uselectionatlas.org/RESULTS/data.php?year=1880&datatype=national& def=1&f=0&off=0&elect=0;   http://uselectionatlas.org/RESULTS/data.php?year= 1888&datatype=national&def=1&f=0&off=0&elect=0;   http://uselectionatlas.org/ RESULTS/data.php?year=1900&datatype=national&def=1&f=0&off=0&elect=0.

22 See http://uselectionatlas.org/RESULTS/data.php?year=1880&datatype=national& def=1&f=0&off=0&elect=0; http://uselectionatlas.org/RESULTS/data.php?year= 1900&datatype=national&def=1&f=0&off=0&elect=0.

23 See http://uselectionatlas.org/RESULTS/data.php?year=1900&datatype=national& def=1&f=0&off=0&elect=0.

24 Booker T. Washington, Atlanta Compromise Speech. http://historymatters.gmu. edu/d/39/.

25 See http://www.thevoterupdate.com/articles/2009/11_10_09_mark_hanna.php.

26 Deborah Davis, *Guest of Honor: Booker T. Washington, Theodore Roosevelt, and the White House Dinner That Shocked a Nation* (New York: Altria Books, 2012).

27 Roosevelt, Letter to Winfield Taylor Durbin, August 6, 1903. In Elting E. Morison, John M. Blum, & Alfred Chandler (eds.), *The Letters of Theodore Roosevelt* (Cambridge, MA: Harvard, 1951–1954), 3: pp. 540–43.

28 Roosevelt, Message to Congress, December 5, 1906; Cooper, p. 210.

29 Brands, p. 589.

30 *Ibid.*

31 Roosevelt, Letter to Julian LaRose Harris, August 1, 1912. *Letters of Theodore Roosevelt* (Cambridge, MA: Harvard, 1954) 7: pp. 584–90.

32 C-SPAN, 2009. http://legacy.c-span.org/PresidentialSurvey/Overall-Ranking.aspx.

6

WOODROW WILSON

Figure 6.1 Woodrow Wilson oversaw the segregation of federal offices in Washington, DC, arguing that it was in the interests of black and white equally.

Harris and Ewing, "Woodrow Wilson," 1919, black and white photograph. Harris and Ewing Collection, Library of Congress, Washington, DC. Public domain, via Wikimedia Commons.

Theodore Roosevelt left the presidency at age fifty on March 4, 1909. Whatever regret or ambivalence he may have felt about his 1904 pledge not to run for re-election in 1908, he was at least pleased with his hand-picked successor, William Howard Taft. Taft had been secretary of war for the last five years of Roosevelt's time in office. He seemed to share most of TR's progressive economic values. But even before Election Day, Taft seemed to drift toward the more conservative, big business elements of the Republican Party. Theodore was worried.

Taft was born in Ohio in 1857, the year before Theodore Roosevelt. He graduated from Yale in 1878, second in his class. His father was a prominent Cincinnati political figure who served as both attorney general and secretary of war in Ulysses S. Grant's administration. The young Taft became a lawyer, judge, and, soon, solicitor general of the United States. After the Spanish-American War, when the United States replaced Spanish colonial rule in the Philippines with its own venture into imperialism, President William McKinley turned to Taft to study conditions in that faraway Pacific archipelago. McKinley later persuaded Taft to become the first civil governor, or governor general, of the new colony. Taft and his family were reluctant to accept the position, but Taft, possessor of a highly conscientious personality, could be relied on, by McKinley and others, to do his duty. He went to the Philippines with the hope of uplifting "our little brown brothers," a phrase reflecting the paternal racism felt by Theodore Roosevelt and many in the post-Reconstruction Republican Party.[1] Although he expressed the common view that nonwhites in the Philippines were "in many respects nothing but grown up children" and "somewhat cruel," he intended his rule to be benevolent. He wanted to bring education to large segments of Philippine society.[2] But, he insisted that that education be modeled on Booker T. Washington's Tuskegee Institute. Brown races, like black, should be educated for agricultural and mechanical vocations, that is, "practical work" but not "higher education." He wrote that we must "heed the lesson" learned during "our reconstruction period when we started to educate the negro," the lesson that educating blacks to the same degree as whites would cause racial tension and violent political turmoil.[3] As appalling as these words may seem today, in the early twentieth century, they contrasted favorably with the more virulent racism of many Southern Democrats.

Taft's thinking about nonwhites was essentially the same as Theodore Roosevelt's. Civilization should be brought to the nonwhite races of the world by the dominant whites. Over time, nonwhites would be fit for higher education and political participation, but not now. Taft estimated that it would take a generation or more for Philippinos to be ready for self-government. This view was consonant with Booker T. Washington's 1895 Atlanta "Compromise Speech" in which he also advocated education for African Americans, first in the practical arts, but forgoing, for the time being, voting rights and governance.[4] Washington rather shrewdly judged how far he could push for black education and advancement in America, especially the South, and believed that the best prospects for African Americans was with the Republican Party of Roosevelt and Taft, whatever its limitations. He allied himself as closely as they would permit with both presidents.

Taft dutifully served as governor general of the Philippines through McKinley's assassination in September 1901, until he returned to the United States in 1904 as Roosevelt's secretary of war. Roosevelt wanted Taft's political support, in Ohio for example, for his 1904 presidential campaign and already sensed that Taft might be a worthy successor. Taft made it clear that he preferred a seat on the Supreme Court, but he was willing to serve as war secretary. In that role, he could still oversee the well-intended American rule of the Philippines and involve himself in other projects of great personal interest, especially the ongoing construction of the Panama Canal. Taft even served briefly as acting secretary of state and was essentially assistant president. When it came time to name Roosevelt's successor as GOP presidential nominee in 1908, Taft was the obvious choice. Again he would have preferred the Supreme Court, but Taft acceded to his friend and mentor Roosevelt and accepted the nomination. Taft realized that as senior cabinet member, he was the logical, available choice.

Taft was elected president in 1908 rather easily. He defeated third-time Democratic nominee William Jennings Bryan with a comfortable majority of the popular vote and a nearly two-to-one Electoral College victory. This was accomplished despite the absence of a Republican black vote in the South. As noted before, disenfranchisement of African Americans through poll taxes, literacy tests, and residency requirements had been a central part of the emergence of the Jim Crow era after Reconstruction. Since most Republican votes in the post-Civil War South were cast by African Americans, declining numbers of Republican votes in Southern states with large black populations illustrate the effectiveness of disenfranchisement. For example, in Louisiana the Republican percentage of the popular vote declined from 52% in 1876 to 26% in 1888 and to 10% in 1904. Similarly, in South Carolina the numbers were 50% in 1876, 17% in 1888, and 5% in 1904.[5] The absence of black votes tempted Republicans to compete for white votes in the South. Though those efforts were not successful, the possibility of winning Southern white support played a role in Theodore Roosevelt's retreat from open contact with Booker T. Washington, his rigidity in dealing with the Brownsville affair, and even his sporadic condemnations of lynching.

William Howard Taft's 1909 Inaugural Address illustrates the convoluted way that race was handled by the Party of Lincoln in the early twentieth century. His speech was well over 5,000 words, the second longest in American history. (Only William Henry Harrison's in 1841 was longer, by another 3,000 words, though edited and pruned by Daniel Webster. Harrison contracted pneumonia from speaking so long on a cold, stormy day and died exactly a month later.) Taft's speech addressed race and voting issues in the context of continuing efforts toward sectional reconciliation ongoing after more than forty years since the end of the Civil War. He spoke of "increasing the already good feeling between the South and other sections of the country" and went on to reference the Fifteenth Amendment to the Constitution, barring voting discrimination on the basis of race. However, he added that "the domination of an ignorant, irresponsible element" should be prevented by constitutional law that would "exclude from voting both negroes and whites not having education or other qualifications thought to be necessary for a proper electorate." He added that "the colored men must base their hope on the results of their own industry, self-restraint, thrift, and business success, as well as upon the aid and comfort and sympathy which they may receive from their white neighbors of the South." There it is. Jim Crow was in full flower. A president from Abraham Lincoln's own Republican Party beginning his presidency supporting literacy tests that had been used to disenfranchise blacks since the end of Reconstruction. Taft returned to the issue later in the speech, affirming that "I have not the slightest race prejudice." He decried "race feeling" but argued that because it existed "the Executive, in recognizing the negro race by appointments, must exercise a careful discretion not thereby to do it more harm than good."[6] That is, where strong prejudice prevailed, blacks should not be appointed to federal positions, such as in the post office, if that upset whites. For their own good, African Americans should be passed over. Consequently, under Taft, some segregation in federal offices began to take hold.

Taft's views were dominant in most of the country, except where attitudes were even more hostile to African Americans. Blacks should not be discriminated against, but they could only vote if they passed educational muster with local officials, and blacks could be discriminated against if and when treating them equally and with dignity might disturb white people. In this context, it is not surprising that black leaders such as W.E.B. DuBois, who thought that Booker T. Washington's policies and those of the Republicans were too deferential to whites, should explore the possibility of voting for a suitable Democrat, if one should ever emerge. In 1912, when Taft ran for re-election, DuBois and others thought that Woodrow Wilson might just be that Democrat.

Ironically, although he came from Union grandparents, Woodrow Wilson was a Southerner with many typical Southern attitudes. He was born in December 1856 in Staunton, Virginia, and lived as a boy and young man in Augusta, Georgia; Columbia, South Carolina—capital of the first state to secede from the Union in 1860, when Wilson was just turning four years old; and Wilmington, North Carolina. Another irony is that both Wilson's parents were from Ohio and their families remained loyal to the Union. His father, Joseph Wilson, was the son of an anti-slavery Ohio state representative, and two of Joseph Wilson's brothers were generals in the Union army. Similarly, his mother, Janet Woodrow Wilson, was the daughter of a Presbyterian minister who remained loyal to the Northern branch of the church when it split during the Civil War. However, Joseph Wilson was an ambitious man who took opportunities that presented themselves, and his racial attitudes moved as his residence did. He and Janet (called Jessie) married in 1849, just as Joseph was being ordained as a Presbyterian minister himself. The couple first lived in Ohio, then in Virginia, where Joseph taught chemistry at Hampton-Sydney College. After several years in higher education, in 1854 the senior Wilson jumped at the offer of a ministry in Staunton, Virginia. The congregation there was large and well-to-do. At the time they moved, the Wilsons had two daughters. Their son, Thomas Woodrow Wilson, was born in Staunton two years later. His parents called him Tommy.

The future president spent only his infancy in Virginia. The year after he was born, Joseph Wilson accepted a better position at a church in Augusta, Georgia. The manse where the minister's family lived in Augusta came with slaves, and Joseph Wilson seemed to embrace easily the Southern view that slavery was sanctioned by God. He seemed to bear no traces of his father's anti-slavery Unionism by the time the Civil War started. The Wilson family's identification with the South would have been reinforced by its close relationship with Janet's brother, Tommy's uncle, James Woodrow. James taught at Oglethorpe University near Atlanta; at the start of the war, he became a professor at the Columbia Theological Seminary in Columbia, South Carolina. During the war, James Woodrow used his scientific knowledge to direct the making of munitions for Confederate forces. Thus Woodrow Wilson was like Theodore Roosevelt in that both had admired uncles on their mothers' side who played important roles for the Confederate States government during the Civil War.

The beginning of that war marked Tommy's first memories. He recollected hearing, just before his fourth birthday, of the election of a man named Abraham Lincoln to something called the presidency. He asked his father what that all meant. The answer was war. During the conflict, Joseph Wilson was a part-time Confederate chaplain. During Sherman's march to the sea in 1864, his church was used as a hospital for wounded rebels. Tommy Wilson would have seen dead and wounded soldiers. He also would have seen Union soldiers detained at the church while being transported to the prisoner-of-war camp at Andersonville, Georgia. And, as an eight-year-old near the end of the war, he might have seen Jefferson Davis retreating through Augusta as a fugitive from Union cavalry.

Tommy was too young to be deeply involved with the war. His major challenge was school. Tommy was not able to read until he was about ten years old. His family and others thought he was "slow." Now we know that he had a form of dyslexia. Once Wilson learned his letters and began to read, a different world opened up to him. With command of language, he imagined himself a powerful persuader, a public speaker of some kind, like his father. He often practiced speaking in his father's empty church. Although he was always a slow and meticulous reader and writer, he worked hard to learn to communicate, both orally and in writing.

Five years after the war, in 1870, when Wilson was about to turn fourteen, his father advanced to a still more prestigious position. The family left Augusta and moved to Columbia, South Carolina, where Joseph Wilson became interim pastor of the First Presbyterian Church of Columbia as well as professor of rhetoric and theology at the Columbia Theological Seminary, the very place where Uncle Jimmy had taught. Tommy still found studying difficult, but with the help of tutors he persisted. He steadily made progress; by the fall of 1873, he was ready to attend Davidson College outside of Charlotte, North Carolina. Admission standards then permitted one with an indifferent but improving track record to be accepted, and the college's ties to the Presbyterian Church made it seem congenial to the son of a minister of that faith. However, Wilson was not particularly taken with Davidson and left after one year, at the same time that his father accepted yet another, better-paying job in Wilmington, North Carolina. After staying home for a year, polishing his skills in speaking and writing and growing increasingly into adulthood, Tommy was ready to resume his studies. It was his father who played the key role in his next step. Joseph Wilson had studied at the Princeton Theological Seminary in New Jersey, where he had become acquainted with James McCosh, the man who now was president of the College of New Jersey, better known as Princeton. Although not as prestigious as the better-known Harvard of Theodore Roosevelt or the Yale of William Howard Taft, it was a distinguished school that already claimed a US president, James Madison, class of 1771. Wilson was admitted, though he still had not obtained a stellar academic record.

Wilson started at Princeton shortly before turning nineteen in 1875. It was there that he began to come into his own. He was accepted in one of the more prestigious eating clubs, and he played on the first-year baseball team. He was a good student, but his involvement in extracurricular activities was his main focus. Those activities included but went beyond socializing and athletics. From the first, Wilson organized and participated in debating groups, working hard to develop his speaking and writing skills. He became editor of *The Princetonian*, the college newspaper founded just when Wilson arrived at college. In writing for the paper, Wilson began to clarify some of his philosophical and political principles. In doing so, he began to put some distance between his father's highly representative Southern perspectives and develop his own independent views. Joseph Wilson, perhaps with the zeal typical of converts, held strongly to prevailing Southern views that opposed universal male suffrage, adding in a letter to Tommy that "I do not refer to the Negroes any more than to ignorant Northern voters."[7] While this statement may indicate no special hostility toward blacks, it does treat blacks as a category of persons among whom no relevant distinctions need be made. The race question aside, Joseph Wilson was clear in his opposition to universal male suffrage. Tommy's emerging view of himself as someone who served people broadly, on the other hand, led him to favor a somewhat more inclusive suffrage.

On another even more fundamental issue, daylight was emerging between the views of the two Wilsons. Southerners in the post-Civil War era became even more vigorous in their states' rights views than they had been during much of the prewar period when they effectively controlled the national government. But Wilson was an admirer of Alexander Hamilton and was coming to believe in a strong, active federal government that concerned itself with the welfare of the American population as a whole. Though Tommy Wilson partly departed from his father's Southern orthodoxy, he was judicious in expressing his differences with his father and the South directly. He often said the South was "the only place in the world" where nothing had to be explained to him.[8] He varied from its traditions only in measured ways. Thus when he was assigned the universal male suffrage side of a debate at Princeton, he declined to participate.

Oddly, Wilson's choice not to debate this question stands in great contrast to his student essays stressing the centrality of oratory and debate in good government. His intellectual passion and power were beginning to focus on speaking and persuasion, "the control of other minds by a strange personal influence and power."[9] Those skills could be put to best use in debate, and debate in turn could create responsible government. In considering the most effective forms of governing, forms that would put issues out in the open and reduce the influence of corruption and bosses that seemed so prominent in the Republican Party during the Grant era, Wilson argued for debate's central role. It could elucidate "the severe, distinct, sharp enunciation of underlying principles" and provide for "the unsparing examination and telling criticism of opposite positions."[10] He also became intrigued with the British parliamentary form of government, in which debate was central. In fact, his later writing on *Congressional Government* argued that cabinet officers in the American government should be members of Congress so that there would be more extensive debate about executive policies and less separation of power. In this way, his identification with his father included an emphasis on the oratory and persuasion so central to Joseph Wilson's successful ministry but stopped short of accepting all of his father's political and social beliefs.

Wilson's complex identification with his father is seen in his evolving career choices. In one of his student essays Wilson argued that one of the best occupations in which to put oratory and persuasion to good use was the law. Joseph Wilson wholeheartedly supported his son's interest in the law and assumed that the law would be his profession, since the ministry apparently would not be. Wilson actually had more interest in politics than in what he considered the grimy practice of law. While at Princeton, he had become involved in a presidential election for the first time, the 1876 contest between Republican Rutherford B. Hayes and Democrat Samuel J. Tilden. Wilson strongly favored the reform-minded Tilden, who won a popular majority but eventually lost the presidency in the Electoral College by one vote. Despite his increasing fascination with politics, in line with his own earlier student writings and his father's wishes, Wilson enrolled in the University of Virginia law school in Charlottesville after graduating from Princeton at age twenty-two in 1879.

The study of the law was as unsatisfactory to Wilson as he had feared. He persisted through his first year of law school in Charlottesville but became ill during his second. He left the university in the middle of that year, one semester short of completing his law degree. Living at home for the next year and a half, he continued his legal studies on his own. Still, Wilson was thinking more and more independently. In some of his writings, he opened up a little distance between his father's view on race and his own, arguing that the defeat of the Confederacy and the ending of slavery was a good thing (it unified the country and abolished an ineffective economic system), and that education for African Americans should be welcomed. Part of Wilson's personal development that year was to drop the nickname Tommy and simply go by the name Woodrow Wilson. This change reflected a promise to his mother that he would honor her and her family by doing so.[11]

Eventually Wilson's legal studies paid off. He was able to pass the bar exam in the state of Georgia. At age twenty-five, he embarked on a law career, without a lot of enthusiasm and without a law degree. That career took the form of a partnership with another young lawyer, Edward Renick, in Georgia's state capital, Atlanta. Wilson soon found the practice of law at Renick & Wilson as uninspiring as the study of law. More and more his interests turned to politics and public affairs. He came to believe, however, that one needed independent wealth, such as that enjoyed by his contemporary Theodore Roosevelt, to support a political career. It seemed unlikely that that was going to come from a legal career. With his personal independence growing ever faster, he decided that if he could not actually become a politician, he would at least study and teach about politics and public affairs by entering academia. He would not be a minister like his father, uncle, and grandfather, nor would he be a lawyer. He would be a professor. Since his father and uncle had also taught, the departure was still a modest one.

Wilson had written numerous essays at Princeton and had published a highly regarded article called "Cabinet Government in the United States" just after he graduated in 1879.[12] Coincidentally, the editor of the journal that published his paper, *International Review,* was a young Harvard professor and Theodore Roosevelt confidant, Henry Cabot Lodge. Lodge would make Wilson's life miserable in later years. For the present "Cabinet Government," emphasizing debate and closer ties between Congress and the executive, formed an important part of Wilson's political thinking. It also helped secure his admission to a new center for graduate study in Baltimore, Johns Hopkins University. Wilson was admitted in the fall of 1883, after only a year with Renick & Wilson.

Once he started graduate school, Wilson's career moved quickly. On the basis of his college essays and the writing he had done after law school, Wilson had a firm foundation for a doctoral dissertation. He achieved that milestone in two years and turned his dissertation into his first book, *Congressional Government,* published in 1885, the year he earned his PhD.[13] The book explored in detail the way the Congress of the United States operated and argued that Congress should be the center point of debate and government. It also explored different nations' forms of government, showed admiration for the British parliamentary system, and again emphasized debate and increased legislative involvement with the executive branch. It instantly made Wilson a star in the scholarly firmament and launched a distinguished academic career.

1885 was a big year for Woodrow Wilson. He found love and work, the two requirements, according to Sigmund Freud, of a happy life. The object of his affections was Ellen Axson, the daughter of a Presbyterian minister he had met in Rome, Georgia, that minister being a friend of Wilson's father. Woodrow first saw her in church in the spring of 1883, when he was still working as an attorney. He was smitten. Ellen apparently reciprocated Woodrow's affection, and their relationship ripened quickly by the standards of the day. They were engaged within five months, just at the time that Wilson left Georgia for Johns Hopkins. Wilson's desire to find employment quickly, so that he could move beyond financial dependence on his father and get married, had energized his graduate work. Woodrow and Ellen were married in June of 1885, the month Wilson earned his PhD.

The work part of the love and work formula also fell into place when Wilson was offered a teaching job at Bryn Mawr College, a new school for women outside of Philadelphia. Wilson was an immediate success as a lecturer, especially in introductory level courses that best employed (and helped develop) his rhetorical skills. During his three years there, he grew not only his resume, but his family. Appropriate, perhaps, to a professor at a women's college, he and Ellen produced three daughters. They arrived in short order: Margaret in 1886, Jessie in 1887, and Eleanor in 1889. By the time Eleanor was born in 1888, the Wilsons had moved to Connecticut, where Woodrow had become a professor at Wesleyan College (now Wesleyan University). He published his second book, *The State,* in 1889.[14] It was more comparative than *Congressional Government* but developed some of the same themes. Along with his continued success as an instructor, now of male undergraduates, Wilson's new book propelled him to academic stardom. He was clearly a significant scholar of government and an enormously gifted teacher. It was not long before his *alma mater* took serious note. Princeton offered him a job, and Wilson joined the faculty there in 1890.

The 1890s were wonderful years for the Wilsons. Woodrow was an enormously popular teacher. Students constructed their schedules and designed their curricula around the possibility of getting into one of his lecture courses. He took on several extra teaching assignments, including lecturing at Johns Hopkins and New York University Law School, to supplement his income, and he continued his scholarly output. He was by now a major figure in academia. Princeton responded when Wilson was offered jobs elsewhere, and soon he was the highest paid professor on campus. It stretches the truth only slightly to say that Woodrow Wilson was now among the rich and famous, at least among the professoriat. His rising status made him an obvious choice for his next position. After twelve years in the study and in the classroom, in 1902 Woodrow Wilson was named president of Princeton University.

Wilson's tenure as college president started well. His induction was attended by J. P. Morgan, Mark Twain, and Booker T. Washington among other luminaries. The new president of the United States, Theodore Roosevelt, who admired Wilson (the sentiment was mutual), was to attend, but a streetcar accident derailed those plans. Still, there was plenty of glitter even in T.R.'s absence. (The two presidents soon became reacquainted at an Army-Navy football game hosted at Princeton.) Booker T. Washington's attendance is notable. While Wilson believed in education for African Americans, he was in the mainstream in focusing on the kind of vocational education offered by Washington at Tuskegee. No black students were attending Princeton when Woodrow Wilson became president, and during his tenure there he affirmed the practice of excluding them. He wrote a young black man from South Carolina who inquired about coming to Princeton that he was better off trying Harvard, Brown, or Dartmouth.[15] Like many others, he argued that it would be uncomfortable and self-defeating for black students to attend college alongside white students. Separation was better for both races. Booker T. Washington was well aware of these views. He capitalized on them to secure ample funding from wealthy Northerners to educate African Americans in the white South. Since he did not challenge or threaten white political hegemony, he was permitted to proceed with his educational project. As we have seen, while some black leaders were growing increasingly uneasy with Washington's moderate or even submissive approach to race relations, Washington and others following his lead went about preparing future generations of young African Americans for increasingly significant roles in American society.

Wilson's presidency at Princeton did not last long by the standards of the day. (One point of contrast is the tenure at the University of Richmond of Frederic Boatwright, president from 1895–1946.) He quickly came into conflict with the dean of the new Princeton graduate school, Andrew West. West wanted to keep the emerging new branch of the university physically separate from the undergraduate campus; Wilson wanted them integrated as closely as possible. This would allow better interaction between graduate and undergraduate students and allow him, the president, more control. West wanted control equally badly. It turned out that West played academic politics better than his president. Getting a large donation to the university for his vision of the graduate school, West split the alumni and trustees. Wilson eventually was forced to capitulate on this issue. He realized that his days as an effective president of Princeton University were numbered.

However, Wilson had a soft landing. By 1904, his writings on government and his leadership of a major American university began to attract the attention of politicians, particularly those in the Democratic Party, with which Wilson had long been affiliated. In speeches around the country, Wilson took aim at the Bryan wing of the party. He thought its policies far too radical. Wilson was soon identified as a spokesman for more conservative Democrats, even though he was progressive in many of his views. It became apparent when Bryan ran unsuccessfully for the presidency for the third time against William Howard Taft in 1908 that the energy that the "Boy Orator of the Platte" had generated in 1896 and 1900 was exhausted (though Bryan was still only forty-eight years old). Wilson seemed appealing to many party leaders. He was untainted by scandal. He was a Southerner but was not associated with the former Confederate government in any way, and besides, he had been teaching and presiding in Yankee states for twenty years. Though he was sympathetic to the common man, he seemed the kind of moderate who could recenter the party and bring it back toward the winning Grover Cleveland formula. With his fortunes at Princeton becoming increasingly vexed, Wilson was careful not to discourage speculation about his political availability. At this point, George Harvey, editor of *Harper's Weekly,* based like Princeton in New Jersey, sounded out Wilson as to his availability to run for Governor in 1910. Wilson signaled his availability and also that, despite his reputation for rectitude, he would not disrupt the operations of the Democratic Party machine in New Jersey. With that assurance, he was duly nominated for governor and resigned as president of Princeton.

While some in the party knew of Wilson's eloquence, many more were bowled over by his oratory. His speech accepting the nomination for governor was so inspiring that the delegates would not let him stop speaking. With his prepared address completed, Wilson fell back on rhetorical skills that he had been honing for twenty-five years. He concluded:

> When I look upon the American flag before me, I think sometimes that it is made of parchment and blood. The white in it stands for parchment, the red in it signifies blood—parchment on which was written the rights of men, and blood that was spilled to make those rights real. Let us devote the Democratic party to the recovery of these rights.[16]

This was oratory that could rival Bryan's, but it came with a fresh (though actually older) face that was decidedly more moderate. Wilson was elected and immediately became a national political figure and a leading contender for the Democratic presidential nomination in 1912.

Wilson's performance as governor only strengthened his credentials for national office. He disappointed the machine bosses in New Jersey with a decidedly reformist program. By 1912, those bosses were as anxious to get him out of state as Republican bosses in New York had been anxious to get rid of Governor Theodore Roosevelt in 1900. Thus party leaders in and out of New Jersey, for different reasons, supported Wilson's campaign for the 1912 presidential nomination. Gaining the nomination would not be so simple. Champ Clark of Missouri, speaker of the House of Representatives, was the first choice of many party regulars, especially those uneasy with the high-minded and somewhat self-righteous professor from Princeton. As the balloting began at the Democratic Convention in Baltimore, Clark was in the lead with Wilson a somewhat distant second. On the ninth ballot, the New York Tammany Hall machine swung its support to Clark, who gained a clear majority of the delegates. However, party rules then required support from two-thirds of the delegates. (This stipulation gave the South veto power over the nomination.) In the past, once a candidate received a majority, other delegates quickly came to his support and gave him the nomination; Clark, however, was not so fortunate. William Jennings Bryan was still a force within the party and the leader of its liberal wing. Bryan viewed Clark, with support from Tammany, as the candidate of Wall Street and swung his support to Wilson. Finally, on the forty-sixth ballot, Wilson received the nomination.

Racial dynamics played a significant role in the presidential election of 1912. As November approached, Democratic prospects looked excellent because of the split between progressives and conservatives within the Republican Party. Theodore Roosevelt, having become disillusioned with his chosen successor, William Howard Taft, challenged him for the GOP nomination. When Taft won with business and conservative support, Roosevelt immediately formed the Progressive Party. That organization famously became known as the Bull Moose Party when Roosevelt declared he felt "as fit as a bull moose" after being shot in the chest on the campaign trail. But while the Republican Party, the Party of Lincoln, had been the party supported by African Americans since the Civil War and Reconstruction, neither Roosevelt nor Taft inspired African American support. As discussed in Chapter 5, Roosevelt's handling of the Brownsville incident in 1906, his backing of "lily white" Southern delegations to the Progressive convention, and Taft's implicit endorsements of literacy tests in his inaugural address made some black leaders look elsewhere.

What might such leaders expect from Wilson? He was a Democrat whose roots were in the South. He had kept Princeton an all-white university. His earlier writings seemed to wax nostalgic about slavery. For example, in an 1893 book on the Civil War era, he commented that "domestic slaves were almost uniformly dealt with indulgently and even affectionately by their masters." He added that field hands "were comfortably quartered, and were kept from overwork by their own laziness" and "slack discipline." In 1901, he wrote that the founders of the Ku Klux Klan "formed a secret club for mere pleasure of association, for private amusement."[17] He did acknowledge that in later years some bad Klan actors went beyond "pranks." That year he also wrote that former slaves were "unschooled in self-control" and "insolent and aggressive."[18] Later he called Theodore Roosevelt's appointment of an African American as collector of the Port of Charleston "an unwise piece of bravado" that would be "too much" for whites.[19] Biographer Scott Berg says that Wilson, like many other white Americans at the time, was "indubitably racist."[20] His past didn't seem very promising from the point of view of African Americans.

Despite these storm clouds on the race relations front, three prominent African American leaders decided to support Woodrow Wilson. Personal contact with Wilson had encouraged them. One was Alexander Walters, bishop of the African Methodist Episcopal Zion Church. Walters contacted Wilson, who quietly welcomed his support. William Monroe Trotter, editor of the *Boston Guardian* and founder of the National Equal Rights League, met with Wilson and was warmly welcomed by him. Perhaps the most important African American leader to lean toward Wilson was W.E.B. DuBois, one of the founders of the new National Association for the Advancement of Colored People, the NAACP. DuBois was critical of Taft because of his segregationist leanings and his failure to oppose lynching more strongly. He regarded Booker T. Washington as too conservative and too willing to surrender black political rights. DuBois had no illusions about Woodrow Wilson. He was aware of his Southern background, some of his earlier more conservative views, and some of the Southern racists involved in his campaign. Nevertheless, he felt that Wilson might move the Democratic Party at least some distance from its Southern tether and offer some hope of progress to blacks. The fact that Wilson had Booker T. Washington as a guest at his Princeton inauguration, to the discomfort of several family and friends, seemed to be a good sign. DuBois, editor of the NAACP's monthly periodical *The Crisis*, endorsed Wilson, writing that "He will not advance the cause of the oligarchy in the South, he will not seek further means of 'Jim Crow' insult, he will not dismiss black men from office, and he will remember that the Negro in the United States has a right to be heard."[21] Another prominent individual concerned with black rights and supporting Wilson was a white man, Oswald Garrison Villard, grandson of famed Civil War era abolitionist William Lloyd Garrison. Villard edited the influential *New York Evening Post*. Wilson's response to overtures from all four men was vague and cautious, but he did promise to see that justice and fair dealing prevailed for all Americans. Wilson walked a very fine line, encouraging and even inviting black support, but doing it quietly so as not to offend his white Southern backers.

One of Wilson's most prominent white Southern supporters was Josephus Daniels, editor of North Carolina's *Raleigh News & Observer*. Daniels had become attached to Wilson in 1909 when Wilson gave a speech lauding Robert E. Lee at the University of North Carolina. Although Daniels supported Wilson for a variety of reasons, the importance of race was uppermost. As he wrote in the Raleigh paper, the South

> is seeking not merely a sectional but a national policy on this subject; for she knows that short of a national policy on the race question, she will never be secure . . . The subjection of the Negro, politically, and the separation of the Negro, socially, are paramount to all other considerations in the South short of the preservation itself of the Republic.[22]

In 1912, Daniels served as Wilson's campaign manager. Though Daniels, like Wilson, was progressive in his views on many issues—including education, public works, and further regulation of trusts—he was a racist even by North Carolina's standards. Afraid of growing Republican and Populist political strength, in his role as editor Daniels fanned the flames of race fear and race hatred on behalf of Democrats and white supremacy. Shortly before the election, Daniels criticized Theodore Roosevelt for having had Booker T. Washington to dinner at the White House eleven years earlier—deviations from white supremacist doctrine were not to be forgiven or forgotten.

With support from both some black leaders and many Southern white supremacists, Wilson was easily elected in November of 1912. While his popular vote was actually less than Bryan's in 1908, the rupture among the Republicans gave Wilson a decisive electoral vote victory. Aside from matters of race, Wilson had staked out a decidedly progressive agenda. He called it the New Freedom. In fact, on domestic issues, it was similar in many important regards to Theodore Roosevelt's "New Nationalism." Both opposed the rapidly growing power of corporations, and both sought protection for the laborer and the common man. Once Wilson was elected, the question became, who would have Wilson's support on race: white Southerners, black hopefuls, or neither one? The answer was white Southerners. Wilson biographer John Milton Cooper wrote in 2010 of "what a powerful civil rights president he might have been if he had put his heart and mind into the cause. But they were not there."[23] That much became clear early in Wilson's first term.

While Wilson himself may have been more moderate on race than many of his Southern supporters, he appointed a number of them to key cabinet posts and largely let them have their way on race. Three such supporters of particular note are Daniels himself, who became secretary of the navy; Albert Burleson of Texas, postmaster general; and Georgia native William McAdoo, secretary of the treasury. (McAdoo later married and then divorced one of Woodrow Wilson's daughters. He was supported by the Ku Klux Klan in the 1924 race for the Democratic presidential nomination.) Their influence was felt quickly. The most dramatic changes occurred in post offices and railway cars delivering mail. Burleson insisted on segregating employees in his department. Josephus Daniels noted in his diary the arguments the postmaster general made:

> It often happens that there are four railway mail clerks in one [railroad car] and when this happens, the white men have to do all the work. It is very unpleasant for them to work in a car with Negroes where it is almost impossible to have different drinking vessels and different towels, or places to wash.

Burleson apparently went on to say that "the segregation would be a great thing as he had the highest regard for the Negro and wished to help him in every way possible, but that he believed segregation was best for the Negro and best for the service."[24]

The idea that segregation would be a help for black people was one that had much currency among many whites in the South. Conflict would be avoided if blacks were kept separate, to the benefit of both races. Starting with the post office, segregation spread rapidly to other branches of the federal government. Political writer Bruce Bartlett cites a study showing that:

> "By the end of 1913, segregation had been realized in the Bureau of Engraving and Printing, the Post Office Department, the Office

of the Auditor for the Post Office, and had even begun in the City Post Office in Washington, D.C. This involved not only separated or screened-off working positions, but segregated lavatories and lunchrooms . . . In the office of the Auditor of the Navy . . . a separate lavatory in the cellar was provided for the colored clerks."[25]

Although the actions taken toward segregating the federal civil service were undertaken by Wilson appointees rather than by Wilson himself, he acknowledged the new reality in a 1913 letter to Oswald Garrison Villard. He argued that segregation would remove racial "friction, or rather discontent and uneasiness."[26] He also made the usual argument that far "from being a movement *against* the Negroes" it was for their own good. Predictably, black leaders and others who decried the segregationist policy were harshly critical of Wilson and his administration. Booker T. Washington said, "I have never seen the colored people so discouraged and bitter as they are at the present time."[27] In contrast, Southern political leaders applauded Wilson, one writing of "the necessity of preserving the integrity and supremacy of the white race."[28]

While ignoring racial issues as much as he could, Wilson embarked on one of the most successful and otherwise progressive periods in American history. With the backing of a Democratic Congress, one that included Northern and Western liberals as well as Southern conservatives, Wilson succeeded in lowering tariffs, thereby offering big businesses less protection from competition; instituting federal income taxes in line with the recently adopted Sixteenth Amendment to the United States Constitution (ratified a month before Wilson took office); establishing the Federal Reserve System in December 1913; and passing the tough Clayton Antitrust Act in the fall of 1914.

The fact that these momentous and progressive changes to the American economy left Jim Crow untouched was no surprise to W.E.B. DuBois. The segregationist initiatives of Wilson and his cabinet were entirely foreseeable, but DuBois had hoped that it might have been different. Still, some black leaders thought that given Wilson's overtures to them in 1912, he might be responsive to hearing directly about their concerns. A group led by William Monroe Trotter, the Boston editor, met with Wilson in November of 1913 and then again in November of 1914. Trotter recalled that prior to the election in 1912, "The Governor had us draw our chairs right up around him, and shook hands with great cordiality . . . and used such a pleased tone that I was walking on air."[29] But the results of neither meeting moved Wilson to slow down increasing segregation in the United States government. The 1914 meeting was especially disastrous from Trotter's point of view. Wilson was in a state of great emotional distress in the wake of his wife's death in August. Ellen Wilson had been a steadying influence on the president for thirty years. In his meeting with Trotter, Wilson lost his temper on hearing the group's complaints and lectured them about how his policies were for their benefit. Wilson regretted losing his temper but refused to see Trotter again. He never opened himself to understanding the

Figure 6.2 African American editor William Monroe Trotter suffered Woodrow Wilson's wrath when he asked the president to make good on his vague promises to help black citizens.

Photographer with the Boston City Council, "William Monroe Trotter," 1915, black and white photograph. Public domain, via Wikimedia Commons.

injustice of what his administration was doing and how blacks were affected by it. Somehow Wilson could not rise above his basic racist beliefs and feelings to see or hear beyond the comfortable Southern narrative that segregation was a kind necessity. It was not a necessary evil but rather a policy and practice that would protect blacks but also white supremacy—two good things in Wilson's world view.

Things got worse just a few months later. In 1905, Thomas Dixon, who had been a student with Woodrow Wilson at Johns Hopkins in the 1880s, published a novel, and then a play based on the novel, called *The Clansman*.[30] The novel critiques white carpetbaggers during the Reconstruction era and is an emotional brief for continued segregation and white supremacy. It portrays the Ku Klux Klan as a group formed to protect whites from other misguided whites who would let loose black savagery. The play formed the basis for D. W. Griffith's monumental and highly racist film, *The Birth of a Nation*, released in 1915.[31] The influential film, seen by many across the nation, shows blacks in ways that reinforce ugly Southern stereotypes of African Americans. It also glorifies the Ku Klux Klan as the defender of white people from the barely suppressed passions of blacks. Dixon persuaded Wilson to show it at the White House in February 1915, perhaps hiding its racist intent from the president. The fact that Wilson agreed to show such a film further poisoned already strained relationships with the NAACP and other black leaders. Whether Wilson actually said of the film, as is widely quoted, "It is like writing history with lightning. And my only regret is that it is all so terribly true," is dubious.[32] Nonetheless, Wilson declined several opportunities to express any condemnation of the film, in part because he did not want to appear unduly influenced by the protests of, among others, William Monroe Trotter. In effect, Wilson let his showing of *The Birth of a Nation* stand as a statement supporting its message.

Later in 1915, Wilson's emotional equilibrium was restored after meeting, wooing, and marrying a wealthy and strong-minded Washington widow, Edith Bolling Galt. Wilson was as giddy, and distracted, as a teenager during his courtship of Galt, but she proved to be a forceful protector of the president during the remainder of his administration. None of this improved matters on the racial front. Not surprisingly, black leaders did not support Wilson's re-election in 1916. Nevertheless, Wilson won a narrow electoral victory, defeating Republican Charles Evans Hughes. Hughes received the endorsement of the Progressive Party after Theodore Roosevelt refused their nomination and threw his support to Hughes. Thus, the nation's choice was between two Progressive candidates. However, neither one addressed the concerns of African Americans. (It is interesting to note, in comparing the results of the 1916 and 2008 elections, the impact of the switch during the twentieth century of the Democratic vs. Republican parties on race issues. Only ten of the forty-eight states belonging to the Union in 1916 voted the same way in those two elections. The "Solid South" and the Plains States were Democratic in 1916 but voted for Republican John McCain in 2008. Most of the Northeast and Midwest states were Republican in 1916 but voted for Democrat Barack Obama in 2008. As we shall see, the 1960s Civil Rights and Voting Rights Acts were a major impetus for the Southern states' change in political party alignment.)

A major issue benefitting Wilson's re-election effort was the Democratic Party slogan, "He kept us out of war." World War I had broken out in Europe in the summer of 1914, Wilson's second year in office. The president worked strenuously to keep the United States neutral between the Allies, led by Great Britain, and the Central Powers, led by Germany. One concern was racial. Wilson feared that the European war was already decimating the white race and that the problem would only get worse if the United States entered the conflict. Nevertheless, German U-boat attacks on American shipping finally propelled the United States into war in the second month of Wilson's second term. In an eloquent speech in April 1917, pledging to fight to "make the world safe for democracy," Wilson asked for, and received, a congressional declaration of war against Germany.[33]

The war again put issues of race on the forefront for both blacks and whites. African Americans had served proudly and effectively in the 1898 Spanish-American War, including with Theodore Roosevelt on San Juan Hill. They had hoped that their service would enhance their status and increase the respect accorded to them by white Americans. For the most part, there was no such acknowledgment. The efforts of black soldiers did little to slow the pace toward Jim Crow. In fact, the idea of trained black soldiers returning to the United States frightened many whites. When the United States mobilized for World War I, many of the same fears of black men with guns, who knew how to use them, haunted many whites. At the same time, African Americans were divided on whether and how to support the war effort. A. Philip Randolph and Chandler Owen, editors of the black socialist newspaper *The Messenger,* argued that it made no sense for African Americans to fight to make the world safe for democracy when America wasn't safe for African American democracy. Brandeis University professor Chad Williams quoted one African American resident of Harlem who, anticipating Muhammad Ali's quip during the Vietnam War that he had no quarrel with "them Viet Cong" and that "no Viet Cong ever called me Nigger," remarked that "The Germans ain't done nothing to me."[34] On the other hand, most African Americans supported the war effort, believing that it was an opportunity to show white Americans that they were competent and valuable citizens and deserved to be treated even-handedly, just as Woodrow Wilson had promised that they would be in 1912.

Large numbers of African Americans did serve in World War I. Most were segregated into all black units, as had been the case for well over a century, since the last integrated regiments fought for American freedom under General George Washington during the Revolutionary War. The presence of black soldiers and increasing racial tensions led to outbreaks of violence in East St. Louis, Illinois, in July of 1917. Though such disturbances were called "race riots" by most Americans, they in fact were essentially terrorist attacks, or pogroms, against blacks. In the East St. Louis case, black neighborhoods were burned to the ground, as had happened and would happen again in other black urban areas in the early twentieth century. Thirty-nine African Americans and nine whites were killed. A month later, a group of black soldiers got into a shootout with whites in Houston, Texas. Almost assuredly provoked by fearful and resentful whites, three blacks and fifteen whites died in the struggle. The army, dominated by racists and racist attitudes, investigated the incident, hung thirteen black soldiers, and sentenced forty-one to life imprisonment. Later, sixteen more black soldiers were sentenced to death in the Houston case.

At this point, Woodrow Wilson went partway in changing the national discourse on race in a positive direction. He personally reviewed and commuted some of the sentences of the black soldiers involved in the Houston shootings. In doing so, he wrote that he wanted his clemency to recognize African Americans' loyalty to the fight for "which so many of them are now bravely bearing arms at the very front of great fields of battle."[35] Still, the African American experience in World War I and its aftermath is a continuing story of Jim Crow racism that Wilson did little to change. Blacks were excluded from the US Marine Corps and typically restricted to service positions in the United States Navy. The experience in the army was somewhat better. Though segregated in separate and unequal quarters both inside and outside military bases, black officers were trained in significant numbers. However, a particularly sensitive issue involved avoiding any situation where black officers might command white enlisted men. As blacks were trained for higher ranks, that problem became more acute; within Wilson's administration, there was some uncertainty as to how to handle it. Secretary of War Newton Baker, though a native of West Virginia, was not as bigoted as some of his cabinet colleagues. He elevated several black assistants. But the army, though technically under Baker's supervision, often moved in the opposite direction. The highest-ranking black officer at the time, Colonel Charles Young, the third black graduate of West Point, could easily have been made a general, but this would put him in command of lower-ranking white officers. Consequently, Wilson was willing to let the army derail Young on the specious grounds of health problems related to high blood pressure.

In spite of all the obstacles imposed by racial fears and Jim Crow traditions, several hundred thousand African Americans were trained and fought in France during the war. Many were assigned to heavy labor support operations, but there were two all black combat units, the 92nd and 93rd divisions. Since the US Army didn't know quite what to do with black combat units and the racial tensions that their presence might generate, some were put under French command. The French took the concept of equality, borrowed ironically from Thomas Jefferson's words in the Declaration of Independence, more seriously than did Americans. They were happy to have African American units fight with their own black units from their African colony, Senegal. Although fighting with French-speaking units imposed an additional burden on black American soldiers, this obstacle too was overcome. One of the most successful units of the 93rd Division was the 369th Infantry Regiment from New York. They became known as the "Harlem Hellfighters." Members of this and other units received some of the highest French military honors, including the Croix de Guerre (Cross of War) and the Palme en Bronze (Cross of War with Palm).

The success of black soldiers might have been a rallying point for African Americans and a turning point in white America's relation to them. After the war ended, the 369th Regiment marched proudly in a parade up Fifth Avenue in New York before huge crowds and inspired hope among their compatriots. But as in the case of the Spanish-American War, black hopes were soon dashed. One preview of their disappointments might have been gleaned from Wilson's dealing with race issues during his trips to Europe at the end of 1918 and the first half of 1919. Soon after the armistice ending World War I began on November 11, 1918, Wilson traveled by ship to Europe to press for a League of Nations and to fashion a treaty formally ending the war. He worked tirelessly with his British, French, Italian, and Japanese allies, among others.

The Japanese proposed that the League commit itself to equal treatment of citizens of all member nations and oppose discrimination based on "race or nationality." Wilson wanted any language about racial equality as vague as possible, knowing that it would cause problems at home and perturb European, especially British, colonialism abroad. Even though most nations supported a racial equality statement in the League covenant, Wilson successfully blocked it. He wanted issues of race ignored as much as possible, although he privately indicated to the Japanese that the League would surely stand for the equality of nations. The Treaty of Versailles was finally signed, with a League of Nations, in the famous Hall of Mirrors on June 28, 1919—without a word about racial equality.

When Wilson returned to America after being away for most of six months, he faced not only a battle to persuade the Senate to ratify the Treaty but a host of postwar domestic tensions. These included fear spreading from the 1918 influenza pandemic that killed millions around the world; fear of Bolsheviks and anarchists in the United States; and fear of black insistence on recognition and equality, made more pressing and powerful by their important contributions to winning the war. One manifestation of these anxieties was an increase in lynchings in the United States during the summer of 1919. While Wilson might have forcefully spoken out against lynching, as he had the previous year, he was too preoccupied by challenges to League ratification to attempt to intervene. In one speech, he decried racial violence but failed to address it with any real conviction or substance. Any hope that Wilson might give further attention to racial issues was shattered, as was Wilson himself, by a serious stroke that the president suffered in September 1919 on his national speaking tour while trying to rally support for the League. For the remaining year and a half of his presidency, Wilson was seriously disabled and hidden from public view. Edith Wilson inserted herself as a go-between, shielding Wilson from other government officials who needed to work with him. She often spoke for him and handled on her own many of his routine affairs. Woodrow Wilson would never lead again.

The 1920 presidential election saw a repudiation of the progressive policies of both Theodore Roosevelt and Woodrow Wilson. Race issues were largely ignored in the campaign. On the tenth ballot, the Republican convention nominated a relative "dark horse," Warren Harding, a Senator and former newspaper editor from Ohio. Harding pledged a "return to normalcy," a rejection of both progressive policies and the international involvement for which Wilson had argued in supporting the League of Nations. The Democrats were deadlocked until the forty-fourth ballot. At first, the leading candidates were two Wilson cabinet members—Attorney General Mitchell Palmer and former Treasury Secretary, and Wilson son-in-law, William McAdoo. Wilson chose not to support McAdoo, who led until the final few ballots. The eventual winner was Ohio Governor James Cox, like Harding a former newspaper editor in their home state. It is of interest that the 1920 election was the only one that included two major party vice presidential candidates, Massachusetts Governor Calvin Coolidge for the Republicans and Assistant Secretary of the Navy Franklin D.

Roosevelt for the Democrats (Roosevelt was only thirty-eight years old and had not yet been attacked by polio), who eventually became president. The election was not close. Tired of the Democrats, the nation overwhelmingly reasserted the old Republican majority of McKinley, Theodore Roosevelt, and Taft. Harding won 60% of the popular vote to Cox's 34%, still the largest popular vote percentage margin of victory in US history.

Woodrow Wilson's years in office were tragic in a number of respects. Still, Wilson is generally ranked as one of the greatest American presidents. His progressive achievements in the first two years of his administration, his effective leadership in World War I, and his idealism about the constructive role that America could play in the world after that war are inspirational to many. He was eloquent, honest, and dignified. On the other hand, his rigidity, attributable in part to poor health, ruined his most cherished project, the League of Nations. But it is in race relations that his failings seem most antithetical to American values. John Milton Cooper views them as "Woodrow Wilson's greatest tragedy." He suggests that Wilson's upbringing led him to oppose mixing religion and politics and may have diverted him from fully appreciating "African Americans as fellow children of God." That separation of religion and politics was "the North Star by which he steered on his life's spiritual and intellectual journey [and it] may have prevented him from reaching his full stature as a moral leader and rendering still finer service to his nation and the world."[36] While Wilson's failings on race may have constituted a personal tragedy, they were a political disaster for millions of African Americans. Progress for blacks in the United States would await another quarter of a century and a second world war.

Notes

1 James Bradley, *The Imperial Cruise: A Secret History of Empire and War* (New York: Little, Brown, 2009), p. 115.

2 *Ibid.*

3 *Ibid.*, p. 121.

4 Booker T. Washington, Atlanta Compromise Speech, September 18, 1895. http://historymatters.gmu.edu/d/39/.

5 See http://uselectionatlas.org/RESULTS/data.php?year=1876&datatype=national&def=1&f=0&off=0&elect=0; http://uselectionatlas.org/RESULTS/data.php?year=1888&datatype=national&def=1&f=0&off=0&elect=0; http://uselectionatlas.org/RESULTS/data.php?year=1904&datatype=national&def=1&f=0&off=0&elect=0.

6 William Howard Taft, Inaugural Address, March 4, 1909. http://www.bartleby.com/124/pres43.html.

7 John Milton Cooper, Jr., *Woodrow Wilson: A Biography* (New York: Knopf, 2009), pp. 29–30.

8 A. Scott Berg, *Wilson* (New York: Putnam, 2013), p. 38.

9 H. W. Brands, *Woodrow Wilson* (New York: Times Books, 2003), p. 6.

10 *Ibid.*, p. 8.

11 *Ibid.*, p. 12.

12 Woodrow Wilson, Cabinet Government in the United States. *International Review, VII,* 1879, pp. 146–63.

13 Wilson, *Congressional Government: A Study in American Politics* (Boston: Houghton Mifflin, 1885).

14 Wilson, *The State: Elements of Historical and Practical Politics* (Boston: D.C. Heath, 1889).

15 Berg, p. 156.

16 John Wesley Westcott, *Woodrow Wilson's Eloquence* (Washington, DC: Library of Congress, 1922), p. 23.

17 Bruce Bartlett, *Wrong on Race: The Democratic Party's Buried Past* (New York: Palgrave Macmillan, 2008), pp. 96–97.

18 *Ibid.*, p. 97.

19 Berg, p. 157.

20 *Ibid.*

21 Cooper, p. 170.

22 Bartlett, p. 100.

23 Cooper, p. 410.

24 Bartlett, p. 102.

25 *Ibid.*, p. 103.

26 Berg, p. 309.

27 *Ibid.*

28 Bartlett, p. 105.

29 *Ibid.*, p. 108.

30 Thomas Dixon, Jr., *The Clansman: An Historical Romance of the Ku Klux Klan* (New York: Doubleday, 1905).

31 D.W. Griffith, *The Birth of a Nation* (David W. Griffith Corp, 1915).

32 Cooper, p. 272.

33 Wilson, Declaration of War Speech, April 2, 1917. http://www.ourdocuments.gov/doc.php?doc=61.

34 Chad Williams, African Americans and World War I, Africana Age, 2011. http://exhibitions.nypl.org/africanaage/essay-world-war-i.html.

35 Berg, p. 485.

36 Cooper, p. 411.

7

HARRY S. TRUMAN

Figure 7.1 Harry Truman shaking hands with Air Force Sergeant Edward Williams. Truman never agonized about the justice of desegregating United States armed forces, knowing it was right.

Acme, "President Harry S. Truman shaking hands with African American Air Force Sergeant Edward Williams," 1950, black and white photograph. Harry S. Truman Library, Independence, Missouri.

C-SPAN's 2009 ratings by historians of American presidents rank only Abraham Lincoln ahead of Democrats Lyndon B. Johnson and Harry S. Truman as chief executives who "pursued equal justice for all."[1] Ironically, both Truman and Johnson came from backgrounds that would make them extremely unlikely to play central roles in the advancement of African American prospects in the mid-twentieth century. Yet Harry Truman has been called an "unsung civil rights hero," and Lyndon Johnson is well-remembered for adopting the words of the best-known Civil Rights anthem of his era and emphatically declaring "and we *shall* overcome" in his famous 1965 speech urging Congress to pass the Voting Rights Act.[2] The leadership of these two presidents on issues affecting African Americans reflects, among other things, major upheavals in the alignment of the two major political parties in the United States on matters of race and equally dramatic changes in their own moral development.

The distance that Harry Truman had to travel can be seen in the difference between his own efforts for blacks as president and his mother's attitude toward Abraham Lincoln. Martha Ellen Young Truman was ninety-two when her son became president. Her daughter, the president's sister, accompanied her to Washington within a month of Harry taking office. Many writers have said that her pro-Confederate sensibilities made her refuse to sleep in the Lincoln bedroom, although what she actually said about where she would and would not spend the night in the White House is unclear. But her reported antipathy to the sixteenth president rings true. Mrs. Truman and her husband John were brought up in the western part of Missouri, close to the border with Kansas. The parents of both Martha and John owned slaves and both lived through some of the most tumultuous years in one of the most fought-over parts of the country. The Kansas-Nebraska Act of 1854 opened the nearby territory of Kansas to "popular sovereignty," a policy whereby residents of a territory would vote to decide whether it should be slave or free. This legislation led directly to what is commonly called "Bleeding Kansas," violent raids by pro-slavery gangs on anti-slavery settlements, and vice-versa, well before the start of the Civil War. In 1856, so-called "Border Ruffians" attacked abolitionists in Lawrence, Kansas. Not long after, anti-slavery crusader John Brown, who later planned his famous 1859 raid on Harper's Ferry in Virginia, led a retaliatory attack at a place called Pottawatomie Creek, chopping to death several men and boys. The most violent attack also took place in Lawrence during the war. In 1863, Confederate cavalry officer William Quantrill led a guerilla force that killed well over 100 people. Both of Harry Truman's parents were affected by the violence, but his mother had particularly bitter memories. She remembered Union soldiers robbing and burning nearby farms when she was nine years old. Two years later, in 1863, Union forces ordered all civilians out of their homes in Jackson County, Missouri. The family sought refuge in nearby Kansas City. Martha would identify with the Confederate cause her whole life.

Harry's father, John Truman, was also from Jackson County. He and Martha were married in 1881 and soon moved about 100 miles south to Lamar, Missouri, near both the Kansas and Oklahoma borders. They made their living as farmers and soon started a family. Their first child, a son, died in infancy. Their second, the future president, was born on May 8, 1884, the year that Grover

Cleveland became the first Democrat to be elected president since before the Civil War. Another son, Vivian, was born in 1886, and a daughter, Mary Jane, arrived in 1889, much to the surprise of her two older brothers. Harry had no idea that the noise from his parents' bedroom meant that he had a baby sister. Martha Truman initiated another life-changing event for Harry the next year, about the time he turned six years old. Harry had always had very poor vision. He once described himself as "blind as a mole."[3] Mrs. Truman took Harry off to nearby Kansas City and paid ten dollars for a pair of eyeglasses.

The good news was that Harry could see much better. The bad news was that he looked very strange to many of his peers. Not many children had spectacles in 1890s Missouri. Furthermore, Mrs. Truman did not want Harry engaging in rough and tumble play with other young boys. Barred from sports and other typical male activities, Harry took to reading and music. He got up every morning at five o'clock to practice the piano; he even imagined that he might someday become a professional musician. He also read voraciously, especially military history and biography. Much of what he read made him want to be a soldier, but he knew his eyesight might prevent him from serving. When he was somewhat older, his poor eyesight and glasses also became something of an obstacle in attracting girls. He was extremely shy and for the most part spent time alone or interacting with his siblings or nearby cousins.

The Trumans moved several times during Harry's childhood. For three years, they lived on Harry's grandmother's large family farm in Grandview, Missouri, before moving to nearby Independence so Harry could attend church and go to school. Independence was in most respects a Southern town. It honored Robert E. Lee and Stonewall Jackson. A favorite song was "Dixie." Most important, it was completely Southern in its racial attitudes, customs, and sensibilities. African Americans lived in segregated neighborhoods, in a place called Nigger Neck. Many words that today are considered among the worst racial slurs were commonplace. Whites, for instance, referred to blacks as "coons" routinely. Harry Truman was socialized into an almost reflexively white supremacist community where segregation was simply the way the world worked.

Shortly after arriving in Independence, Harry noticed a striking young girl in his Sunday school class. He especially admired her "most beautiful blue eyes" and "golden curls."[4] A year younger than Harry, she was Bess Wallace, who would marry Harry almost twenty years later. Their relationship developed very slowly and was interrupted repeatedly by family circumstances. It took five years for Harry to summon the courage to talk to Bess. They did, however, attend the same school from fifth grade until high school graduation and remained in intermittent contact thereafter.

During Harry's childhood years, John Truman's fortunes rose and fell. He worked both as a farmer and as a livestock and commodities trader. The family was comfortable but never well-off. Compared to Bess Wallace's family, for example, the Truman's circumstances were very modest. Nevertheless, Harry's memories of his childhood were quite happy. Some combination of a sunny inborn temperament and a rapidly developed buoyancy and optimism gave him an upbeat outlook that served him well throughout his life. One specific childhood memory was of the joy that he, his family, and many of their neighbors shared in 1892 when Grover Cleveland was elected to a second term as president of the United States. Harry was eight. Though Cleveland had been the governor of New York, as a Democrat he had strong support in Western Missouri with its strong pro-Southern sympathies.

Throughout his school years, Harry worked intensely on his piano playing, becoming especially adept at performing classical pieces by Beethoven, Chopin, and Mozart. He also continued his immersion in books and, thanks to some dedicated teachers, became a talented writer. In high school, Harry took a job at a drug store in the central square in Independence, keeping the building clean and organized and assisting on a wide range of essential chores. He worked every morning before school and on weekend afternoons. His assignments included providing glasses of whiskey for church members who opposed public saloons but would take a drink hiding behind shelves in the drug store. This was all part of Harry's education and maturation. His work allowed him to become known around town as a reliable and agreeable young man with good future prospects. To his regret, after several months, Harry's father insisted that he stop work at the drug store and concentrate on his studies.

During his high school years, Harry aspired to go to West Point. However, his bad eyes made him ineligible. But if a military future was unlikely, politics was another area that captured his attention. John Truman was involved in local politics and was able to get sixteen-year-old Harry a position as a page at the 1900 Democratic National Convention, held that year in Kansas City. Harry was constantly on the go, keeping busy running errands and delivering messages. He loved every minute of it. The huge convention hall held 17,000 people, creating an electric atmosphere that Harry never forgot. That year, for the second time, the Democrats nominated William Jennings Bryan, "the Boy Orator of the Platte." Bryan had lost to Republican William McKinley when he ran for president in 1896 at the age of thirty-six. At that time he barely met the Constitution's thirty-five-year-old age requirement. Four years later, Democrats hoped that a more seasoned forty-year-old Bryan could prevail. As it turned out, William McKinley had presided over a strong economy in his first term and was easily re-elected, with Theodore Roosevelt as his running mate. Nevertheless, young Harry Truman, like his father, became enthralled by Bryan and always regarded him as a hero. Bryan's fight for the common man proved to be a model for Harry throughout his political career.

Though Harry could not go to West Point, he wanted to move beyond the uncertainties and difficulties of farm life. After graduating from high school in 1901 with Bess Wallace, he enrolled in a business college in Kansas City. However, his father's business dealings soon took a bad turn, and Harry was called home to help support the family. During the next several years, he worked on the family farm and also took jobs in Kansas City as a postmaster, a bank clerk, and on road construction. He enjoyed being on his own, but had lost contact with Bess, whose father, though prosperous and respected, committed suicide in 1903. Bess, her mother, and three younger brothers then moved to Colorado for a year. When the year was up, they returned to Independence and lived at Bess's grandmother's house on 219 North Delaware Street. It was to be Bess' only home for the rest of her life—before, during, and after her marriage to Harry Truman.

In 1905, Harry joined a local National Guard unit and served for two three-year terms. One attraction was that the Guard was a way for Harry to enjoy male companionship. He could get away with fellow members for several weeks at camp in the summer and attend occasional meetings the rest of the year. However, keeping up with his National Guard responsibilities became more difficult just the year after he joined. By 1906, his father had given up on several other jobs and gone back to the farm. He needed Harry and his younger son Vivian to help out. Harry was twenty-two. It looked like he was going to be a farmer for a very long time. For most of the next ten years, Harry worked on the farm, doing his share of physical chores, including plowing, planting, and harvesting, depending on the season. He also did most of the clerical work, including keeping the books and paying bills.

Through most of these years, Harry was out of touch with Bess Wallace. There were, however, occasional sightings. Some of his cousins lived on North Delaware Street in Independence and were neighbors of the Wallace's. In 1910, he joyfully reported seeing her, ever so briefly, on a visit to his relatives. As more frequent visits from the farm in Grandview to Independence transpired, Harry and Bess engaged in a prolonged exchange of letters. Their correspondence covered a range of subjects—music, Charles Dickens, and politics, among others. Within a year of the 1910 encounter, Harry declared his love for Bess in a letter and proposed marriage. She declined. It is not entirely clear why. One factor might have been that Bess's mother, a widow for nearly ten years, needed her help with both her own elderly parents and with the younger Wallace brothers. Another concern was that Harry's life prospects seemed meager given the Wallace's elevated social status. Still, Harry persisted. He and Bess continued their correspondence.

In the fall of 1912, Harry happily noted the election of Woodrow Wilson, the first Democrat to be elected in twenty years, since Cleveland's second victory in 1892. Late the next year, Bess wrote Harry a letter in which she agreed to a secret engagement. No date was set. Harry was about to be thirty years old, and while the timing was uncertain, he finally had expectations of marrying the woman who had first entranced him since the day in Sunday school that he first noticed her, some twenty years earlier.

The year 1914 brought momentous changes to both the world and the Truman family. In August, war in Europe began, a war which would be known first as The Great War and, later, World War I. For the time being, under Woodrow Wilson's leadership, the United States remained neutral. In November of that year, John Truman died. With his father's death, Harry was able to engage in activities outside the farm, but he was still very much tied to it. He worked long days and at times became quite discouraged about his future prospects. He invested in a mining company and an oil business; neither one succeeded. Although he knew that farm life was not for him, the family farm ironically provided some financial cushion. During the war, both food prices and the value of land rose, and a productive farm was worth a considerable sum. In the meantime, Harry continued to see Bess and continued with his various lines of work. It was becoming increasingly likely that the United States would be drawn into the European conflict. Although in 1916 Woodrow Wilson ran successfully for re-election on the Democratic Party slogan, "He kept us out of war," mounting German U-boat attacks on American shipping made US entry more likely. Finally, on April 2, 1917, less than a month after his second inauguration, the president asked Congress for a declaration of war against Germany.

Harry Truman could easily have stayed out of the armed forces in World War I. At thirty-three, he was over the draft age. As a supporter of a family involved in food production, critical to the war effort, there would have been no stigma at all if he had just continued farming. In fact, he had some difficulty getting into the Army. His poor eyesight made him ineligible for service, but the chance to fulfill his lifelong soldiering dreams, and perhaps to leave the farm, drove him to find a way to enlist. Harry also realized that military service might provide a foundation for a political career. In due course, he passed the physical, sliding by the vision test by memorizing the eye chart. He joined his old National Guard unit, which soon became incorporated into the Army as the 129th Field Artillery Regiment. Now, as he and Bess faced the reality that Harry would soon be shipped "over there" and would likely see combat, she pleaded with him to get married. This time Harry declined. He wrote that it would be unfair for "me to ask you to tie yourself to a prospective cripple—or a sentiment." [5] But both Bess and Harry pledged their love and fidelity and agreed that they would marry when he returned from war.

Truman's experiences as a soldier changed his life. Shortly after he enlisted, he caught up with his old Guard unit, found himself elected lieutenant, and began training in Kansas City. Soon the 129th moved to Doniphan, Oklahoma, where it continued drilling. During that time, Harry made some lifelong friends. One of the most important was Eddie Jacobson, who had worked in a Kansas City clothing store before joining the army. Together with Jacobson, a sergeant, Truman ran the regiment's canteen. Mostly because of his friend's business acumen, the canteen was extremely well-run and made money for the many troops who had invested in it. Harry Truman's stock with his men rose to new heights. He was already respected for his straightforward likeability and steadiness. Now, providing his men with everything from food, drinks, and cigarettes to haircuts and clothing, Harry's stature as a leader took off as the canteen did. Doubts he had about his ability to measure up receded, for the time being.

Training was difficult during the cold Oklahoma winter of 1917–18, but in March troop transport trains took the 129th from Doniphan to New York City to await a ship for France. For the most part, Truman was not impressed with New York. Displaying the deep ethnocentrism of his Western Missouri upbringing, he called the city "Kike Town" and complained about the number of Jews in that part of the world. Despite the fact that his close friend Eddie Jacobson was Jewish, in 1918 Harry felt free to make derogatory comments about Jews as a group. Such words were part of the culture. But the layover in New York didn't last long. On March 29, the ship *George Washington*, which would later carry Woodrow Wilson to France at the end of the war, left American shores, bound for Europe. Harry Truman and 129th Field Artillery were aboard.

Arriving in the French port of Brest two weeks later, Harry encountered new challenges. First, he had to learn how to operate the French 75-millimeter field piece, the most effective artillery weapon on either side during the war. Without a college education, Truman found the mathematics, surveying, and engineering the piece entailed very challenging. Typically, he persisted and mastered the weapon. Even more challenging was the leadership assignment he faced. Newly promoted to captain, on the basis of his excellent work in Oklahoma, Truman was ordered to take command of the regiment's unruly Battery D, 2d Battalion. Battery D had already overwhelmed two other captains, and it seemed to be ungovernable. Truman's quick success is startlingly reminiscent of Ulysses S. Grant's success in taking command of the 21st Illinois Volunteer Regiment in 1861. Both units had run off previous commanders. In both cases a small, somewhat odd-looking man confronted his troops. In Truman's case, his eyeglasses would have made him seem particularly out of place. In both cases, swift, sure, but fair disciplining of noncommissioned officers gained the leader respect. In Truman's case, he talked to the men and, more importantly, listened. He gave them time to say what was on their minds. In short order, Truman was seen as having "personal magnetism." One soldier said that whatever that quality was, "he had it."[6] When it came time to move out, Battery D did it in record time.

Once the 129th approached the front, the effectiveness of their training met its most stringent test. Hauling heavy weapons up mountains in the cold and dark, sometimes under fire, the men were stressed to the breaking point both physically and mentally. However, the unit didn't panic or run away, as others had, and Captain Truman was "cool under fire."[7] The unit marched for over a week, typically eighteen to twenty miles each night. In late September, the regiment finally engaged and opened fire at the enemy. Their job was to aim over the American lines at the German enemy and then move forward as their own infantry attacked. They had to keep up so as to fire over their men rather than at them. The work was dangerous and difficult. At one point in their movement forward, Truman saw a German artillery unit preparing to fire on an American regiment. Disobeying orders, Truman calmly waited until the Germans had set up, so that they could not simply run away, and then ordered his men to fire at the enemy, surely saving the American regiment. Throughout the days of combat, Truman's steady, clear-headed leadership made him the undisputed, and highly admired, chief of Battery D.

Shortly before the 129th was about to attack again on November 11, Captain Truman was told to hold his fire. An armistice would take effect at 11:00 AM that morning, the eleventh hour of the eleventh day of the eleventh month. The war was over.

After the Allies' sudden victory, it would take nearly five months for Truman and his men to get back to the United States. Demobilization was a slow process, and the transporting of American troops back home across the Atlantic became a logistical nightmare. The months waiting in France for an Atlantic crossing were in some ways as demanding as combat. The young troops were bored and restless and faced multiple temptations in Paris and in the countryside. Keeping them in good order severely tested Truman's leadership capacities, but he managed successfully.

Captain Harry Truman finally got back to Kansas City and Independence in May of 1919. He was thirty-five years old and a much more experienced, confident, and resourceful man than he had been two years earlier. Now he focused on two things: marrying Bess Wallace and starting a career in politics. Bess and Harry wrote numerous letters during the war, and their engagement survived their separation. The marriage was a sure thing. It took place the month after Harry returned to Independence. Bess's mother wanted her daughter and new son-in-law to move into the house on North Delaware. Partly because there was no better alternative, they did. Now happily married, Harry turned to politics. He knew his career would be aided greatly by an important alliance he made during the war. Besides Eddie Jacobson, he had formed a close friendship with Jim Prendergast, the nephew of Kansas City Democratic Party political boss Tom Prendergast. If Truman was to have a political career in Jackson County, he would have to have the blessing of Mr. Prendergast. That Harry had helped Jim Prendergast out of several jams in Europe would count for a great deal.

Though Truman saw politics as the way to move forward in the world, the presidential election year of 1920, held only eighteen months after his return from France, offered slim prospects for a Democrat. Nationwide, the Republican tide was strong. The country wanted to "return to normalcy." The national current ran as strongly through Missouri as anywhere else. The state was well into its century-long reign as the USA's "bellwether." In twenty-six presidential elections between 1904 and 2004, Missouri voted with the winner twenty-five times (it voted for the loser, Adlai Stevenson, only in 1956). Like thirty-six out of forty-seven other states, Missouri chose Warren G. Harding and Calvin Coolidge over James Cox and Franklin D. Roosevelt. Truman would wait for a more propitious year.

While 1920 was a year for Harry Truman to bide his time, it was a year of hope and optimism for African Americans. The Democrats and Woodrow Wilson had been voted out. The Democratic majorities in both the House of Representatives and the Senate had gradually diminished since that party's sweep in 1912, and Congress elected in 1920 had strong Republican majorities in both houses. The Party of Lincoln was in firm control of the federal government once again. Warren Harding had promised that the Republicans would undo the segregation of federal offices institutionalized under Woodrow Wilson and the Southern Democrats in his cabinet. Time would tell.

For Harry Truman, while a political career could wait, earning a living could not. Harry needed to find a way to support his new bride. He had not had much success so far. He soon decided to join his war-time buddy Eddie Jacobson in opening a men's clothing and dry goods store, commonly called a haberdashery. The success of the Jacobson and Truman canteen during the war forecast success. Both men borrowed considerable sums of money to get the operation up and running. However, the postwar economic slump doomed their enterprise. By 1922, they were bankrupt and heavily in debt.

That year Truman did finally step into politics, in part because a political position came with a salary. As a candidate for office, Truman had several things going for him. He had joined various civic and veterans groups after his return to Independence. Such associations, along with those he had made doing business, provided potential political contacts that could be exceedingly helpful. Furthermore, his military experience lent him stature as a leader and provided still more connections. Childhood shyness was long gone. Harry Truman knew he could lead. Most important, perhaps, Truman knew that he had to work through his wartime friend's uncle, Thomas Prendergast. In fact, Truman's connection with Jim Prendergast was the final element in the mix that brought Truman favor with "Boss" Prendergast. However, it was not the only thing. The Boss thought that Truman's war record and civic networks might be just the thing to make him a successful candidate for judge in Jackson County. In 1922, Harry ran and won. Along with another elected judge and a third presiding judge, Truman became one of the political leaders of his home county.

As judge, Truman did all he could to serve his constituents. He oversaw the construction of schools and hospitals in the county and gave particular attention to road building and maintenance. Throughout his term, he realized that there were certain corrupt practices with which he would have to go along to maintain his position. At nearly forty years old, Harry was not naïve. He would do the best he could, as honestly as he could, for as long as he could, for Jackson County, but he would have to work within the constraints of the Prendergast machine. It turned out that his initial stint as county judge lasted only two years. In 1924, the Republican presidential ticket, now headed by Calvin Coolidge, easily carried Missouri and the national election. Truman was out of a job.

As it turned out, African Americans were also facing lost hopes. Despite pledges from the Republican Party, neither Warren Harding nor Calvin Coolidge, Harding's successor to the presidency when he died suddenly in 1923, followed up on GOP pledges to undo Wilson-era segregation. The Republican Party's longtime concern for African Americans had started to erode with black disenfranchisement in the South starting in the 1890s. As noted earlier, both Theodore Roosevelt and his successor William Howard Taft had made appeals to white Southerners once black Southerners could no longer vote. Republican concerns for African Americans ebbed. Although the elections of Harding in 1920 and Coolidge in 1924 offered hope, not much good happened. Both presidents were largely passive. They did not see a role for the federal government in combating racism. Since a Democratic administration had proved so antithetical to their interests, African Americans' prospects were, for the moment, bleak.

Despite his 1924 setback, Harry Truman's reputation as an effective and comparatively ethical political leader earned him another chance for a political position. He successfully operated under a tight budget, enhanced law enforcement, and continued to maintain county roads. Consequently, Boss Prendergast supported Truman for the position of presiding judge of Jackson County in 1926. The term was for four years. Truman won easily and was re-elected for another four year term in 1930. By that time, the nation was in the throes of the Great Depression, and Republican politics were largely discredited in Missouri and elsewhere. Perhaps the time was right for Truman to practice politics on a larger stage. Since it was customary for presiding judges to move on after two terms, Truman thought that 1932 would be an opportune moment to run for a higher position, specifically governor of Missouri. It seemed very likely that Franklin D. Roosevelt would be elected president by a wide margin that year and might well sweep a Democratic governor into the Missouri state house.

This time Boss Prendergast said no. He had other protégés in mind. However, he promised to support Truman for a seat in the House of Representatives in the midterm elections of 1934. Harry would be fifty that year and might finally be able to move beyond politics at the county level. However, Prendergast changed his mind and named someone else for the congressional seat. Harry Truman's career looked stalled. He would either have to accept a minor county position or find another line of work. It seemed that he would live and die an obscure figure chewed up by the Prendergast machine. Then something completely unexpected happened. Franklin Roosevelt had brought in an overwhelmingly Democratic Congress in 1932. As the midterm elections of 1934 approached, it seemed that popular New Deal policies would increase those large margins and that the incumbent Republican senator in Missouri might be vulnerable. "Boss" Prendergast decided to go after that seat. For various reasons, his first several picks to run against the Republican declined. Harry Truman was tabbed as Prendergast's man almost by default. He had to compete in a primary against two other Democratic contenders, but he succeeded in cementing his identity as a strong New Deal supporter and won the nomination handily, with overwhelming support from Jackson County. The general election against the sitting GOP Senator Roscoe Patterson wasn't close. It was a bad year for the GOP. Truman won with just under 60% of the vote.

At long last, Harry Truman went to Washington. He knew full well that his election was based on some very good luck and good timing and that getting re-elected in 1940 would not be easy. Still, though feeling like "a country boy arriving on the campus of a great university," he applied himself with his usual diligence and hoped for the best. He didn't receive much attention from the president, who hardly needed to worry about the aspirations of a junior senator whose vote he could count on in any event, but he did his job honorably.[8] Though he failed to pass any legislation, he was dutiful to the party and, with continued good fortune, might have won re-election handily.

By 1940, however, the stars no longer aligned in Harry Truman's favor. First, Tom Prendergast had been convicted of tax evasion. The Prendergast machine was finished. Also, Franklin Roosevelt had made some political mistakes after being overwhelmingly re-elected in 1936. One biographer entitles a chapter "Hubris" to describe FDR's second-term overreaching.[9] He tried to "pack" the Supreme Court with New Deal sympathizers and campaigned against members of his own party whom he deemed insufficiently supportive. In 1940, he was running for an unprecedented third term against a charismatic and persuasive Republican, Wendell Willkie. The possibility of the United States becoming involved in World War II strengthened Republican isolationists; Roosevelt was clearly in for a tough fight. Even if Roosevelt won, it wasn't clear that his coattails would help re-elect Truman. However, Truman's luck held. Democrats mocked corporate lawyer Willkie, who tried to capitalize on his modest "Hoosier" roots, as the "barefoot boy from Wall Street." Furthermore, Willkie actually supported FDR's international perspective. That stance helped Roosevelt win handily, by about five million votes. Though his margin was much less than his eleven million vote edge in 1936, it was a large enough victory to help re-elect Harry Truman to the Senate, with a narrow 51% of the vote, much less than in his 1934 election.

Franklin Roosevelt's New Deal politics not only set the stage for Harry Truman's elections to the US Senate in 1934 and 1940, they also greatly altered African American political loyalties. That sea change is suggested in the title of historian Nancy Weiss's book, *Farewell to the Party of Lincoln.*[10] As we have seen, African American leaders had become disillusioned with the Republican Party by late in Theodore Roosevelt's presidency, and even more so by the politics and policies of William Howard Taft. Still, the black voices supporting Woodrow Wilson in 1912 were in the minority. Those voices soon felt betrayed by Wilson's racism and his cabinet officers' segregation of several departments of the federal government. They generally welcomed the return of the Republicans following Warren Harding's election in 1920. When Harding and then Calvin Coolidge turned out to be not much better than the Democrats, blacks once again seemed to be lost in a political wilderness. Still searching for a potential president who might support them, many African Americans thought they might have found one in New York Governor Al Smith, the 1928 Democratic candidate for president against Herbert Hoover. Smith opposed many of the factions in the party, including Southerners, which blacks also opposed. Though Smith, like Wilson, quietly encouraged black support, he never spoke out for the concerns of and justice for African Americans. In the end, it did not really make any difference. Partly due to his Roman Catholicism, Smith was overwhelmed by Herbert Hoover in the 1928 election. The Ku Klux Klan also played a role in Smith's defeat. In the early 1920s, the Klan had emerged as a reinvigorated force in Democratic politics, strongly backing Woodrow Wilson's son-in-law and Treasury Secretary William McAdoo. The Klan and many Southerners were nearly as prejudiced against Catholics and Jews as against blacks, as shown in slogans using alliterative KKK phrases, such as "Kill Koons, Kikes and Katholics." Not surprisingly, Al Smith lost five former Confederate states that had not, with one exception, voted for Republicans since Reconstruction.

By 1932, continued disaffection with Republicans, who were led once again by Herbert Hoover, led many blacks away from the GOP. However, they moved away more slowly than other groups that year.[11] While Hoover and Republicans were disappointments during the early years of the Depression, the 1932 Democratic Party ticket of Franklin Roosevelt and John Nance Garner of Texas offered little inspiration to African Americans. Roosevelt was a wealthy patrician from New York, with additional connections to Georgia from his time spent in Warm Springs, where during the 1920s he worked to recover from polio. He showed little interest in African Americans. Garner was the prototypical Southern Democratic politician who cared little about the status of blacks, other than keeping them in their place. Roosevelt and Garner won easily in 1932 and then again overwhelmingly in 1936, winning every state except Maine and Vermont. That election showed a huge swing of black voters to the Democrats, despite FDR's apparent indifference to their aspirations. Roosevelt's New Deal policies, often opposed, incidentally by Vice President Garner, were of tremendous help to African Americans, who had been disproportionately hurt by the Great Depression. FDR and Garner won 71% of the black presidential vote in 1936. Never again would Republicans win the black vote.

When FDR ran for a third term in 1940—winning and also helping re-elect Harry—the political calculus for African Americans was somewhat complicated. The good news was that John Garner had been replaced as vice president. The new VP was a former Republican and former secretary of agriculture, Henry Wallace. Wallace was an emphatic liberal whose family had taken black agronomist George Washington Carver into their home in Iowa when Henry was a boy. He was completely free of race prejudice and might be counted on to support African American interests. The bad news was that Roosevelt's shrinking popular support, especially among isolationists, made him even more dependent on Southern Democrats. Roosevelt would not disturb that constituency unless forced.

These concerns would not have been pressing on Harry Truman as he looked toward his second term in the US Senate. One matter that did demand his attention was mobilization for possible war or for at least supporting Great

Britain and the Allies in the event of war. After several tense but peaceably resolved conflicts with Nazi Germany in 1938, armed conflict finally broke out in September of 1939 when Hitler invaded Poland. By 1940, France had surrendered and Great Britain, fighting alone, was buckling under German attacks. British Prime Minister Winston Churchill reached out to Franklin Roosevelt for any kind of aid. Roosevelt finally resolved to make the United States the "Arsenal of Democracy" and help England as much as he could within the constraints of laws pledging American neutrality. One thing Roosevelt did, with the support of Southern senators, was to begin building American ships, planes, and other war materiel. As always in wartime, the possibility of corruption and profiteering by companies manufacturing arms was a significant concern. It was one that brought Harry Truman onto the national stage.

Harry Truman, as farmer, businessman, and county judge, had always been concerned about making sure that quality goods were sold at fair prices. This interest led him to be named chair of a Military Affairs Senate Subcommittee charged with investigating corrupt practice by wartime manufacturers. Although Franklin Roosevelt worried that such investigations would constrain or even derail war readiness, he acceded to the work of the subcommittee. Starting in early 1941, Harry Truman and other committee members visited defense plants around the country, held countless hearings, and issued numerous reports. They investigated shoddy housing for war workers in New Jersey and wasteful defense spending everywhere. When the Japanese attacked Pearl Harbor on December 7, 1941—"a date which will live in infamy"—the United States was propelled into World War II. Then Truman's work took on added importance.

Thanks to what became known as the "Truman Committee," a War Production Board was established. Throughout most of the conflict, the war-related work of business, unions, and government was scrutinized meticulously. The committee's activities drew on many of Harry Truman's most deeply-rooted personal qualities. He was scrupulous, fair, honest, and diligent. Though not charismatic, he was well-liked and respected by nearly all of his colleagues. In March of 1943, a drawing of Truman was on the cover of *Time* magazine. Inside was a story called "Billion Dollar Watchdog," which characterized the Truman Committee as "watchdog, spotlight, conscience and sparkplug to the economic war-behind-the scenes."[12] In the spirit of William Jennings Bryan, Truman saw himself as protecting the little man against large, impersonal organizations. He was seen by the public as the ultimate patriot, protecting both the nation as a whole and its ordinary citizens. Harry Truman was no longer the obscure "Senator from Prendergast," but a man of substance. He was named as one of the ten most important American figures in the war effort.

The early work of the Truman Committee coincided with another development in preparing for war that profoundly affected the welfare of African Americans in both the short run and the long run. Thanks to New Deal labor laws and the demand for workers in war-related industries, the Brotherhood of Sleeping Car Porters (BSCP) and its black president, A. Philip Randolph,

Figure 7.2 A. Philip Randolph successfully pressed Presidents Franklin D. Roosevelt and Harry S. Truman to take steps for racial justice.

John Bottega, NYWTS staff photographer, "U.S. civil rights leader A. Philip Randolph," 1963, Library of Congress, Washington, DC. Public domain, via Wikimedia Commons.

had gained considerable influence in American politics and the national econ-omy. Randolph was dissatisfied with the unequal treatment of blacks in the labor force and sought ways to pressure President Roosevelt to correct those injus-tices. FDR felt that action on behalf of blacks would distract from the needed focus on military preparation and his "arsenal of democracy" policies. It would be even more disruptive than the Truman Committee since it would antagonize Southerners who had thus far supported the president's efforts. Roosevelt at first attempted to dodge Randolph's demands. However, Randolph had an ally in the president's wife, Eleanor Roosevelt, who had long been more vigorous than her husband on questions of equal rights. She became a helpful liaison between Randolph and FDR. During several meetings with either the president or First

Lady, Randolph explained that over 100,000 African Americans would march on Washington, DC, if nothing were done to address racial injustices. It became clear to both Roosevelts that Randolph would move ahead if nothing were done. Only days before the scheduled march, the president yielded to Randolph's pressure and issued an executive order affirming that the policy of the United States was "that there shall be no discrimination in the employment of workers in the defense industries or government because of race, creed, color or national origin." Furthermore, a Committee on Fair Employment Practice was established.[13] In some ways, Randolph's achievement was limited. The executive order did not apply to hiring outside of the defense industry. Furthermore, it fell short of African American leaders' demand that the American military itself be desegregated. However, it marked the first substantial action taken by an American president in the interests of civil rights since the Grant administration of the previous century. Harry Truman would have been aware of these developments in 1941 but would have had no way of knowing that in the years ahead they would continue to shape him, and the nation.

The transformation of Harry Truman from taken-for-granted political commoner to major national figure began in 1941 and crystallized in 1944, the year he turned sixty. As Franklin Roosevelt contemplated running for a fourth term, so that he could see the world war through to its conclusion, party elders grew increasingly concerned about the president's health. Whoever was vice president might have to step into the president's big shoes at a moment's notice. Vice President Wallace had a mystical streak that worried many, and he was far too liberal for large segments of the Democratic Party. Conservatives wanted to dump Wallace and replace him with James Byrnes, a South Carolinian who had served in the US Senate and on the United States Supreme Court. However, Byrnes, though close to FDR, would offend many liberal Northern Democrats, especially those concerned about racial issues. Roosevelt kept party members guessing, dropping a number of names. He finally settled on Harry Truman as Wallace's replacement. Truman was considered a moderate. He would be open, fair, and competent. At the Democratic convention in Chicago, Truman hesitated when he heard that Roosevelt had picked him. But his resistance was overcome when FDR shouted over the telephone to an aide in a convention hotel room, loud enough so that he knew Truman would hear, "Well, you tell the Senator if he wants to break up the Democratic Party in the middle of the war, that's his responsibility."[14] Truman would have been happy to remain in the Senate, but the pressure was irresistible. Some said that his selection constituted "the second Missouri Compromise." After some tense moments, the convention endorsed FDR's choice. The Democratic ticket in 1944 would be Franklin D. Roosevelt and Harry S. Truman. Their Republican opponents would be New York Governor Thomas E. Dewey, a moderate-to-liberal presidential candidate, with conservative Governor John Bricker of Ohio as his running mate.

During the campaign, Truman and Roosevelt only met once. Truman was shocked at how ill the president appeared. He campaigned extensively and became vice president-elect in November when FDR won election to a fourth term. Roosevelt's health had become an issue, though he too campaigned vigorously. Health and increasing national weariness with the New Deal and government regulation reduced FDR's margin of victory. Still, he won by 3.5 million votes. The final outcome was not close.

On January 20, 1945, Harry Truman was sworn in as vice president of the United States. He would serve for eighty-two days. During that period of time, he met with the president alone only twice and was kept in the dark about major developments in US end-of-war planning. Remarkably, he was not informed about the ongoing "Manhattan Project," the effort by American scientists to build an atomic bomb before the Germans did. On the afternoon of April 12, Truman's life, and the life of the country, changed suddenly. Late that day, Truman was in the Capitol building attending to the business of being president of the Senate. He had started to settle down, probably for a drink, with old friends from Congress when he got a message to call the White House right away. He was told to come over to the Executive Mansion as rapidly and quietly as possible. He tried to imagine small matters that might demand his attention, but he likely anticipated the worst, however difficult that would be. When he reached the White House, Truman was escorted to the second floor living quarters. He met the First Lady, who told him simply, "Harry, the President is dead." Truman asked Eleanor Roosevelt whether there was anything he could do for her. She replied, "Is there anything *we* can do for *you, Harry*? For you are the one in trouble now."[15]

Truman could only partly imagine how true that was. The next day he told the press, "Boys, if you ever pray, pray for me now. I don't know whether you ever had a load of hay fall on you, but when you told me yesterday what had happened, I felt like the moon, the stars and all the planets had fallen on me."[16] What manner of president was Harry Truman likely to become? And what might be expected of him in regard to African Americans and civil rights? His overall leadership challenge was daunting. He was succeeding one of the most powerful and beloved presidents in history who had served the nation for twelve years, with the nation mourning his death. The United States was involved in one of the deadliest wars of its history in both Europe and the Pacific. While a successful end to the war seemed likely, there was no guarantee. Also, the postwar world would present enormous challenges, both economically and diplomatically. And Harry Truman had none of Franklin Roosevelt's charisma. Yet he was intelligent, diligent, even-handed, direct, and willing to fight hard for what he believed. The aristocrat would be replaced by a plain-speaking common man. Truman's energy was a surprise to many. Secret Service agents at the White House had in large measure been able to loaf for twelve years. President Roosevelt was bound to a wheelchair and obviously did not go for bracing walks. Harry Truman took rapid early morning strolls, without the Secret Service if he could escape their notice. The White House would be a different kind of place. President Truman would be active and outspoken to the point of being combative for an agenda very much like Franklin Roosevelt's.

Truman's dispositions on race issues were harder to forecast. He may have shared a kind of casual racism with other Missourians, but there were clear limits. As noted earlier, the Ku Klux Klan was a political force in 1922 when Truman first ran for election as county judge. And in 1924 it might have helped him win re-election, even with the national Republican sweep. Truman attended one meeting of the Klan to see for himself what it might do for him and to him. When members asked him to pledge never to appoint Catholics to county offices, he knew he could never be part of it. He had commanded Catholics and Jews in combat. He would not desert them for political gain. This moment may have been one that crystallized in Truman's own mind the conviction that he would deal with individual people fairly and not discriminate on the basis of race or religion. Later, in the Senate, he had supported anti-lynching laws and opposed poll taxes. On the other hand, some of his initial presidential appointments disappointed black leaders. James Byrnes was appointed secretary of state. By virtue of there being no vice president once Truman assumed the presidency, Byrnes was next in line for the White House. One black newspaper derided Byrnes as a "Dixie Race-Baiter."[17] Truman also appointed a Texan, Thomas Clark, as his attorney general. However cheered Southern segregationists were by these appointments, Truman soon came out swinging, as no president had since Grant, for equality and civil rights. Somewhere in Harry Truman's development, basic moral principles recognizing the equality of human beings and the rightness of fair treatment became not only clear but central to his political philosophy.

It did not take long for this side of Harry Truman to be revealed, much to the dismay of his Southern friends in the Democratic Party. The war in Europe came to a successful conclusion within one month of Truman taking office. The surrender of Nazi Germany was a pleasant birthday present for the president on May 8, 1945. By July of 1945, Truman knew that the United States had developed atomic weapons that would almost surely win the war in the Pacific. While he was undoubtedly preoccupied with these momentous developments, he initiated strong action for civil rights. In a message to Congress in June, Truman asked for the restoration of funding for what was now called the Fair Employment Practices Committee (FEPC). In his message to Congress, Truman said that discrimination in employment against "properly qualified people because of their race, creed or color is . . . un-American in nature" and "has a tendency to create substandard conditions of living for a large part of our population." Southern Democrats blocked that change, but in September Truman kept up the pressure. He pushed for the FEPC to be made permanent. This time the full power of the Southern Democratic filibuster was revealed. Truman's new proposal was blocked.

For the time being, Truman accomplished what he could on his own. He appointed an African American judge to the Customs Court, the highest appointment ever of a black citizen by a US president. He also appointed a white Republican known to be sympathetic to civil rights and equal justice to the Supreme Court. None of this helped Truman's political prospects. The post-war world presented the United States with nearly overwhelming challenges, both domestically and internationally. Inflation and labor unrest threatened to paralyze a return to prosperity, and Communist expansionism in Eastern Europe had the potential to start another costly war. Many of Truman's fellow Democrats deserted him. Arkansas Senator William Fulbright, known in later years for his enlightened views on many issues, toed the Southern line on race issues. He suggested that Truman appoint a Republican secretary of state and then resign the presidency so that the new appointee could become president.

Fulbright and his Southern colleagues had no idea how persistent and resil-ient Harry Truman would be on matters of civil rights and equal justice, no matter the political price. His resolve was strengthened by what he saw as a shameful and dangerous postwar climate for returning African American sol-diers. In February of 1946, just five months after the end of the war, black vet-eran Isaac Woodard was beaten by police in South Carolina. Although details of the incident are not entirely clear, we know that Woodard was discharged from the service in Augusta, Georgia, and boarded a bus for his home in North Caro-lina. In a small town in South Carolina, the bus driver reported that Woodard had been disruptive. He was pulled off the bus by the local sheriff and severely beaten. He was taken to a hospital, where it took several weeks for his family to locate him and take him home. Woodard was blinded by the beating for the rest of his life. It took some months for the news of the attack on Woodard to reach Truman. When it did, Truman launched an investigation; his administra-tion brought charges against the sheriff. The case came to trial in South Carolina but was ineptly handled by the local US Attorney. The defense lawyer cautioned the jury that if the sheriff were found guilty "then let this South Carolina secede again."[18] He was acquitted in thirty minutes. Though the outcome was a set-back for Truman, he never wavered in his commitment to take what action he could for racial justice. Other equal rights violations in the South only deepened his determination.

During the months that the Woodard case unfolded, Truman's political stock sank badly. While he was given high marks for the way he stepped into office after FDR's death, by the summer of 1946 his approval ratings had dropped into the mid-thirties. The public seemed to feel that the range of problems facing the country was overwhelming the president. In the 1946 midterm congressional elections, the Republican Party routed the Democrats and took control of both houses of Congress for the first time since the Hoover administration. Despite being in a very tight spot, and despite the fact that a greater proportion of the remaining Democrats in Congress were now Southern, Truman kept pushing for African Americans and justice. Within a month of the election, he issued an Executive Order establishing a presidential committee on civil rights. His charge to the committee employed vintage direct, hard-hitting Truman rhetoric. He told them: "I want our Bill of Rights implemented in fact. We have been trying to do this for 150 years. We are making progress, but we are not making progress fast enough."[19] In fact, the energy Truman put into this issue was remarkable. Little good had come out of his efforts thus far, either for him or for black Americans. Still, Truman gave the whole problem one of the most sustained pushes in American history. In the face of setbacks, his efforts would endure.

Fortunately, in 1947 there were other encouraging developments in American race relations. When the major league baseball season opened in April, the Brooklyn Dodgers lineup included the first African American player since before the Jim Crow era, Jackie Robinson. A few months later, Larry Doby pinch-hit in a game for the Cleveland Indians, becoming the first black player in the American League. (Doby would always refer to Jackie Robinson as Mr. Robinson. Both became all-stars.) In October of 1947, Harry Truman continued his own efforts. He became the first president to speak to the NAACP. His speech emphasized not only the immorality of segregation, it also explained the negative economic impact of discrimination in employment and education and the international loss of respect that America garnered for its racist ways. For the 1940s, this was tough talk.

Truman's push continued into 1948, a presidential election year. A number of events came together that year to bring momentous changes for all Americans, including African Americans. The first was one of the most harrowing episodes of the Cold War. Conflict between the Soviet Union and the United States had broken out almost immediately after the end of World War II. West Berlin was a flash point. The western portion of the German capital was still occupied by French, British, and American forces. It had become a source of tension with the Russians, as it was a free outpost entirely surrounded by Communist-controlled East Germany. In May of 1948, Russians attempted to wrest control of West Berlin from the Allies by blocking access to the isolated city by road and rail. Truman immediately organized the famous "Berlin Airlift" to bring vital supplies to beleaguered West Berliners. The airlift was an eventual success, but it underscored the fact that dangerous conflict with the Soviet Union would be ongoing.

One of Truman's responses to the Soviet action was to institute a peace-time draft in July. Here A. Philip Randolph once again loomed large. Because of the way black soldiers had been treated in World War II, and even more pointedly because of the way they had been treated after the war, Randolph urged African Americans to resist the draft. Truman felt the overpowering wrath of Randolph in 1948 just as Franklin Roosevelt did in 1941. Pressure from the civil rights leader along with Truman's own growing concern for justice led to another far-reaching executive order, number 9981, abolishing segregation in the armed services.[20] Although full implementation was long in coming, the executive order changed the American military, and with it American society, profoundly and unalterably.

In addition to issuing the executive order desegregating the armed forces, Harry Truman pressed for civil rights legislation throughout 1948. He mentioned the issue in his January State of the Union address and promised he would

Figure 7.3 The Chicago Defender celebrated President Truman's desegregation of the military and noted yet another lynching.

Front page, *The Chicago Defender,* January 31, 1948.

follow up on the report of his committee on civil rights, aptly titled "To Secure These Rights," that had been issued the previous October.[21] He submitted specific legislative proposals in February. As the Democratic Convention of 1948 approached, the combination of Truman's press on civil rights and his resistance to Soviet aggression, along with all the economic growing pains of the postwar years, threatened to tear the Party apart. Henry Wallace, FDR's extremely liberal third-term vice president, announced he would run for president against Truman on the Progressive Party ticket. When Truman backed a strong civil rights platform at the Democratic National Convention in July, saying he believed it was his duty under the Constitution, Southern delegates had had enough. In a matter of days, they held their own convention in Birmingham, Alabama, and nominated racist South Carolina Governor Strom Thurmond for president on something called the States' Rights Democratic Party ticket, known less formally as the Dixiecrat ticket. Thus Truman faced not only the Republicans, who renominated New York Governor Thomas E. Dewey, who had lost to FDR in 1944, but splinter tickets from the Democratic Party on both left and right.

Consonant with his civil rights initiatives, in the middle of 1948, Harry Truman made another momentous decision. Despite strong opposition from his highly respected Secretary of State George Marshall, Truman decided to recognize the new state of Israel. While doing so may have helped him with Jewish voters, Truman's humanitarian instincts, as well as his decades-long friendship with Eddie Jacobson, were major factors. Truman's identity as an egalitarian who would rise above and oppose persistent prejudices was in full flower.

Going into the fall election, almost all political observers, and all polls, predicted that Harry Truman would be soundly defeated. Truman never accepted that view. In one of the most memorable political campaigns in US history, Truman traveled by train around the country, giving both long and short speeches at whistle stops and large cities, generally blasting the "do-nothing 80th Republican Congress." In truth, while the eightieth Congress had done little to advance Truman's agenda, it was Southern Democrats who blocked strong Republican efforts on civil rights. This did not stop Harry Truman from ripping into the GOP, so much so that one man listening at a whistle stop shouted, "Give 'em hell, Harry," giving the president a new nickname he was proud to carry. Truman's commitment to racial equality and nondiscrimination was underscored when he gave a speech in Harlem toward the end of the campaign. Literally and figuratively, Harry Truman showed up for African Americans.

In the end, thanks to Truman's vigorous campaign, overconfidence on the part of Republicans, and the country's overall satisfaction with New Deal policies, Truman and the Democrats won decisively in the November election. Truman won the popular contest by over 2 million votes and the Electoral College by more than 100 votes. He narrowly missed winning an absolute majority of the popular vote as Thurmond, Wallace, and other candidates polled over 2.5 million votes. Black votes put Truman over the top in close states such as California, Ohio, and Illinois. On the other hand, Truman lost four Southern states to Thurmond that he might have won easily had he not pushed so hard for civil rights. Also, Henry Wallace's large vote in New York probably cost Truman that state and its forty-seven electoral votes, the biggest prize of all.

As Truman entered his own full term in January of 1949, Southern Democrats still held enough seats in Congress to defeat any legislation in favor of racial equality. It was not even possible to pass anti-lynching laws. Truman did the best he could with executive orders. For example, he caused the Civil Aeronautics Administration to desegregate dining facilities at Washington National Airport. Still, further progress for black Americans would have to wait for another day.

Harry Truman's hard-won full term was marked by immense challenges. Communists took over in China in 1949. The Korean War broke out in 1950. American fears and even paranoia about Communism scuttled any legislative progress for almost all of Truman's agenda. His approval ratings going down steadily, to a record low of 22% in early 1952, Truman decided not to run for re-election. That year the Republicans easily won the presidency with World War II hero General Dwight D. Eisenhower as president and California Senator Richard M. Nixon as vice president. Harry Truman and Bess retired to Independence and largely avoided the political spotlight until his death nearly twenty years later. Further progress on civil rights in the 1950s would await the surprising leadership of Democratic Senator Lyndon B. Johnson from Texas.

Whether sung or unsung, Harry Truman is a true hero in the story of presidential leadership and African Americans. Despite being raised in a Southern-leaning town in the Jim Crow era and having at least an early flirtation with the Ku Klux Klan, somewhere deep in his character was a strong sense of right and wrong, justice and injustice, and basic fairness. He brought that sense to American race relations. Psychologically, Harry Truman is one of the lowest presidents on the so-called Big Five trait of "openness."[22] He can also be characterized as low in cognitive complexity. Fortunately, he was ready to act when right and wrong were clear to him. The combination of a somewhat dogmatic morality and an inclination to lead and to fight for what he believed was right led him to act decisively for desegregation and against racism. In his Second Inagural, Lincoln asked the nation to go forward "with firmness in the right as God gives us to see the right."[23] No president did so with more conviction and firmness in the right regarding African Americans than Harry S. Truman.

Notes

1 See http://legacy.c-span.org/PresidentialSurvey/Pursued-Equal-Justice-For-All.aspx.
2 Bruce Bartlett, *Wrong on Race: The Democratic Party's Buried Past* (New York: Palgrave Macmillan, 2008), p.131; Lyndon B. Johnson, Voting Rights Speech, March 15, 1965. http://www.greatamericandocuments.com/speeches/lbj-voting-rights.html.
3 David McCullough, *Truman* (New York: Simon & Schuster, 1992), p. 41.
4 See http://www.whitehousehistory.org/history/white-house-first-ladies/first-lady-elizabeth-truman.html.
5 See http://millercenter.org/president/truman/essays/biography/2.
6 McCullough, p. 118.
7 *Ibid.*, p. 123.
8 Robert Dallek, *Harry S. Truman* (New York: Times Books, 2008), p. 10.
9 Jean Edward Smith, *FDR* (New York), ch. 17.
10 Nancy J. Weiss, *Farewell to the Party of Lincoln: Black Politics in the Age of FDR* (Princeton, NJ: Princeton University Press, 1983).
11 *Ibid.*, p. 32.
12 See http://content.time.com/time/magazine/article/0,9171,774390,00.html.
13 H.W. Brands, *Traitor to His Class: The Privileged Life and Radical Presidency of Franklin Delano Roosevelt* (New York: Random House, 2008) p. 712.
14 McCullough, p. 314.
15 Dallek, p. 17.
16 McCullough, p. 353.
17 Bartlett, p. 136.
18 See http://recollectionbooks.com/siml/library/blindingIsaac.htm.
19 Bartlett, p. 139.
20 See http://www.trumanlibrary.org/9981.htm.
21 See http://www.trumanlibrary.org/civilrights/srights1.htm.

22 Steven J. Rubenzer and Thomas R. Faschingbauer, *Personality, Character, & Leadership in the White House: Psychologists Assess the Presidents* (Washington, DC: Brassey's, Inc., 2004), p. 26.

23 Abraham Lincoln, Second Inaugural Address, March 4, 1865. In Don E. Fehren-bacher (ed.), *Lincoln: Speeches and Writings 1859–1865* (New York: Library of America, 1989), pp. 686–87.

8

LYNDON B. JOHNSON

Figure 8.1 Martin Luther King, Jr. and Lyndon B. Johnson were wary allies in pushing for civil rights and voting rights legislation.

Yoichi Okamoto, "President Lyndon B. Johnson meeting with civil rights activist Martin Luther King, Jr.," January 18, 1964, black and white photograph. Courtesy of the LBJ Library, Austin, Texas. Public domain, via Wikimedia Commons.

The year 1963 was pivotal in African Americans' struggle for freedom and equal rights. At first, much of the focus was on Birmingham, Alabama, often regarded as the most brutally segregated city in the United States. Black leaders Fred Shuttlesworth of the Alabama Christian Movement for Human Rights (ACMHR) and Martin Luther King, Jr. of the Southern Christian Leadership Conference (SCLC) organized a series of nonviolent protests aimed at downtown business interests. Their activities included boycotts of segregated stores, protest marches, and sit-ins. Their most notorious opponent was Commissioner of Public Safety

Eugene "Bull" Connor. Connor had been active in suppressing blacks in the city for years, including canceling a parade in 1951 honoring twenty-year-old baseball star and Birmingham native Willie Mays. But Shuttlesworth, King, and others were savvy enough to know how to use Connor's belligerence for their own interests. Predictably, Connor filled the city jails with protesters. In April, one of those jailed was King, who wrote his memorable essay "Letter from a Birmingham Jail" while incarcerated. In the letter, King explained the necessity of nonviolent direct action, the difference between just and unjust laws, and the importance of white people aiding rather than resisting the moral imperative of equality.[1] Later, as events in Birmingham lurched toward complete chaos and mass violence, Connor turned fire hoses and snarling German shepherds against black children.

Finally, the federal government stepped in to help restore order. President John F. Kennedy had resisted the politically perilous path of introducing civil rights legislation, but he understood that his hand was being forced. Vice President Lyndon B. Johnson urged Kennedy to confront directly the fundamental American principles involved, including the "self-evident" truth that "all men are created equal." In June, Kennedy spoke out. Addressing the nation about events in Birmingham, the president stated that Americans were "confronted primarily with a moral issue, as old as the Scriptures and as clear as the American Constitution."[2] He asked Congress to pass a civil rights bill.

African American leaders kept the pressure on that spring and summer, culminating in the massive March on Washington in August, where Martin Luther King gave his famous "I Have a Dream" speech. Segregationists in Congress fought back. By late in the fall, they had bottled up the president's legislation in the House of Representatives Rules Committee. Then, on November 22, 1963, John F. Kennedy was assassinated in Dallas. If a civil rights act was to become law, it would be up to the leadership of the new president, Lyndon B. Johnson of Texas.

The world into which Lyndon Johnson was born over a century ago, in 1908, is difficult to imagine. Time had barely touched the Texas hill country since the Lone Star State was admitted to the Union in 1845. In many areas, there were no paved roads and no electricity. Outhouses were more plentiful than indoor plumbing, and meals were prepared over hot wood cookstoves. What is now an hour's drive east to Austin, the state capital, was then a journey that took over a day by horse. Lyndon's father, Samuel Johnson, was a popular political figure and ambitious rancher and businessman whose fortunes rose and fell during Lyndon's childhood. His mother, Rebekah Baines Johnson, attended Baylor University and was one of the few female college graduates in the region. The Johnsons were married in 1907, when Sam was a representative in the Texas state legislature. He was a populist Democrat of the William Jennings Bryan persuasion, rather than the pro-business Grover Cleveland wing of the Party. Sam and Rebekah's first child arrived a year after their wedding and was named

Lyndon Baines Johnson. The future president was the oldest of five, having three younger sisters and a brother.

Because of financial setbacks, Sam Johnson gave up his seat in the Texas legislature and returned to ranching the year after Lyndon was born. He and Rebekah had different aspirations for their young son. Rebekah thought of herself as superior to the average local resident and had high ambitions for Lyndon. She wanted him to be a well-educated, cultured young man and pushed him toward music and dance. Sam thought she was making the boy too feminine, and Lyndon apparently agreed. He refused dancing lessons and endured the silent treatment from his mother for more than a week. Lyndon was entranced by his father's expansive personality and was thrilled when Sam was again elected to the state legislature in 1918. The ten-year-old Lyndon began accompanying Sam Johnson to Austin and found himself mesmerized by legislative activity both on the floor and behind the scenes. During the next five years, he received an extensive tutorial in political wheeling and dealing. He was impressed with his father's tolerance and integrity, particularly his staunch opposition to the reviving Ku Klux Klan in the South.

Lyndon attended high school in Johnson City and graduated in 1924. Despite his mother's wish that he go to college, Lyndon set out for California with several friends. The glitter of Hollywood was compelling. Maybe he'd somehow strike it rich during the Roaring Twenties on the Pacific coast. Youthful dreams were deflated within two years, however, and a sobered Lyndon Johnson returned home to Texas. He worked on a construction crew for a time but then came to the viewpoint that perhaps his mother was right and that going to college made sense.

That fall, 1926, Johnson enrolled in Southwest Texas State Teachers College in San Marcos. Even though tuition was only seventeen dollars a semester, attending was a financial burden. Johnson took several part-time jobs to pay the bills, but he was also extremely active in college life. He joined the debate team and edited the school newspaper. One of his campus jobs was delivering messages for the school's president. Johnson was tireless and ingratiated himself both with the president and influential faculty members, especially Professor Harry Greene in the political science department. The college president became so dependent on Johnson's assistance that he took Lyndon with him on trips to Austin to lobby for state funding. Greene's influence led Lyndon to use his status as newspaper editor to get press credentials that admitted him to the floor of the 1928 Democratic National Convention in Houston. Just as Harry Truman was captivated by seeing William Jennings Bryan nominated in Kansas City in 1900, Lyndon Johnson had an early taste of political stardom when he watched Franklin D. Roosevelt of New York nominate his state governor, Al Smith, for president. Johnson would also have noted the extreme Jim Crow segregation practiced by Southern Democrats at the convention in Houston. Blacks were separated from whites at the convention by chicken wire.[3] Smith was nominated but fared no better in 1928 than Bryan had in 1900. He lost badly to Herbert Hoover in the general election.

While Johnson would have preferred to complete his senior year at San Marcos, he simply couldn't afford it. He would have to find a way to earn money. That way turned out to be a teaching job in the dusty south Texas town of Cotulla. Like many such small Southern towns, it was highly segregated, not between white and black, but between white and Mexican. Johnson was assigned to teach at a Mexican school. His charges were twenty-eight students in the fifth through eighth grades. They came from extremely impoverished homes, most lacking running water. Typical teachers spent as little time with their pupils as possible. Johnson said that whites treated the Mexicans "just worse than you'd treat a dog."[4] However, something about these young children touched Lyndon Johnson. Perhaps his own family's poverty, possibly the way they were discriminated against. For whatever reasons, Johnson threw himself into helping his students with characteristic energy. Working harder than anyone else, and using his own meager paycheck to buy equipment for the school, Johnson made a legendary impact on those he taught and those with whom he worked. Years later they would talk about the future president as if he were a gift from above. And years later it would become plain that Cotulla affected Lyndon Johnson as deeply as he affected it.

Unfortunately for the Mexicans of Cotulla, Johnson was able to return to college after one year as a teacher. After two summers and one academic year of intense study at San Marcos, Lyndon Johnson earned his college degree in 1930, at about the time of his twenty-second birthday. He soon got a teaching job and, although he needed the work and teaching was a respectable and satisfying calling, politics was still a powerful magnet. That fall he worked tirelessly for Welly Hopkins, a candidate for the Texas state senate. After Hopkins won, Johnson went on to teach public speaking and debate at a Houston high school. Then in 1931, Lyndon Johnson's life changed. The US congressman from his district died and was succeeded by a wealthy candidate named Richard Kleberg. Welly Hopkins, among others, recommended Johnson as Kleberg's legislative secretary. Kleberg was impressed and offered Lyndon the position. It did not take long for him to accept.

Johnson and Kleberg arrived in Washington, DC, in December of 1931 after traveling in luxury on a Pullman car. Johnson had never experienced such opulence. He liked what he saw. He soon took up residence in a city hotel occupied by many other congressional aides. Herbert Hoover was president and America was mired in the second year of the Great Depression. There seemed little that progressive or populist Democrats could accomplish, but Lyndon used his time and prodigious energy to make contacts and build relationships. Among Texas congressmen, he befriended Sam Rayburn and other liberals. Rayburn was a bachelor, twenty-six years Johnson's elder, and the two struck up a father-son like connection. Johnson also became acquainted with a more conservative Texas congressman, John Nance Garner, who had just become speaker of the

House of Representatives. Although Johnson could be pushy, rude, and aggressive among peers or underlings, he was deferential to the point of obsequiousness with his elders. In addition to building links to other congressmen, Johnson became active in an organization of congressional aides called the "Little Congress." Johnson soon became its leader and greatly increased its membership. The club debated the political issues of the time and hosted prominent speakers. Among them was New York Congressman Fiorello La Guardia, nicknamed "The Little Flower." When LaGuardia was elected mayor of New York City in 1933, he invited Johnson and other Little Congress members to visit the Big Apple and attend a show at Radio City Music Hall.

Within a year of Johnson's arrival in the capital, the political situation changed drastically. The Hoover administration had lost its credibility and the nation's confidence. The situation wasn't helped when Hoover authorized Army Chief of Staff Douglas MacArthur to drive out the so-called Bonus Army from government property in Washington. That army was composed of World War I veterans who had been promised a bonus for combat service in Europe. They had only received half their pay when they encamped in the capital city starting in the spring of 1932. Some in the government feared Communist influence and believed the protesters were a threat to national morale, if not national security. With cavalry, infantry, and back-up tanks, MacArthur and his troops destroyed the shanties and tent cities where the impoverished veterans had been living.

Hoover's perceived callousness and ineptitude led to his losing the presidency in a landslide to Democrat Franklin D. Roosevelt in November of 1932. Lyndon Johnson knew FDR's running mate well. The new vice president would be John Nance Garner of Texas. Amidst the growing depression, FDR took office on March 4, 1933, promising that "This great Nation will endure as it has endured, will revive and will prosper." He famously reassured Americans that "the only thing we have to fear is fear itself—nameless, unreasoning, unjustified terror which paralyzes needed efforts to convert retreat into advance."[5] For Lyndon Johnson and other Democrats, the doors of opportunity opened for constructive action. The First Hundred Days of the New Deal had begun.

After the political excitement of the early months of the Roosevelt administration, Lyndon Johnson diverted some of his attention to distinctly nonpolitical matters. He frequently traveled back to Texas with Congressman Kleberg. On one of those trips he met Claudia Alta Taylor, the young daughter of another wealthy Texan, Thomas Jefferson Taylor. She was nicknamed Lady Bird and immediately attracted Lyndon Johnson. She in turn said she felt like "a moth drawn to a flame."[6] Lyndon proposed the day after they met and pursued her relentlessly. Lady Bird was both repelled and compelled by Lyndon's insistence. Upon the advice and consent of her father, she soon relented and married Johnson in November 1934, just over two months after they first met.

Back in Washington, Johnson showed his political skill in outmaneuvering Vice President Garner in exerting control of Texas political patronage. After Garner was defeated by a news leak orchestrated by Johnson, he complained bitterly about this young congressional secretary. The vice president asked, "Who in the hell is this boy Lyndon Johnson; where the hell did Kleberg get a boy with savvy like that?"[7] Perhaps Johnson was too nimble for his own good. Congressman Kleberg rather abruptly fired him in 1935. There were several possible reasons, but one was Lyndon's relentless scheming to gain more control within Kleberg's office and to take more credit for what that office accomplished for constituents. That Kleberg was more conservative than the New Deal policies that Lyndon worked to implement was another factor.

All of a sudden the restless, pushing, manipulating, and cajoling twenty-six-year-old was out of a job. Friends such as Sam Rayburn saw to it that that did not last long. Franklin Roosevelt had established the National Youth Administration (NYA) with the goal of helping young men and women in the grip of the Depression get training and find employment. The state of Texas needed an administrator. Rayburn and others pushed for Johnson in conversations with the president and also the First Lady, Eleanor Roosevelt. Though Johnson was very young for such a position, the Roosevelts had heard enough about him to be impressed with what he could accomplish. Lyndon got the appointment. He and Lady Bird happily moved to Austin to start Lyndon's new job.

For most of the next two years, LBJ worked for the NYA. As usual, he did so with unparalleled energy and effectiveness. The national head of the program thought Lyndon's Texas program was the best in the country. Thousands of young people got schooling, training, and work on such projects as state parks. Johnson's program provided uplift for blacks as well as whites. African Americans were given equal opportunity under Lyndon Johnson. Both the president and First Lady in Washington took note. Before long, Lyndon Johnson was back in that city. In 1937, the congressman for Lyndon's district in Texas died. Though Johnson was initially not on the prognosticators' lists of possibilities to fill the seat, he went after it. His campaign strategy was simple: Roosevelt, Roosevelt, and Roosevelt. The president had just been re-elected by the largest popular vote margin in history. He won every state except Maine and Vermont. Johnson knew that Texans liked FDR and his New Deal policies, so he told as many voters as he could in as many ways as he could that he did, too. He traveled day and night throughout the district and touched, literally, as many people as he possibly could. Though a relative unknown at the start of the special election campaign, he won easily. Lyndon Johnson was sworn in in May of 1937 as congressman for the tenth district in Texas. He was twenty-eight years old.

Not surprisingly, the new congressman from Texas was not the typical House of Representatives freshman. His years as Richard Kleberg's secretary and his leadership of the Little Congress had given him unequaled DC experience. His work with men and women in the Texas NYA had expanded his contacts. Most critically, he was the protégé of Sam Rayburn. Now Rayburn had been elected majority leader in the House and was one of the nation's most powerful political figures. He invited Johnson to attend "Board of Education" meetings in his office on late afternoons, where like-minded congressional leaders met to discuss policy and politics and perhaps share some good whiskey. The first-term senator from Missouri, Harry S. Truman, was a group regular. Johnson also found favor with the most powerful Democrat of all, President Franklin Roosevelt. Shortly after LBJ had won his congressional seat, the president had traveled to Texas and invited Lyndon to join him for a portion of his trip. Back in the capital, the president made it known to his staff that Johnson should be supported. One of the president's most powerful staffers, Tommy Corcoran, was designated to remove obstacles for Lyndon. The congressman in return worked in his usual exhaustive and exhausting way for FDR's programs. He oversaw the addition of roads and electric power to his district and helped arrange loans for needy constituents. Those efforts paid off for the president. Corcoran said that Johnson was one of the most effective congressmen he had ever seen.

Johnson's campaigning as a fervent FDR supporter and his efforts for the New Deal have to be understood in terms of questions about Johnson's character and beliefs that have challenged biographers for years. The most important puzzle is what Johnson really believed, especially about civil rights for African Americans, and liberal policies more generally. Johnson's ambition was towering, and everything else was subordinate to that. Robert Caro, in *The Path to Power,* the first of his masterful four volumes collectively entitled *The Years of Lyndon Johnson,* discusses the way LBJ's peers viewed him during his years in the Little Congress. Caro summarizes their assessment that Johnson's outsized ambition "was unencumbered by even the slightest excess weight of ideology, of philosophy, of principles, of beliefs." Caro seems generally to accept their characterization that whatever LBJ's beliefs, "they would have not the slightest influence on his actions."[8] Through most of his career, Johnson would blow with the wind, especially by telling those who could help him with their power or their money exactly what they wanted to hear. Biographers Robert Dallek (1991) and Randall Woods (2006) have more sympathetic views. Dallek argued that Johnson was a "visceral New Deal liberal with a practical talent for accommodating diverse interests,"[9] but in a chapter entitled "The Liberal as Conservative," Dallek acknowledges that during most of his congressional career, LBJ began pulling to the right on civil rights and other issues. Over most of the twenty years following his election to Congress, Lyndon Johnson's behavior did not auger favorably for the well-being of African Americans.

Johnson's record in Congress supports an affirmative answer to the eternal question of whether money is the root of all evil. As an outspoken supporter of New Deal policies, Johnson steered construction work to his district, much of which was done by the company known as Brown & Root (now a subsidiary of Halliburton). The brothers Herman and George Root, cofounders of the business, were generous supporters of Lyndon Johnson. They benefited from federally funded road and bridge projects in Texas, and their gratitude to Congressman Johnson was made tangible through substantial campaign gifts. Since the Brown brothers were deeply conservative, Lyndon Johnson had to be more selective in his support for New Deal and other liberal policies that might perturb the flow of money from the Browns. That arrangement worked well for both parties for many years, for as long as Lyndon Johnson was in Congress.

The next move in Johnson's political career came in 1941. One of Texas' two senators, Morris Sheppard, died in April of that year. Several influential liberals urged Johnson to run for the seat. With the financial backing of the Brown brothers, Johnson entered the race, promoting himself as a strong supporter of Franklin Roosevelt and national unity during the perilous months ahead that might mean America's entry into World War II. The president could not endorse one Democrat over another but did signal his admiration for the young congressman, stating that "I can only tell you what is perfectly true—you all know that he is a very old and close friend of mine."[10] FDR needed support from people like Johnson, as he barely won congressional authorization to expand the peace-time military draft. Roosevelt's backing almost did the trick for Johnson, but a recount of dubious validity gave the primary victory to Johnson's opponent. LBJ was never so casual about vote counting again.

Johnson returned to the House of Representatives. He was there on December 7, the infamous date of the Japanese attack on Pearl Harbor that plunged the United States into the ongoing war. Since Johnson had supported the draft, he felt an obligation to join the service himself. Taking a "leave of absence" from Congress, an arrangement by which he did not have to give up his seat, Johnson managed to enter the Navy Reserve as a lieutenant commander. Such a post would not ordinarily involve leaving the country or actual combat, but Lyndon insisted on traveling to the Pacific to see things for himself. He planned to visit General Douglas MacArthur in Australia. While the general was suspicious of Johnson's motives, LBJ won MacArthur over. Lyndon soon arranged to go on a fact-finding mission in a B-26 bomber. The plane unexpectedly came under attack from Japanese Zero fighter planes and absorbed extensive damage. It was fortunate that the American plane did not crash. Johnson was remarkably calm during the tensest moments. One crew member described him as "cool as a cucumber."[11]

Lyndon's war-time naval experience lasted only six months. The president called congressmen who had taken leave back to the capital. He needed their help managing the war and its associated politics. LBJ returned to DC in the middle of 1942 to participate in the midterm elections. He also had to attend to some personal matters. Lady Bird by then had a second miscarriage and become increasingly unhappy with the reality that Lyndon had had and was still having extramarital affairs, both serious and casual, with other women. To help ease the increasing tension between them, Lyndon managed to purchase an Austin radio station that Lady Bird could manage. Over many years, the station made the Johnsons wealthy. (When Lady Bird did finally have children, daughters Lynda Bird Johnson born in 1944 and Lucy Baines Johnson born in 1947, the family's finances were in good order.)

Despite efforts by Johnson and others, the Republicans made serious inroads into Democratic majorities in the 1942 midterm elections. Still, Lyndon Johnson remained loyal to President Roosevelt and was one of only a small minority of congressmen to vote to sustain FDR's veto of a 1943 tax cut bill favoring the wealthy. When the next presidential election took place in 1944, an end to the war seemed in sight, Democratic prospects were brighter, and Franklin Roosevelt was elected to an unprecedented fourth term as president. Sam Rayburn was now speaker of the House, and Johnson retained his seat in Congress. But national and Southern political dynamics would undergo dramatic changes in the next months and years, and Lyndon Johnson changed along with them. First, FDR died on April 12, 1945, and Harry Truman became the nation's thirty-third president. Then World War II ended with Allied victories in Europe in May and the Pacific in August. Much like the "return to normalcy" that Warren Harding offered after World War I, the country seemed to yearn for simpler, more traditional times after World War II. However, the country was beset by labor unrest, increasing fears of Communism, and the sense that Harry Truman, though he stepped in brilliantly after FDR's death, was hapless in addressing the nation's problems. These circumstances contributed to a political "perfect storm" for Democrats when the Republicans won both houses of Congress in the 1946 midterm elections.

Lyndon Johnson understood which way the political winds were blowing. Tacking with those winds to the right, LBJ voted for the anti-labor Taft-Hartley Act of 1947, which was passed over President Truman's veto. More notably, he began to support repeated actions by the racist, segregationist Southern Democrats in Congress, including voting against the Fair Employment Practices Commission set up under FDR. He also consistently voted with the South to oppose anti-lynching and anti-poll tax legislation. Congress had never been effective in supporting 1870's Fifteenth Amendment to the US Constitution, which guaranteed citizens the right to vote regardless of race or color. That amendment specifically stated that "The Congress shall have power to enforce this article by appropriate legislation," but since Reconstruction nothing had been done to actually put the article in force in the South. The fair-minded Lyndon Johnson of Cotulla and the Works Progress Administration did nothing to help.

In this context, Lyndon Johnson decided to try again for the Senate in 1948. Although Harry Truman's chances of being elected to a term as president in his own right seemed nil that year, the Senate seat in Texas would surely stay with the Democrats. For LBJ, the challenge was winning his party's primary. His opponent was the popular conservative governor, Coke Stevenson. Even though Lyndon had ceased being a New Deal supporter and joined other Southerners in opposing civil rights and President Truman's desegregation of the armed services, he was nowhere near as extreme as the racist Stevenson. Typically, Johnson campaigned furiously for the nomination. However, five days after the primary, voting tabulations showed Stevenson winning by just under 400 votes. This time, however, the Johnson forces were prepared to make sure the final count was in their favor. Late reporting precincts tipped the balance and LBJ was declared the winner by eighty-seven votes. When the outcome was contested in federal court, it fell to US Supreme Court Justice Hugo Black to make a ruling. Black was a liberal who would have been repelled by Coke Stevenson's politics. It is also likely that he was pressured by the more traditional Democrats like Sam Rayburn and perhaps even President Truman. In the end, Black decided to let the state count stand. Johnson's eighty-seven-vote primary victory prevailed. In November, he easily defeated his Republican opponent. That same day, much to the surprise of most political observers, Harry Truman won a clear victory over Thomas Dewey in the presidental race. His victory included a decisive win in Lyndon Johnson's Texas.

When Johnson took up his Senate seat, he quickly realized that he would have to take a less belligerent approach than he had in the House. The United States Senate, "the world's greatest deliberative body," valued deference and decorum. Lyndon Johnson had always learned the rules rapidly, and at age forty—a relatively young member—he easily fell into the role of fawning son. Instead of Sam Rayburn, LBJ's Senate father-figure was the distinguished Richard Russell of Georgia, one of the most powerful men in the Senate. A bachelor like Rayburn, Russell grew very fond of the hospitality and consideration of both Lyndon and Lady Bird Johnson. Russell became as influential a mentor for Johnson in the Senate as Rayburn had been in the House.

Although Johnson veered to the right of Harry Truman on domestic issues, he stuck by him on foreign policy, effectively bridging the gap between liberal and conservative branches of the Democratic Party. This positioning, the support of Russell, the canny advice of the young Senate aide Bobby Baker, and LBJ's typically relentless work ethic combined to see him elected as party whip following the midterm elections in 1950. He was now the second-ranking member in the Senate Democratic hierarchy. This was a remarkable achievement for a young freshman senator who had held his seat for only two years. It demonstrates as powerfully as anything else Johnson's effectiveness both in advancing himself and the causes he was supporting at any given time.

The early 1950s were a remarkable time in American politics. The two major parties were not nearly as polarized as they are today. There were liberal or at least moderate but also conservative wings in each party. Unfortunately for African Americans, relative comity between the two parties meant that justice for blacks was once again a back-burner issue. Being divisive, it was largely ignored. Also, foreign policy, in the aftermath of World War II, was largely nonpartisan, with the prevailing sentiment that "politics stops at the water's edge." Still, some Republicans, led by senators such as Joseph McCarthy of Wisconsin and the newly elected California Senator Richard Nixon, hammered away that the Democrats were soft on Communism. Tensions arising from the start of the Korean War in the summer of 1950 made matters worse. In April of 1951, the fissures deepened when President Truman fired General of the Army Douglas MacArthur for publicly contesting Truman's limited war approach in Korea. Lyndon Johnson and Sam Rayburn stood by the president. LBJ's support further strengthened his growing stature as a centrist stalwart within the Democratic Party.

The 1952 elections led to a further remarkable advance in Lyndon Johnson's already rapid political ascendancy. That year brought a Republican victory in the presidential race for the first time since Herbert Hoover was elected in 1928. Dwight D. Eisenhower, a political moderate, became the thirty-fourth president of the United States. At the same time, the GOP regained control of both houses of Congress. One of the Democratic casualties in the Senate races was the former majority leader, Ernest McFarland of Arizona, who lost to an unapologetic conservative named Barry Goldwater. That opened the position of Senate minority leader to Lyndon Johnson. Two short years later, in 1954, Democrats regained control of both houses of Congress. Sam Rayburn of Texas was once again speaker of the House, and Lyndon Johnson of Texas became the majority leader in the Senate, one of the least senior in that body's history. In the spirit of bipartisanship, Republican President Eisenhower, Democratic Speaker Rayburn, and Majority Leader Johnson worked effectively together to advance the president's agenda. In doing so, however, Johnson often managed to amend "Eisenhower bills" to the liking of Democrats. By this time, if not much earlier, LBJ could imagine himself in Ike's seat. Why couldn't he be president? It was not at all clear that Eisenhower would run for re-election in 1956, and by this time Lyndon was seen as a powerful Democrat who could unite the party as its presidential candidate. Somehow he would have to reassure liberals about his position on civil rights, but he had many assets, principally his unparalleled effectiveness as what Robert Caro called "master of the Senate."[12]

Any speculation about a political future was put on hold in July of 1955 when LBJ suffered a massive heart attack. He was overweight, he drank too much, he smoked several packs of cigarettes a day, and he worked feverishly. Under strict medical supervision, LBJ made a speedy recovery. Ironically, President Eisenhower also suffered a heart attack in September of that year. While Johnson tried to deflect speculation about his chances, he positioned himself carefully. In November he gave a passionate speech in Texas proposing a set of policies he called "A Program with a Heart."[13] It put forth a laundry list of New Deal-like proposals and advocated an end to the poll tax. As often happened in Lyndon Johnson's complex political evolution, speaking in his home state caused him to take a step away from Southern racial orthodoxy. Some months later, in early 1956, LBJ took another such step, refusing to sign the so-called Southern Manifesto that accused the US Supreme Court of the "abuse of judicial power" in unanimously outlawing school segregation in the 1954 Brown vs. Board of Education decision.

As 1956 unfolded, many prominent Democrats supported Johnson for the presidential nomination. Lyndon himself thought he might emerge as a compromise candidate in a deadlocked convention, especially when former President Truman came out against the front runner, Adlai Stevenson, who had lost to Ike in 1952. In the end, Democrats chose Stevenson. Then LBJ nominated Massachusetts Senator John F. Kennedy, whom he knew might be a rival in 1960, for vice president. He graciously referred to Kennedy as "the fighting sailor, who wears the scars of battle." But Kennedy lost the VP nomination to Tennessee Senator Estes Kefauver. In the general election, the Republican ticket of Eisenhower and Richard Nixon handily beat Stevenson and Kefauver.

Looking to the future, Lyndon knew that in order to be elected president he still needed to overcome the stigma of being a Southerner who opposed equality for African Americans. Congress had not passed a civil rights bill since 1875 during the Grant administration. Johnson decided that leading Congress to do so might disarm liberal opposition to his presidential ambitions and pave the way to victory. As in the past, the United States Senate was likely to be the graveyard of any attempts to enact civil rights legislation. However, in 1957, a strong bill originally proposed by President Eisenhower had passed the House of Representatives by a better than two-to-one margin. Now it would be up to Lyndon Johnson to steer it through the Senate. There was no reason to think he would succeed where so many others failed, but his tactics turned out to be brilliant. First, he persuaded Western senators to back civil rights in exchange for Southern support for a much-favored dam in Hells Canyon on the Snake River on the Idaho-Oregon border. He then promised Southern senators that he could engineer a bill that was essentially toothless. Next he got his friend and mentor Richard Russell of Georgia to hold off on a Southern filibuster. Johnson implied that if Russell helped him become president, he would protect Southern interests.

Even with all of this maneuvering and manipulation, the legislation looked dead. Provisions for desegregating public accommodations—hotels, restaurants, and movie theatres—were more than Southern Manifesto senators could swallow. LBJ arranged to delete this portion of the bill in exchange for Dixie support for voting rights. Although allowing blacks to vote was potentially the most powerful threat in the bill to institutional racism and white supremacy, the right to vote was so fundamental to American law and values that it was difficult to overtly oppose. There was, however, a potential saving grace for the South. If there was language stating that those charged with violating the new law would have the right to trial by jury, the South might be able to accept it. No white jury would convict voting registrars or other election officials of violating such a law. Now, however, a proposed trial by jury amendment enraged liberals. This time LBJ got help from Senator Frank Church, a liberal from Idaho who wanted to deliver on the Hells Canyon Dam. Church thought that the trial-by-jury amendment might be acceptable to Northerners if it were itself amended to demand that juries be integrated.

Getting this amendment to the amendment passed demanded a kind of political theatre that only Lyndon Johnson could have directed. Senator Joseph O'Mahoney of Wyoming took the floor to support the trial-by-jury amendment. Senator Church, much to O'Mahoney's feigned surprise, popped up and asked O'Mahoney if he would accept a friendly amendment to the amendment demanding desegregated juries. Following prevailing Senate norms of decorum, O'Mahoney agreed and continued to argue for trial-by-jury, as amended. Then

Senator John Pastore of Rhode Island interrupted with a range of questions and objections and then acted as if he had been persuaded by O'Mahoney's brilliance. It sounds farcical, but it worked. When the amendment to the amendment passed with the support of key Northerners such as John F. Kennedy of Massachusetts, Richard Russell held back an extended filibuster, and the entire bill eventually passed the Senate, 72–18. Many black leaders and other liberals thought the bill was next to worthless. A. Philip Randolph thought it was "worse than no bill at all."[14] Still, some liberals thought it was a step forward and provided a foundation for further legislative action. African American leader Roy Wilkins of the NAACP eventually came around to support it. The national press generally gave Lyndon Johnson credit for masterful leadership in the cause of equal rights. But had he earned enough credibility with civil rights supporters in the Democratic Party to gain the 1960 nomination for president?

What happened next is difficult to understand. LBJ had always been extremely active in going after what he wanted. He was generally a whirlwind of passionate movement. But he was strangely passive as the 1960 presidential race took shape. He knew that there would be several contenders, including the very liberal senator Hubert Humphrey of Minnesota and the more moderate John Kennedy of Massachusetts. Adlai Stevenson was still the hero of many in the party, including its elder stateswoman, Eleanor Roosevelt. Lyndon desperately wanted to be nominated but thought his best chances were to lay low and hope, as he had in 1956, that a deadlocked convention would turn to him. However, John Kennedy's victories over Hubert Humphrey in primaries in Wisconsin and West Virginia effectively wrapped up the nomination. Finally, just days before the convention, LBJ publicly announced his candidacy and challenged Kennedy to a debate before the combined Massachusetts and Texas delegations. He had nothing to lose. However, Kennedy's charm and wit won the day. When Johnson criticized "some Senators" for missing quorum calls, Kennedy deftly quipped that he assumed Johnson was not talking about him. In short order, the convention, as expected, nominated Kennedy, and it appeared that LBJ's presidential ambitions would be permanently frustrated.

However, things changed quickly. The morning after JFK's nomination, he asked Johnson to be his running mate. Kennedy had calculated that he needed to carry Texas and other Southern states to beat Richard Nixon and that LBJ could help him do it. As vice president under Kennedy, Johnson would have much less power than he already had as Senate majority leader. None other than fellow Texan John Nance Garner had said that the vice presidency wasn't worth a bucket of warm spit, or words to that effect. But the deciding factor was that as vice president he would be a heartbeat away from being president, and no other path to the top job looked possible. Johnson accepted Kennedy's offer.

In November of 1960, Kennedy and Johnson defeated Nixon and Henry Cabot Lodge by the narrowest of margins. Lyndon Johnson thus became the thirty-seventh vice president of the United States. The next two years, ten months, and two days were desperately and increasingly unhappy ones for

Johnson. The relations between JFK and his vice president had always been strained. Johnson felt shut out; the more he felt that way, the more unstable he seemed to become, and the more Kennedy kept him at a distance. When Johnson was included in meetings, he veered between pontificating and dominating or remaining stubbornly silent, claiming he had not been given enough information to express an opinion. However, as African Americans and their supporters kept pressuring the federal government—by organizing Freedom Rides through the South in 1961, by demanding the admission of James Meredith to the University of Mississippi in 1962, and by urging the government to order federal marshals to push Governor George Wallace away from "the school house door" so that black students could enroll at the University of Alabama in 1963 —Kennedy increasingly looked to Johnson for advice. When he could, the vice president spoke eloquently about civil rights. As part of the Civil War Centennial in 1963, Johnson gave a speech at Gettysburg, Pennsylvania. It was late May. With obvious passion, he said "One hundred years ago, the slave was freed. One hundred years later, the Negro remains in bondage to the color of his skin." He continued in words reminiscent of Martin Luther King Jr.'s "Letter from a Birmingham Jail." He said that the Negro today asks for justice and whites respond by asking for patience. "To ask for patience from the Negro is to ask him to give more of what he has already given enough." He concluded saying that blacks and whites must work together—"There is no other way."[15] Suddenly the vice president seemed to be as energized as he had been in the Senate. Just days later, his urgings helped nudge the president toward giving the kind of speech about civil rights that Johnson had been advocating in recent meetings.

Though moved, Kennedy was still reluctant to take action on behalf of civil rights beyond enforcing the law and protecting black citizens from violence. He finally changed his mind on June 11, the day that the Justice Department forced Alabama Governor George Wallace to stand aside and admit black students to the University of Alabama. That evening Kennedy addressed the nation, saying that America faced "a moral crisis as a country and as a people" that it "is as old as the Scriptures and is clear as the American constitution." He declared that "it is time to act in the Congress, in your state and local legislative bodies and, above all, in all of our daily lives."[16] He then outlined the central features of what would eventually become the Civil Rights Act of 1964.

That summer, Lyndon Johnson tried to advise President Kennedy, and his brother Robert Kennedy, the attorney general of the United States, how best to work with Congress to pass his legislation. However, there was enough ill will between LBJ and the Kennedys to once again sideline the vice president. When both Kennedy and Johnson and their wives traveled to Texas in late November 1963 to try to heal rifts between liberal and conservative factions in the state Democratic Party, the Civil Rights Bill was stalled in both houses of Congress.

On the afternoon of November 22, the president was shot in a Dallas motorcade. Johnson was rushed to a small but secure room in Parkland Hospital to await word on Kennedy's condition. He and Lady Bird waited there for over thirty-five minutes. Johnson deflected his Secret Service agent's insistence that he leave Dallas immediately on Air Force One. He first wanted to hear official word of the president's condition. He was unusually calm and clearly prepared to take decisive action, no matter what he learned. He was aptly described as decisive and "adamant."[17] Finally, John F. Kennedy's closest aid in Dallas, Ken O'Donnell, came into the small room and said simply, "He's gone."

The new president and First Lady, the dead president's body, and the rest of the Kennedy entourage, including the bereaved Mrs. Kennedy, returned to Washington on Air Force One that afternoon, arriving after dark. During the next several days, the nation was riveted in its grief by television coverage of President Kennedy's funeral. LBJ begged Kennedy's staff to stay with him, saying that he needed them more than JFK did. But he also quickly took command and addressed the nation two days after Kennedy's burial at Arlington Cemetery. He eulogized the late president and expressed his "determination to continue the forward thrust of America that he began." He echoed the resolve Kennedy expressed in his 1961 inaugural address—"but let us begin"—and firmly declared "my fellow Americans, let us continue." Any doubts about where Lyndon Johnson stood on civil rights were quickly dispelled. He spoke of Kennedy's "dream of equal rights for all Americans, whatever their race or color" and put that issue at the top of his agenda. In challenging Congress to advance on a number of fronts, he signaled his first priority:

> First, no memorial oration or eulogy could more eloquently honor President Kennedy's memory than the earliest possible passage of the civil rights bill for which he fought so long. We have talked long enough in this country about equal rights. We have talked for one hundred years or more. It is time now to write the next chapter, and to write it in the books of law. I urge you again, as I did in 1957 and again in 1960, to enact a civil rights law so that we can move forward to eliminate from the Nation every trace of discrimination and oppression that is based upon race or color. There could be no greater source of strength to this Nation at home and abroad.[18]

As Johnson well knew, rhetoric from the bully pulpit would not be enough. The wheels of Congress, especially in the Senate, moved ever so slowly, if at all. Throughout its history, it seemed as if it had only two speeds: "slow" and "stop." LBJ was determined to harness the potential momentum from Kennedy's death to increase its velocity. Several weeks before the assassination, JFK's Civil Rights Bill had been passed by the House of Representatives Judiciary Committee and referred to the Rules Committee. There it might have died a slow, lingering death. The House Rules Committee Chair was Howard Smith of Virginia, an ardent segregationist. Smith simply sat on the bill, refusing to let the committee debate and vote on it. There was one way to bypass Smith. The House had a procedure called a "petition to discharge" by which a majority of the whole

House could force a vote to take a bill from a committee and bring it to the floor of the entire body for debate. Many congressmen, no matter how they felt about civil rights, were reluctant to force the House to circumvent its usual procedures. Finally, however, responding to pressure from President Johnson, House leaders lined up the necessary votes for a discharge petition. Chairman Smith, to avoid the humiliation of such a step, allowed the Rules Committee to vote on the bill, and it was finally brought to the House Floor on January 30, 1964. It took less than two weeks for the House to pass the bill and send it to the United States Senate and an uncertain fate. The final vote was 290 in favor and 130 opposed. Most of the "no" votes were cast by Southern Democrats. The House Republicans, at least for a time, reclaimed their legacy as the "Party of Lincoln" and supported the bill by a four-to-one margin.

The Civil Rights Bill was handed to the Senate in the middle of February. As in the House, a key step in its passage was preventing it from being buried in a committee chaired by a segregationist Southern Democrat. In this case it was the Judiciary Committee; its chair was Senator James Eastland of Mississippi, one of the most rabid anti-black members of Congress. With Johnson pulling many of the strings in the background, a plan of attack unfolded. Normally, a bill such as this one would be read twice by the majority leader and then automatically referred to the Judiciary Committee. The new majority leader, succeeding Lyndon B. Johnson, was Mike Mansfield of Montana. Mansfield arranged a delay between the first and second readings of the bill. Since there was no precedent for handling a bill before a delayed second reading, Mansfield took it directly to the Senate floor, bypassing Eastland and Judiciary. Still, the legislation itself and any amendments could be filibustered to death, and the South was prepared to talk forever to prevent an up or down vote. It would take a two-thirds vote for "cloture" by the whole Senate to cut off debate. In the case of a civil rights bill, never had such a vote been successful.

By now, President Johnson and key Democratic leaders such as Senator Hubert Humphrey of Minnesota and the late president's brother, Attorney General Robert F. Kennedy, realized that the Civil Rights Bill could only pass with support from Republicans. More specifically, they needed support from conservative Midwestern Republicans. Even more specifically, the minority leader himself, a Midwestern conservative named Senator Everett Dirksen of Illinois, needed to be brought on board. Among the many difficulties was that the probable Republican candidate for president that year, the man who would face Lyndon Johnson in the November election, was Senator Barry Goldwater of Arizona. Goldwater was adamantly opposed to cloture and the Civil Rights Bill itself. Would Dirksen and others be willing to oppose the party's likely presidential nominee and nominal leader?

Johnson and Humphrey thought they knew how to appeal to Dirksen. First, Dirksen needed to be persuaded to read the political writing on the wall. The nation, and the state of Illinois, were strongly in support of civil rights. Second, Dirksen had senses of both pride and history. He would not want to be on the wrong side of a turning point in the nation's progress. Hubert Humphrey began the courting of Dirksen on a Sunday talk show program on March 8. Although Dirksen had expressed reservations about some parts of the bill, Humphrey said, "He is a man who thinks of his country before he thinks of his party . . . and I sincerely believe that when Senator Dirksen has to face the moment of decision where . . . leadership will be required, . . . he will not be found wanting." [19] Johnson told Humphrey to keep the pressure on, telling him "You drink with Dirksen," "You talk to Dirksen," "You listen to Dirksen." [20] Later Humphrey confided that "I would have kissed [his] ass on the Capitol steps" to get Dirksen on board. [21]

The president joined in with his own offensive. Former LBJ aids claimed that Johnson sketched for Dirksen an imaginary scenario with black and white children playing together, being told that Everett Dirksen made it all possible. In one conversation taped in the White House, Johnson told the senator that he had seen the Illinois state "exhibit at the World's Fair, and it said 'the Land of Lincoln.' So you're worthy of the Land of Lincoln. And the Man from Illinois is going to pass the bill, and I'll see that you get proper attention and credit." [22] When the time came for a vote to impose cloture and break the Southern filibusters, Dirksen told his colleagues, "Stronger than all the armies is an idea whose time has come. The time has come for equality." [23] Finally, in mid-June, the Senate voted 71–29 to cut off debate and days later voted 73–27 for the final bill. At long last, Lyndon Johnson signed the 1964 Civil Rights Act into law on July 2, 1964. LBJ was at the peak of his power and popularity.

In August, the 1964 Democratic Convention in Atlantic City, New Jersey, nominated Johnson for a full presidential term of his own. He squeezed as much drama as he could out of his choice of a running mate, but there was little surprise when he finally selected Senator Hubert Humphrey of Minnesota. By that time, a badly divided GOP had nominated Barry Goldwater for president and a little known New York congressman, William Miller, as his running mate. Goldwater's nomination was the harbinger of the Republican Party's enduring turn to the right and the extinction of a species known as "liberal Republican," represented for many years by Governor Nelson Rockefeller of New York. When Goldwater concluded his speech accepting the party's nomination by declaring that "extremism in the defense of liberty is no vice," and "moderation in the pursuit of justice is no virtue," he confirmed both Republican and Democratic perceptions that he was a dangerous extremist. [24] In November 1964, negative views of Goldwater and support for the man continuing the legacy of John F. Kennedy gave Lyndon Johnson one of the biggest election victories in American history. His 61% popular vote total stands as the largest ever. Johnson also pulled in an overwhelmingly Democratic Congress, dominating Republicans 295–140 in the House of Representatives and 68–32 in the Senate. It appeared that Lyndon Johnson would be able to have his way in his own elected term as president.

Figure 8.2 Hosea Williams and John Lewis two minutes before they were assaulted by Alabama state police. The racial violence in Selma dramatized the significance of Lyndon Johnson's "And We Shall Overcome" voting rights speech.

Spider Martin, "Two Minute Warning"—Hosea Williams and John Lewis confronting troopers in Selma, Alabama, on Bloody Sunday, March 7, 1965, black and white photograph. Courtesy of the Spider Martin Civil Rights Collection (SMCRC), Austin, Texas.

There were some clouds on the horizon. One was that Goldwater carried five Deep South states: South Carolina, Georgia, Alabama, Mississippi, and Louisiana. The South, opposing equal rights for African Americans, was on its way to becoming a bulwark of a very conservative Republican Party. Second, in August Johnson had asked for and received congressional approval to take military action in South Vietnam to counter the danger of it falling to Communist North Vietnam. Johnson was taking his initial steps into what would become known as the "quagmire" of the long war in Vietnam.[25] At the moment, however, those concerns were outweighed by the huge election victory for Johnson and congressional Democrats. In January of 1965, when the president was inaugurated for a full term of his own and the overwhelmingly supportive eighty-ninth Congress came to power, it was time for LBJ to press ahead with one of the most expansive domestic agendas in American history.

The achievements of Lyndon Johnson and the eighty-ninth Congress in 1965 and 1966 are among the most impressive and far-reaching the nation has ever seen. Like the domestic accomplishments of Woodrow Wilson and Franklin Roosevelt during their first two years in office, they took giant steps toward a more progressive society. In LBJ's case, the legislation for his "War on Poverty" helped advance what he called "The Great Society." He succeeded in urging Congress to pass bills that supported housing and education and established

Medicare and Medicaid. For African Americans, his most important accomplishment was passing the Voting Rights Act of 1965.

Although the Civil Rights Act of 1964 took monumental steps forward, the South had managed to keep African Americans from wielding their most powerful weapon, the right to vote. In county after county and precinct after precinct, voting registrars and others had found ways to subvert the Fifteenth Amendment to the Constitution, ratified in 1870 with the vigorous support of President Ulysses S. Grant. Johnson felt that there was little he could do. Even with his swelling majorities in the House and the Senate, it would be too much to ask Congress to pass a second civil rights bill in consecutive years. As had happened in 1963, however, black leaders acted independently to apply nonviolent force. Once again, Alabama was the chosen venue. Civil rights workers in the small city of Selma had formed the Dallas County Voters League in an effort to register blacks. Little headway had been made when Martin Luther King, Jr. and others organized a voting rights march from Selma to Montgomery, the state capital of Alabama and formerly the first capital of the Confederacy, some forty miles to the east. When the march started out on March 7, 1965, on what has become known as Bloody Sunday, the marchers were attacked by riot police with tear gas, clubs, and whips and turned back. The assaults were televised. While some white spectators at the scene cheered, most of the nation was horrified by the violence and injustice. As in Birmingham, two springs before when JFK was president, pressure built. A second march was attempted two days later. Like the first, to avoid violence, it was turned back. Black and white leaders implored President Johnson to nationalize the Alabama National Guard.

On Saturday, March 13, the president invited Alabama Governor George Wallace to the White House. Wallace got what had become the famous "Johnson Treatment." LBJ would lean into a man and make him bend backward so as not to have the president's long nose in his face. He would stab his finger into the man's chest and plead, cajole, and threaten. Whatever it took. In Wallace's case, the president had the shorter governor sit in a low, soft sofa so he could pull his rocker up to Wallace and lean over him. He wouldn't accept Wallace's pleas that he didn't have the power to keep law and order. "Don't you shit me, George Wallace," fumed the president.[26] He asked Wallace whether he wouldn't rather have a marble monument carrying the words "George Wallace, He Built" rather than a cheap sign saying "George Wallace, He Hated." Johnson then got Wallace to join him in meeting reporters and told them that the governor had promised to protect the marchers. Martin Luther King, Jr. now announced that he had organized a march that would begin a third time on Tuesday, March 16. Johnson asked to address both houses of Congress on the evening before.[27]

As the president drove to the Capitol that night, March 15, 1965, few knew exactly what he would say, and almost no one could anticipate the passion with which he said it. It was as if all of his anger at witnessing inhuman treatment of blacks and Mexicans for much of his life welled up to override any mere political calculation. Something as deep and genuine as any part of Lyndon Johnson took over. He began by stating, "I speak tonight for the dignity of man and the destiny of democracy." He spoke of the fundamental right to vote and argued that it was time to act to secure that right. "This time, on this issue, there must be no delay, no hesitation, and no compromise with our purpose. . . . The time for waiting is gone." He declared that black people's struggle to secure their rights "must be our cause too. Because . . . really it is all of us, who must overcome the crippling legacy of bigotry and injustice." Then pausing, the president segued into the most memorable words of his powerful speech, declaring his commitment emphatically with the words of the song that had become the anthem of the civil rights movement: "And we *shall* overcome."[28] The high-water mark of the civil rights era had been reached.

Just as in the previous year, overcoming the South's last ditch efforts to preserve segregation and white supremacy would take all of the president's energy and tactics of persuasion. He began the struggle that very night on the way out of the Capitol. He shook hands with House Judiciary Committee Chairman Emmanuel Celler. "Manny," he said, "I want you to start hearings tonight." When the elderly Celler said he would start the next week, LBJ glared at him and said "Start them *this* week, Manny." For good measure, he told him to work nights and weekends.[29]

It took several months, but the monumental 1965 Voting Rights Act was passed and signed into law on August 6, 1965. President Johnson spoke once again on that occasion: "[T]his is . . . a victory for the freedom of the American nation. And every family across this great, entire searching land will live stronger in liberty . . . and will be prouder to be American."[30]

By this time, President Lyndon Johnson had passed his peak as trusted and admired leader of the United States. On April 7, 1965, just over three weeks after his "And we *shall* overcome" voting rights speech, the president spoke at Johns Hopkins University about the need to fight Communism in Southeast Asia. He argued that the United States must give further aid to the South Vietnamese in their battle against the Viet Cong and North Vietnam.[31] By that summer, the conflict in Vietnam was routinely called "war." A major escalation had begun, and LBJ's political fortunes began to sink. Furthermore, the passage of the Voting Rights Act did not seem to improve race relations. More radical black leaders began to eclipse Martin Luther King, Jr. and American cities burned. While LBJ promised that the country could afford "guns and butter," inflation began to loom as an economic issue. In the midterm elections of 1966, Democrats lost three Senate seats and an eye-popping forty-seven seats in the House of Representatives. Much of the loss was blamed on "white backlash," opposition to the civil rights movement, and reaction to perceived black militancy. Johnson and the Democrats were clearly on the ropes.

Not a great deal was accomplished for civil rights during Lyndon Johnson's last two years in office. Opposition to the war in Vietnam increased so much that Johnson announced at the end of March of 1968 that he would focus entirely on the search for peace and, "accordingly," not run for re-election.[32]

The good will that came from that announcement did not last long. Four days later, Martin Luther King, Jr. was assassinated in Memphis, Tennessee. In June, Robert F. Kennedy, the late president's brother, was shot in Los Angeles on the night he won the Democratic presidential primary in California. He died two days later. The country was reeling.

As the fall presidential election shaped up, war in Vietnam was the dominating issue. The Republicans nominated Richard Nixon in Miami Beach and, in the bitter and tumultuous convention that author Norman Mailer called the "siege of Chicago," Democrats nominated Hubert Humphrey.[33] Alabama Governor George Wallace entered the race as a third party candidate. With Johnson and the war deeply discredited, Humphrey trailed badly going into the fall campaign. However, late in the campaign, he broke with LBJ in his support of the war and his prospects grew brighter. The election ended up being very close. Nixon followed a so-called Southern strategy, appealing to a "silent majority" who wanted "law and order," commonly seen as a code term signaling opposition to advances for African Americans. He won, but by less than one percent of the popular vote. The flight away from the Democratic Party in the South was dramatic. Although Humphrey narrowly defeated Nixon and Wallace in Texas, he won 30% or less in most other states of the former Confederacy. George Wallace carried the Deep South states of Georgia, Alabama, Mississippi, Louisiana, and Arkansas. Nixon carried Virginia, the Carolinas, Tennessee, and Florida.

When Johnson turned the presidency over to Richard Nixon in January 1969, few mourned his departure. Historians still give him low marks for his handling of the war in Vietnam. He seems forever haunted by the ghost of John F. Kennedy, as many influential writers assert that Kennedy would have somehow avoided dragging the country into the horrors of that war as Johnson did. This question will be debated for many years to come. However, LBJ is ranked second only to Abraham Lincoln on the C-SPAN dimension called "pursued equal justice for all."[34] Passing the Civil Rights Act of 1964 and the Voting Rights Act of 1965 demanded the kind of moral and legislative leadership genius that, at his best, Lyndon Baines Johnson gave to the United States.

Notes

1 Martin Luther King, Jr., Letter from Birmingham Jail, April 16, 1963. http://www. africa.upenn.edu/Articles_Gen/Letter_Birmingham.html.

2 John F. Kennedy, Civil Rights Address, June 11, 1963. www.americanrhetoric.com/ speeches/jfkcivilrights.htm.

3 Robert A. Slayton, *Empire Statesman: The Rise and Redemption of Al Smith* (New York: The Free Press, 2001).

4 Robert Dallek, *Lone Star Rising* (New York: Oxford University Press, 1991), p. 16.

5 Franklin D. Roosevelt, First Inaugural Address, March 4, 1933. http://www.bartleby. com/124/pres49.html.

6 Patricia Brennan, *Washington Post,* December 11, 2001. See also Dallek, p. 115, "queer-moth-and-the-flame feeling."

7 Robert A. Caro, *The Years of Lyndon Johnson: The Path to Power* (New York: Knopf, 1982), p. 26.

8 Caro, *The Path to Power,* p. 275.

9 Dallek, p. 10; Randall Woods, *LBJ: Architect of American Ambition* (Cambridge, MA: Harvard University Press, 2006).

10 Charles Peters, *Lyndon B. Johnson* (New York: Times Books, 2010), p. 25.

11 Woods, p. 167.

12 Robert A. Caro, *The Years of Lyndon Johnson: Master of the Senate* (New York: Knopf, 2002).

13 Dallek, p. 491.

14 Caro, *Master of the Senate,* p. 991. Caro's book discusses LBJ's Senate machinations in passing this bill in great detail.

15 Lyndon B. Johnson. http://www.lbjlib.utexas.edu/johnson/archives.hom/speeches. hom/630530.asp.

16 Kennedy, Civil Rights Address.

17 Robert A. Caro, *The Years of Lyndon Johnson: The Passage of Power* (New York: Knopf, 2012).

18 Lyndon B. Johnson, Address to Congress, November 27, 1963. archive.umd.edu/ citizen/lbj1963int.html.

19 Caro, *The Passage of Power,* p. 564.

20 *Ibid.*

21 Charles Peters, *Lyndon B. Johnson* (New York: Times Books, 2010), p. 83.

22 Michael Beschloss, *Reaching for Glory: Lyndon Johnson's Secret White House Tapes, 1964–1965* (New York: Simon & Schuster, 2001), p. 350.

23 Peters, p. 83.

24 Barry Goldwater, Acceptance Speech, Republican National Convention, July 16, 1964. http://www.washingtonpost.com/wp-srv/politics/daily/may98/goldwaterspeech.htm.

25 David Halberstam, *The Making of a Quagmire: America and Vietnam in the Kennedy Era* (New York: Random House, 1965).

26 Beschloss, *Reaching for Glory,* p. 231.

27 Ronald A. Heifetz, *Leadership without Easy Answers* (Cambridge, MA: Harvard University Press, 1994), Chapter 7.

28 Johnson, Voting Rights Speech, March 15, 1965. http://www.greatamericandocu ments.com/speeches/lbj-voting-rights.html.

29 Robert A. Caro, *The Years of Lyndon Johnson: Means of Ascent* (New York: Knopf, 1990), p. xxi.

30 Johnson, Address to the Nation, August 6, 1965. http://millercenter.org/president/ speeches/detail/4034.

31 Johnson, Address at Johns Hopkins University, April 7, 1965. http://www.lbjlib. utexas.edu/johnson/archives.hom/speeches.hom/650407.asp.

32 Johnson, Address to the Nation, March 31, 1968. http://www.lbjlib.utexas.edu/ johnson/archives.hom/speeches.hom/680331.asp.

33 Norman Mailer, *Miami and the Siege of Chicago: An Informal History of the Republican and Democratic Conventions of 1968* (New York: World Publishing Company, 1968).

34 C-SPAN 2009 Historians Presidential Leadership Survey.

CONCLUSION

Figure 9.1 Barack Obama, the first African American US president, was inaugurated on January 20, 2009.

Bart Stupak, "President Barack Obama taking the Oath of Office in Washington, D.C., January 20, 2009." Public domain, from Wikimedia Commons.

When John F. Kennedy was inaugurated as the thirty-fifth president of the United States in January of 1961, African Americans were hopeful that he would soon move forward on civil rights with "vigor," as he was fond of saying. But progress was very slow.[1] Kennedy was reluctant to take action that would be politically costly in the South. As a result, civil rights leaders, including James Farmer, founder of CORE, the Congress of Racial Equality, decided to take matters into their own hands. They organized "Freedom Rides," starting in May of 1961. Although a United States Supreme Court decision in 1960 had outlawed segregated public buses and segregation in restaurants and waiting rooms at interstate bus terminals, the law was ignored in Southern states and seldom enforced by the federal government. So Freedom Riders took direct action. They were black and white men and women who attempted to ride buses together through the heart of the South, from Washington, DC, to New Orleans, traveling through the Carolinas, Georgia, Alabama, Mississippi, and Louisiana. They would refuse to obey segregationist practices observed throughout the region.

Starting on May 4, thirteen riders boarded two buses in Washington. Blacks and whites sat side by side, and some blacks rode in the front of the bus. The trip went smoothly until the buses crossed the Alabama line ten days later. Members of the Ku Klux Klan, and police, knew the riders were coming. Klan members, dressed in their Mother's Day Sunday best, undeterred by police, attacked the buses in Anniston, Alabama. One bus was set on fire. Passengers were nearly killed. As the trips continued and the numbers of riders swelled, they were sometimes barely saved by local civil rights leaders from being burned, beaten to death, or lynched. There slowly emerged an accommodation whereby Freedom Riders were ensured safe passage in traveling from one town or city to another but were arrested and jailed when they sought to use segregated facilities at rest stops. In Jackson, Mississippi, and other towns, the local jails couldn't handle the numbers, and Freedom Riders were moved to state prisons.

The Kennedy administration charged that the Freedom Riders were giving America a bad image and asked for "a cooling-off period." James Farmer responded, "We have been cooling off for 350 years, and if we cooled off any more, we'd be in a deep freeze."[2] The movement continued throughout the summer of 1961, with the Justice Department taking action to at least protect the riders. It would be another two years before President Kennedy proposed bold civil rights legislation.

In August of the Freedom Rides' summer, 1961, a mixed-race boy was born in Honolulu, Hawaii, and named after his Kenyan father, Barack Obama. The boy's mother, Stanley Ann Dunham, was a first-year student at the University of Hawaii. In his memoir, Dreams from My Father, the boy, Barack Hussein Obama, described his mother as "an awkward, shy American girl, only eighteen" when she met his father.[3] A sexual innocent, Ann Dunham was captivated by the charismatic Kenyan and became pregnant. Obama Sr. and Dunham were married in February 1961, six months before the birth of their son, now the forty-fourth president of the United States. Unbeknownst to Ann Dunham, Barack Obama already had a wife and two children back in Africa.

It is difficult to convey the unlikely and unstable early life of the future president. The improbable marriage of his parents was likely doomed from the start. Ann left Hawaii to take courses at the University of Washington in Seattle within a month of Barack's birth.[4] Obama Sr. earned his college degree from the University of Hawaii and left Oahu the next summer. Ann returned with her son, nicknamed Barry, shortly thereafter to continue her college education. The following year, 1963, she met and fell in love with an Indonesian graduate student, Lolo Soetoro. Ann and Obama Sr. were divorced in 1964, and Ann married Soetoro in 1965. He, however, returned to Indonesia the next year. After living either with his mother or her parents in Hawaii until he was six-years old, Barry was then taken to Jakarta, Indonesia, so that Ann could rejoin her husband there. She and Lolo had a daughter, Maya, born in 1970. After four years in Indonesia, the ten-year-old Barry flew back to Hawaii to live—at times with Ann's parents and at times with Ann herself, depending on her travels. Thanks to one of his grandfather's connections, Barry was admitted to the prestigious Punahou School, entering the fifth grade in the fall of 1971.

During Barry's tumultuous first ten years, America was going through one of its own most turbulent decades, the Sixties. In the month that Obama was born, the Soviet Union, under Nikita Khrushchev, confronted the Kennedy administration by starting construction on the Berlin Wall. The civil rights movement was gaining momentum. Martin Luther King, Jr. led the massive 1963 March on Washington the month Barry turned two years old; on the boy's third birthday, the bodies of three young murdered civil rights workers were found near Philadelphia, Mississippi. On his next birthday, in 1965, Congress gave final approval to Lyndon Johnson's Voting Rights Act.[5] Soon thereafter, urban riots and the war in Vietnam became central political issues, ultimately leading to the narrow election of Republican Richard Nixon in 1968 as the thirty-seventh president of the United States.

Nixon's background on civil rights, and his politics and policies relevant to African Americans, like the man himself, contained numerous contradictions. Nixon had been vice president in 1957 when Senate majority leader Lyndon Johnson secured the passage of the first civil rights bill since 1875. Nixon favored a more expansive bill than the one finally passed, but cooperated with LBJ in achieving what was possible. When he campaigned for president in 1960 against JFK, Nixon attracted many prominent black supporters, including baseball legend Jackie Robinson and, at least initially, Martin Luther King, Sr. However, when he ran for president again in 1968, the political landscape had changed considerably. The 1964 Civil Rights Act had unmoored the increasingly less "solid" South from the Democratic Party. Five Deep Southern states voted for Republican Barry Goldwater in 1964. In 1968, according to some interpretations, Nixon followed a "Southern Strategy" that, as noted earlier, appealed to white Southerners, using slogans such as "law and order" that were widely seen as anti-black code words. He worked closely with segregationist icon Strom Thurmond of South Carolina that year, thereby losing Jackie Robinson's support.[6] The Southern Strategy was at least partially successful: Nixon carried five Southern states, including Thurmond's South Carolina. However, in contrast to appeals to his white Southerners, Nixon simultaneously advocated finding a constructive way to promote "black capitalism."[7] Given these contradictions, it was not clear how he would govern.

When Nixon became president, to the surprise of many, he was decidedly progressive on several race issues. Members of Nixon's cabinet and administration worked with local communities throughout the South to speed the desegregation of schools. In little more than a year, desegregation had been accomplished on a broad scale.[8] In his book *One of Us: Richard Nixon and the American Dream,* respected journalist Tom Wicker wrote, "The indisputable fact is that he got the job done—the dismantling of dual schools—when no one else had been able to do it."[9] In addition, on welfare policy, Nixon promoted changes that were arguably in the interests of African Americans.[10] He also pushed the so-called Philadelphia Plan, an "affirmative action" initiative requiring nondiscrimination in awarding federal contracts.[11] Unfortunately, initiatives such as these gave way to increasing focus on ending the war in Vietnam. Nixon and the nation largely turned away from issues relating to black Americans.

Starting in early 1972, or in the middle of Barry Obama's fifth-grade year at Punahou, Richard Nixon began to plan his upcoming re-election campaign. His efforts were led by the Committee to Re-elect the President, also known as CREEP. Nixon was overwhelmingly re-elected that year, largely on the basis of his foreign policy accomplishments. However, not long after the election, the public and the press started to pay increasing attention to the June 1972 break-in at the Democratic Party headquarters in the Watergate complex in Washington, DC. While the break-in had occurred several months before the election, over the next two years, various investigations led to a cascading series of disclosures that culminated in Nixon's resignation from the presidency in August of 1974, a few days after Barry Obama turned thirteen. When Nixon left office, Gerald Ford became the thirty-eighth president of the United States. His straightforward character and centrist policies won the approval of many Americans, but his pardon of Richard Nixon during his second month in office doomed his efforts to be elected president in his own right in 1976. That year Ford lost to a relatively unknown Democrat from Georgia, Jimmy Carter, the thirty-ninth president of the United States. Barack Obama was fifteen years old and in his sophomore year at Punahou.

Jimmy Carter was a different kind of Southern Democrat. Elected governor of Georgia in 1970, he was viewed by many journalists as a representative of the "New South," a South that had put racial divisions behind it. During his campaign for president, Carter often lauded the Civil Rights Act of 1964 as "the best thing that ever happened to the South."[12] Carter won the presidency in significant measure on the basis of regional pride. He carried all of the states of the former Confederacy except Virginia. He also carried much of the Northeast. Commentators noted that his electoral coalition was the opposite of Franklin Roosevelt's. FDR won the Northeast because he hailed from that region, and he won the South because it was reliably Democratic. In direct contrast, Carter won the Northeast because it had become reliably Democratic and the South because he was a Southerner. As president, Carter was a very strong supporter of civil rights and the inclusion of African Americans in government. Appropriately, C-SPAN's 2000 survey of presidential rankings placed Carter fourth on "pursued equal justice for all," after Lincoln, Lyndon Johnson, and Harry Truman.[13]

During Carter's single term in office, Barry Obama graduated from Punahou and started Occidental College. As he acknowledged in *Dreams from My Father,* he did not do good academic work in his last year in high school or at first in college. Part of the difficulty stemmed from lacking a firm sense of racial identity. As he grew into adolescence, he increasingly felt that he didn't belong. Most of his peers in high school were white. He didn't feel fully accepted by them. Additionally, because his father was an African—rather than an American—black man, he never felt fully accepted by many African Americans. It was clear that he was nonwhite and therefore barred from full inclusion in a white world. But African American friends would often remind him in hurtful ways that he really was not one of them either.[14]

Despite these personal confusions, in his early years at Occidental, Obama began to embrace his identity as an African American. He also began using his real first name, Barack, and left his Barry persona behind. At one point, a girlfriend asked if she could call him Barack. He replied that was okay "as long as you say it right."[15] Also at that time, Obama took his first steps into political activism. Like students at many American colleges in the early 1980s, those at Occidental had started protests against the apartheid regime in South Africa. They advocated and then demanded that their schools divest their assets from firms doing business in that country. Obama was chosen to give a speech opening a rally advocating divestment. By this time, he had grown confident in his ability to influence others: "I figured I was ready, and could reach people when it counted."[16]

Obama's political awakening coincided with a sharp turn to the right in American politics. In his sophomore year at Occidental, 1980, Ronald Reagan was elected as the fortieth president of the United States. Reagan overwhelmed Jimmy Carter's bid for re-election, carrying forty-four states. That Reagan would take a different approach to race and policies such as affirmative action was signaled in many ways, direct and indirect. The candidate opened his campaign in Philadelphia, Mississippi, where three civil rights workers had been killed in 1964. He spoke of "states' rights," a term often used in the 1960s to oppose civil rights and voting rights legislation. While defenders of Reagan deny that there were any racial implications in his expressing support for returning power to state and local governments, the symbolism of those words in that place betokened an end to further efforts on behalf of African Americans during the Reagan years. Reagan was not a bigoted man and opposed discrimination, but he had no real interest in blacks as a group and believed that when affirmative action took the form of racial "quotas" it was counterproductive. Democrats demurred.

During the Reagan years, Barack Obama finally began to develop what he called "the comfort, the firmness of identity,"[17] almost as if he were describing a warm, sturdy building. Becoming serious about academics, he transferred to Columbia University in New York City. In his senior year, an aunt from Kenya called to say that his father had been killed in an automobile accident. Obama hadn't seen "the Old Man" in over ten years. Despite the shock and the sense of loss of a parent he barely knew, Barack continued his undergraduate studies, finishing in 1983 with a major in political science. In *Dreams from My Father*, he wrote that that year he "decided to become a community organizer." He wanted to "organize black folks. At the grass roots. For change."[18] But it took some time to actually become a community organizer. There was no apparent way to make a living at it, so Obama worked for the Business International Corporation in New York, then for the New York state branch of PIRG, the Public Interest Research Group. During his time with PIRG, Obama's energy for community organizing and community action took shape in his efforts to protest shabby conditions in the New York subway.

After working for two years in New York, in 1985 Obama moved to Chicago to become more directly involved in community action with a church-based organization called the Developing Communities Project. Much of his time went into improving housing and developing educational and job training opportunities. After close to three years of alternately frustrating and fruitful efforts in Chicago, Obama decided that he could be much more effective in achieving his larger goals—helping poor, powerless people, especially African Americans—if he had a law degree. He applied to and was accepted at Harvard Law School, to enter in the fall of 1988. Before moving to Cambridge, however, he took a trip that changed his life, first to Europe and then to Kenya.

The journey to Africa was a milestone for the twenty-six-year-old Barack Obama. It further complicated but also enriched his sense of family and identity. He spent most of the time with his older half-sister Auma, daughter of his father's first wife Kezia, and also various aunts, uncles, half-brothers, and half-sisters. Obama Sr. had fathered two children with Kezia, Auma and Malik, then Barack Jr. with Ann Dunham, two children with a third wife Ruth, two more children with Kezia (although their paternity is debated), and a final son with a fourth wife—a total of eight. In due course, Barack Obama met all his Obama half-siblings and at least tried to establish some kind of relationship with each one. His African relatives had heard many stories about Barack from Auma and Malik, and he was treated as a prized, long-lost member of the family. As flattering as that reception was, the weeks in Africa revealed to Barack the overwhelming complexities of his extended clan. He was glad to have met its members and to have learned about his father, his grandparents, and others, but he was ready to come back to America.

During the autumn of Obama's return to the United States and his entrance into Harvard Law School, the United States was going through another presidential election between Ronald Reagan's vice president, George Herbert Walker Bush, and his Democratic opponent, Michael Dukakis, governor of Massachusetts. Bush offered a "kinder, gentler" conservative approach, though it was never clear exactly what that phrase meant. Still, Bush won decisively, reflecting both the country's overall satisfaction with Republican leadership under Reagan and Dukakis's shortcomings as a candidate. The GOP had thus won five of six presidential elections, starting with Nixon's two victories in 1968 and 1972, Reagan's wins in 1980 and 1984, and now the Bush succession. Only the first of those Republican victories was close. And only Jimmy Carter's narrow victory in 1976 interrupted the Republican lock on the White House. At the same time, the Republican Party had become decidedly less vigorous in supporting African Americans during the Reagan years. What could be expected under Bush? As it turned out, Bush was moderate or even progressive on civil rights issues. While he vetoed a 1990 civil rights bill on the grounds that it set "quotas," he signed a slightly weaker bill in 1991, which extended protections and legal remedies against employment discrimination. He also signed the landmark Americans with Disabilities Act (ADA) in 1990, extending a range of civil rights protections to many disabled persons.

During the Bush years, Barack Obama worked his way through Harvard Law School. In the summer after his first year, he worked as an associate at the prestigious Chicago law firm of Sidley & Austin, where his mentor was a young attorney named Michelle Robinson. Subsequently, he was elected the first African American editor of the prestigious *Harvard Law Review.* He graduated *magna cum laude* in 1991.[19]

For several years after his graduation, Obama was a visiting professor at the University of Chicago Law School. While teaching constitutional law, he also worked on the manuscript that was published as *Dreams from My Father.* He also found time to date and then marry his former Sidley & Austin mentor, Michelle. That same year, 1992, Obama led a major voter registration drive for African Americans in Illinois. Thanks in part to Obama's efforts, Bill Clinton carried Illinois handily in his successful 1992 presidential race against George H.W. Bush. Clinton became the first Democrat to carry that state since Lyndon Johnson in 1964. While Obama continued his teaching and also joined a Chicago law firm, working on civil rights cases and neighborhood development, Bill Clinton began his presidency. He seemed so comfortable with and sympathetic toward African Americans that he was called the "first black President." Toni Morrison first used the phrase in a 1998 *New Yorker* column: "This is our first black President. Blacker than any actual black person who could ever be elected in our children's lifetime. After all, Clinton displays almost every trope of blackness: single-parent household, born poor, working-class, saxophone-playing, McDonald's-and-junk-food-loving boy from Arkansas."[20] While there has been considerable discussion of exactly what Morrison meant, especially now that the nation has elected an "actual black person," the label did convey a sense of Clinton's abiding concerns for racial justice and the welfare of African Americans. Clinton notably appointed African Americans to six different cabinet positions. No previous president had appointed more than one black cabinet officer.

When Bill Clinton ran for re-election in 1996, Barack Obama took his first steps into electoral politics. He ran successfully for the Illinois state Senate, representing Chicago's Southside. In the state capitol in Springfield, he often worked with Republicans on issues such as ethics reform and health care, as well as his own more partisan agendas of welfare reform and child care. To some extent, working with Republicans was the only way to accomplish anything. The GOP was in the majority and exercised iron control over legislative proceedings. Because elections to the Illinois senate are for alternating two- and four-year terms, Obama had to run for re-election in 1998 but not in 2000. With a state Senate seat to fall back on that year, he ran for the United States House of Representatives. That was a mistake. He was overwhelmingly defeated in the Democratic primary by a four-term incumbent. One important outcome of that failed race was that Barack Obama began to work with the political consultant David Axelrod. Axelrod would be an important member of the Obama team in later years.

In 2000, the same year that Obama decisively lost his bid for a seat in Congress, George W. Bush won the presidency in a manner that was anything but decisive. Democrat Al Gore, vice president under Bill Clinton, won the popular vote, but Bush prevailed narrowly in the Electoral College, based on disputed returns from Florida awarded to him by a Supreme Court decision. While the Bush campaign described their candidate as a "compassionate conservative," the end of the Clinton era worried many African Americans. They had voted overwhelmingly for Gore in the election. However, on racial issues Bush seemed entirely even-handed. His first appointment as secretary of state was an African American man, Colin Powell, and his second was Condoleezza Rice, an African American woman. Powell was well aware of how much things had changed in the United States. In his autobiography *My American Journey,* Powell writes about not being served a hamburger in a local drive-in restaurant in Georgia when he was stationed at Fort Benning in the 1960s after a tour in Vietnam.[21] Bush also appointed blacks to two other cabinet positions, Housing and Urban Development and Education. The Clinton and George W. Bush years showed clearly that the makeup of the federal government at the highest levels had dramatically changed since the 1960s.

During George W. Bush's first term, Barack Obama began to speak out on national issues. In campaigning for re-election to the Illinois Senate in 2002, he urged great caution in rushing into a "dumb war" in Iraq; after his re-election, he continued to speak out against the looming war, saying that it was not too late to change course.[22] But eventually it was too late. President Bush ordered the invasion of Iraq in March of 2003. By that time, Obama's eloquent and analytic style had started to attract national attention. He was ready to embrace it. Even before his 2002 state Senate re-election, Obama began planning a possible entry into the 2004 US Senate race in Illinois. When his strongest primary opponent dropped out of the race due to a divorce controversy, Obama surprisingly won with over 50% of the vote, 29% more than the second-place finisher. That victory was enough to get Obama named as the keynote speaker in July at the Democratic National Convention in Boston, where John Kerry was nominated for president. The keynote speech immediately led the media to put Obama forth as a future presidential contender, even before he actually won his Senate seat. He talked about his mixed-race background and said that "in no other country on Earth is my story even possible." He focused on hope and described his own as embodied in "a skinny kid with a funny name who believes that America has a place for him too." In November, Obama won his Senate seat with 70% of the vote, while George W. Bush narrowly defeated John Kerry for the presidency.

During the next several years, there was a great deal of speculation about who the two major political parties would nominate for president in 2008. That election would be the first in over a half-century in which neither an incumbent president nor an incumbent vice president was a candidate for president. The nomination was wide open for both Democrats and Republicans. Among Democrats, the leading candidate was Hillary Clinton, former first lady and current US Senator from New York. Clinton won an overwhelming Senate re-election victory in 2006 and was the front-runner. Barack Obama, however, was nearly always in the conversation as a promising leader. Both senators had announced plans to run by early 2007.

The race for the Democratic nomination was extremely close. Clinton and Obama each won roughly the same number of delegates and the same number of popular votes in primaries and caucuses. But "super delegates" swung to Obama, and he was nominated at the 2008 Democratic Convention in Denver, Colorado. Hillary Clinton and her husband, former President Bill Clinton, both eventually supported Obama strongly in the general election. The Republican nominee was another senator, John McCain of Arizona. No matter who won, the final outcome would propel a sitting US Senator into the White House. Only Presidents Warren Harding and John F. Kennedy had been elected previously from the Senate. The campaign focused on President Bush's leadership, the war in Iraq, and, increasingly, the financial crisis that became the Great Recession in the fall of 2008. Polls showed that race was not a particularly large factor in the outcome. An October *NBC News/Wall Street Journal* poll showed that while 2% of registered voters said that race made them more likely to vote for Obama, 4% indicated that race made them less likely to vote for Obama.[23] In November, Obama won decisively. In his concession speech, John McCain graciously acknowledged the historic importance of the election of an African American as president of the United States. Barack Obama had come a long way. So had America.

Notes

1 Michael Beschloss, *Presidential Courage: Brave Leaders and How They Changed America* (New York: Simon & Schuster, 2007), 245.

2 Dave Mort, *Bye Bye Miss American Pie* (2008). ISBN 9789780956950.

3 Barack Obama, *Dreams from My Father* (New York: Random House, 1995), p. 9.

4 David Maraniss, *Barack Obama: The Story* (New York: Simon & Schuster, 2012).

5 Maraniss, p. 190.

6 Michael Beschloss, "The Life and Death of a Political Friendship" *The New York Times,* June 7, 2014, B22.

7 Robert E. Weems, Jr. and Lewis A. Randolph, "The National Response to Richard M. Nixon's Black Capitalism Initiative: The Success of Domestic Détente." *Journal of Black Studies, 32,* 2001, pp. 66–83; Tom Wicker "Richard Nixon." In James M. McPherson (ed.), *To the Best of My Ability: The American Presidents* (New York: DK Publishing, 2004), pp. 266–73.

8 Bruce Bartlett, *Wrong on Race: The Democratic Party's Buried Past* (New York: Palgrave Macmillan, 2008), 175.

9 Tom Wicker, *One of Us: Richard Nixon and the American Dream* (New York: Random House, 1991), p. 506.

10 David Gergen, *Eyewitness to Power: The Essence of Leadership, Nixon to Clinton* (New York: Simon & Schuster), p. 63.

11 Bartlett, pp. 176–77.

12 Jimmy Carter, speaking at a Democratic Issues Conference, Louisville, KY, November 23, 1975 (Jimmy Carter Library and Presidential Museum). In a speech in Fort Worth, Texas, on November 1, 1980, President Carter repeated the assertion that the civil rights and voting rights bills of the 1960s were "the best thing that ever happened to the Southland." See also Molly Worthen, "Main on a Mission." *The New York Times Book Review,* June 8, 2014, 22. JC to Vernon Jordan, 1970, "You won't like my campaign, but you will like my administration."

13 C-SPAN 2009 Historians Presidential Leadership Survey. This report shows Carter at fourth in 2000 and Bill Clinton as fifth. In 2009, the two reversed rankings.

14 David Remnick, *The Bridge: The Life and Rise of Barack Obama* (New York: Vintage, 2011).

15 Obama, p. 104.

16 *Ibid.*, p. 105.

17 Maraniss, p. 564.

18 Obama, p. 133.

19 Maraniss, p. 573.

20 Toni Morrison, Talk of the Town, *The New Yorker,* October 5, 1998.

21 Colin Powell, *My American Journey* (New York: Random House, 1995), p. 108.

22 Remnick, *The Bridge.*

23 United States presidential election, 2008.

INDEX